ALFRED DE MUSSET

ALFRED DE MUSSET
From the portrait by Charles Landelle

ALFRED DE MUSSET
1810~1857

❋

A Biography by
HENRY DWIGHT SEDGWICK

Poète! aussi longtemps que marchera
la terre . . . ton nom sera jeune et
fameux!   *Sully-Prudhomme*

Ce poète qui fut toutes nos âmes et
toutes nos jeunesses . . . le Byron
de France.   *Barbey-d'Aurévilly*

The lips of a strange woman drop as
an honeycomb, and her mouth is
smoother than oil: but her end is
bitter as wormwood, sharp as a two~
edged sword.   *Proverbs*

ILLUSTRATED

❋

THE BOBBS~MERRILL COMPANY
PUBLISHERS   INDIANAPOLIS

To
WILLIAM YORK PETERS
This book is
affectionately dedicated

Forsake not an old friend, for the new is not comparable
unto him. A new friend is as new wine: when it is old
thou shalt drink it with pleasure.

CONTENTS

ILLUSTRATIONS

PREFACE

A BIOGRAPHY of Alfred de Musset is so like that of Don Juan, that a reader who does not belong to the generation that in the storm-swept, sun-flecked moods of adolescence, carried *les Nuits* in his pocket and shouted out,

> *J'aime et je veux pâlir,*
> *J'aime et je veux souffrir,*

such a reader, I say, would not guess that Musset's poetry was pure, fresh, transparent, gushing forth direct from his heart. So, on the top of Mt. Helicon, the fountain of Hippocrene bubbles passionately up and bursts forth in pellucid water, flinging iridescent drops into the sunlight, and flows down to the sad-hued olives on the somber slopes below.

In the beginning of the nineteenth century three great European poets sounded the note of sorrow. Keats—

> Now, more than ever, seems it rich to die——

Leopardi—

> *E fango il mondo*——

and Alfred de Musset—

> *Le seul bien qui reste au monde*
> *Est d'avoir quelquefois pleuré.*

Of the three, Keats, it will be asserted by English readers, possessed the greatest genius and the most finished art; Leopardi is, I think, the most poignant, the

11

most solid in his sorrow; but Alfred de Musset, more
than the other two, sang as a wounded bird might sing.
His range was narrow; but self-pity for lost love, even
by Catullus, perhaps, has never been so melodiously, so
piercingly, put into words. All sorrowing lovers, with a
touch of the poet in them, hug their grief till grief itself
is almost as sweet as the lost love; but Musset's feeling
for lost love was far deeper than for love possessed.
He needed the ingredient of anguish for his emotion to
reach its height, and his most hopeless debauchery was
not in women and wine, but in his surrender to a blinded
ideal of lost love and voluptuous pain.

French critics, to gratify their public—for a public
always demands some kind of numerical valuation—
assign the first place in French lyrical poetry of this time
to Victor Hugo, the second to Lamartine, the third to
Alfred de Musset. Let us cultivate appreciation and shun
the vulgarity of such ordination. The value of a lyrical
poet for me lies in his power to express the full emotion
that I imperfectly feel; to loose the disabilities that clog
my appreciation of what my desires, were they ennobled,
might be; to dispel the mist that prevents me from seeing
ideal passion—of love, of suffering, of beauty, of truth—
as Nature's fondlings, the poets, see it. This is what
Musset has helped many to do; and for that reason he is
one of the immortals.

My biography does not concern itself with an appreciation of the poet's soul, but of the muddy vesture in which
that soul was clothed. The conversations reported,
though I can not vouch for their truth, are taken word

for word from letters, with no change other than that
from indirect to direct discourse, or from reminiscences
of persons that knew him. The materials are scanty.
There are the poet's letters in general, his correspondence
with George Sand, his correspondence with Aimée
d'Alton, his biography by his brother Paul de Musset
(1877), and anecdotes and recollections contained in scattered memoirs, by Alton-Shée, Sainte-Beuve, Maxime du
Camp, Madame Jaubert, and a few others. There are
also four romances that contain elements of biography,
La Confession d'un enfant du siècle (1836), by Alfred
himself, *Elle et Lui,* by George Sand (1859), *Lui et Elle,*
by Paul de Musset (1859) and *Lui,* by Louise Colet; there
are the *Lettres d'un Voyageur* and *l'Histoire de ma vie,*
by George Sand; and to this list, I may add that Musset's
Nouvelles and many of his poems concern himself. Then
there are several books and very numerous essays on the
liaison between Musset and George Sand. There is little
else. The more recent biographies by La Vicomtesse de
Janzé (1892), Arvède Barine (Madame Vincens) (1893),
Maurice Donnay (1926) and Émile Henriot (1928), add
little or nothing to our information. I give a brief bibliography in the appendix.

H. D. S.

Dedham, Massachusetts,
    March, 1931.

ALFRED DE MUSSET

Alfred de Musset

CHAPTER I

PAUL DE MUSSET says, "The genealogy of the Musset family will be found in every French peerage." Of this genealogy Alfred de Musset was exceedingly proud, more so than of his genius. He said to his friend Alton-Shée, "You are a peer of the realm, but I will wager that my lineage is nobler than yours." In one of his poems he refers to his armorial bearings: A golden falcon, hooded and belled, gules on field azure; and he is reported to have boasted that Jeanne d'Arc was a great-great-grandaunt of his.

His ancestry was in truth picturesque and befitting a poet. The relationship to Jeanne d'Arc has a touch of fantasy, but not more than usual in remote genealogies. Jeanne's niece married the cousin, or perhaps brother, of the first wife of one of the poet's ancestors, Denis Musset, from whose second wife the poet was descended. The earliest known of the Mussets, Simon, was a lawyer in the service of Charles Duc d'Orléans, the charming poet who was taken prisoner by the English at Agincourt. Simon Musset, by right of an estate belonging to his wife, assumed the title *Seigneur de la Courtoisie*. It was his son Denis, that became of kin by affinity to Jeanne d'Arc. Denis's son Claude, by right of his wife, acquired a second estate, and became *Seigneur de la Courtoisie et de la Bonne-Aventure*. The latter château, whose ruins still exist I believe, was situated on the little River Loir, about five miles down-stream from Vendôme, hard by a ford, the *Gué du Loir,* famous in poetry. It remained in the family till 1847. At the age of twelve, Alfred, who had a talent for drawing, made an excellent sketch of it. Claude's son, Guillaume, in the reign of Henri III, married Cassandre de Peigney, a daughter to that Cassandre Salviati whom Ronsard wooed in vain. Guillaume was in the service of both Charles IX and Henri III. Then came a line of soldiers. Guillaume's son Charles, *le capitaine* Bonnaventure, was killed in Richelieu's wars in north Italy. His son, a second Charles, was captain in the regiment of Gaston d'Orléans, brother to Louis XIII, and was killed in battle. His son, the third Charles, served with distinction under Turenne. His son, the fourth Charles, married into the famous du Bellay family, to which the poet Joachim du Bellay belonged, friend to Ronsard and member of the *Pléiade.* His son Joseph-Alexandre was also a soldier, but with him the family bade farewell to plumed troops and spirit-stirring drums, for though Joseph's son, Victor Donatien, father of the poet, says in a memorial that he was at Marengo, it does not appear to have been in the capacity of soldier.

Victor Musset got his name Donatien from his godfather, the celebrated Comte de Rochambeau, who, with General Washington, compelled Lord Cornwallis to surrender at Yorktown. Victor's elder brother became a soldier, while Victor was destined for the church, but the Revolution altered the direction of his career, and he served the government both under the Republic and under the Empire, in a civil capacity. Victor was fond of letters and, being an admirer of Rousseau, had published an edition of his works. This taste for books and scholarship stood him in good stead, for under the Restoration, because of his liberal opinions, he was dismissed from the service and was forced to earn a livelihood by his pen. He wrote a life of Rousseau, translated books from the English, worked as a hack for booksellers, and was glad enough, under a new minister of war, to obtain employment in that department. Victor Donatien was a social, hospitable man, *"avec un peu de légèreté dans les mœurs,"* a little unorthodox in his morals, who liked to have guests at his table to listen to his stories, but if he was crossed or disagreed with, he became sharp and vehement. As a father he pursued the doctrine of *laisser-aller*.

It was not only in his father's house that Alfred, in his boyhood, breathed an atmosphere of books, but also in the château of the Marquis de Cogners, his father's cousin, the head of the family. This Marquis, whose father had assumed, or suffered to be put upon him, the title which had belonged to the former owner of the seigneurie of Cogners but did not run with the land, had served, as his rank demanded, in the army, but even then had interested himself in literature. In his youth he wrote a story in which the first influences of the Romantic movement are plainly visible: the heroine coming out of a convent pleases a young officer, who is so carried away by his amorous passion that he resents light talk concerning feminine virtue, challenges the evil speaker and is killed in a duel. Other pieces of prose and verse followed.

When Alfred knew the Marquis, he was a very old gentleman, mayor of his village. His old-fashioned manners, dignified, courteous and modest, accorded well with the old château, where Alfred often passed his holidays as a boy.

There was a similar literary atmosphere in his mother's family. Of his mother herself, although she outlived him, we know little. She was a dignified lady, with, I suspect, little humor. In a sketch by Alfred, she shows a face of quiet determination, a little grim, with deep serious eyes, and her expression suggests rather a cold and skeptical outlook on life; but perhaps her son was not successful in the likeness. She seems to have had few or no interests outside her family and housekeeping, and though she was devoted to both her sons, to Paul more than to Alfred, she left them not long after her daughter's marriage, and went to Angers where her daughter's husband lived. There is no evidence that she cared for literature, or for her son's poetry. But her father and her brother differed widely from her in that respect. Her father, Alfred's grandfather, was a distinguished old lawyer, who had played a creditable part during the Revolution. He, too, was something of a poet and man-of-letters; he had helped edit the epistles which the long-vivacious Ninon de l'Enclos had written to the young Marquis de Sévigné, son to the celebrated Madame de Sévigné. During Alfred's boyhood, Grandfather Desherbiers was an old man, nearly destitute and crippled by an accident, and living at Mans, where his son Stephen had procured him a lodging at the prefecture. Paul de Musset says that his grandfather had a prodigious memory and would recite whole plays to his grandchildren, acting each part as he went, that he was charming in conversation, and possessed the French gaiety and the picturesque method of expression that are so limpid and sparkling in the comedies of his grandson, the poet. With his uncle, Stephen Desherbiers, Alfred was always on most intimate and affectionate terms.

CHAPTER II

Victor Donatien de Musset and Edmée-Claudine Guyot Desherbiers had three children: Paul born in 1804, Alfred born December 11, 1810, and Hermine born in 1819. The girl played virtually no part in the poet's life, and except that she took lessons in music of Franz Liszt there is nothing to say of her; Paul, on the other hand, was a close friend throughout Alfred's life, and a passionate champion after his death, and sealed his fraternal affection by marriage with one of Alfred's mistresses and consigned Alfred's love-letters to her for eternal publicity in the Bibliothèque Nationale.

Paul was so much older than Alfred that they were separated during school years; at the age of nineteen he made application to be admitted to the École Polytechnique, but the authorities, men of the Restoration, discovered that his father had written the life and edited the works of Jean Jacques Rousseau, and struck Paul's name off the list. So Paul went as clerk into a banking house. In 1831, after Alfred had evaded an attempt by his father to put him in the War Department, Paul received the appointment and served for eight years. But his interest lay in literature; he wrote novels, studied the careers of various personages of the seventeenth and eighteenth centuries, cultivated social life and amused himself. He was not truthful and seems to me rather vulgar-minded and a snob, but he was a pleasant compan-

22

ion, told anecdotes well, and as confidant of Alfred's
desires and woes counseled him on all occasions, and very
likely wisely, and never was jealous of his brilliant
younger brother.

The Mussets lived in Paris at No. 57 Boulevard Saint-
Germain, near the Hôtel de Cluny, and Alfred was born
there. He was a precocious, sensitive child, and Paul,
who wrote his biography, tells various family anecdotes
about him. The first time that Alfred was taken to church
he asked his mother: "Are we going again next Sunday
to see the comedy of the mass?" At the age of three, he
received some new red shoes, which he admired immensely. While dressing to go out, his mother spent a
tedious time brushing and combing his long curly blond
hair. Alfred became impatient to put on the shoes:
"Hurry, mama, or the new shoes will be old." And one
day—it was at a time when his chief pleasure was to dine
in the country with a greataunt at Bagneux—he was playing with a very young kitten, to its great discomfort, so
the nurse took it from him. He burst out at her in fury
and shouted: "There, take your cat! It will scratch you!
It will tear your dress! The ceiling will fall on your head!
But *I* shall dine at Bagneux!" At four he fell in love, so
Paul says, with a grown-up cousin; when she went away
she said, "Don't forget me." "Forget you!" he cried.
"Don't you know that your name is written in my heart
with a knife?" He was but four years old, also, when
Napoleon came back from Elba, and standing among the
crowd in the Tuileries Gardens, the two little boys, Paul
and Alfred, watched the Emperor with passionate inter-

est, "Cæsar in the midst of the blind tools of his will."
They never forgot the sight and, in their young imagination, worshiped this god among men. Another memory
of that time was of Hungarian hussars, quartered at their
aunt's house at Bagneux. Certainly the storm and stress
of those great years affected the poet's mind; for in the
famous opening pages of *La Confession d'un enfant du
siècle,* he ascribes the tremulous nerves and irritable characters of his generation, their cynicism, pessimism, and
morbid thoughts, their reverence for the spirit that
denies, to the fact that they were begotten by war-worn
fathers, between battles, and borne by mothers peering
through their tears to see if their husbands would ever
come home.

But, apart from his extreme sensitiveness, Alfred's
boyhood was happy. He and Paul had a sympathetic
tutor who taught them history on their walks, and Italian
by conversation, and for geography read them voyages of
Magellan, Vasco da Gama and Captain Cook. But Alfred's extremely nervous undisciplined character showed
itself even then. At times, as often happened in later
life, he seemed to be beside himself. One day he broke the
mirror in the drawing-room with a billiard ball, cut the
new curtains with scissors, and devastated a great map
of Europe. But his imaginative and romantic disposition also showed itself. At their Grandfather Desherbiers', he and Paul found a library like Don Quixote's and
plunged into romances of chivalry, *Jerusalem delivered,
Orlando Furioso,* and also *Amadis.*

When nine years old Alfred was sent, as a day scholar,

to the Collège Henri IV. Here he made the acquaintance, one hestitates to say friendship because Alfred was always more intimate with the other sex than with his own, of several boys who came largely into his later life. One of these was Paul Foucher (whose sister afterward married Victor Hugo), a boy of the same tastes as himself, and the two used to go to the theater together; and, as they walked home from school through the Luxembourg Gardens, they would recite aloud bits of the plays that had caught their fancy. Another was Alton-Shée, though at the time they did not know each other. In their twenties the two were a great deal together, but Alton-Shée says they were familiars rather than friends, as Alfred never opened to him the doors of his inner thoughts, nor to any man, unless it was Alfred Tattet. The poet rarely used the intimate *tu* and *toi* to any man except his brother. A third schoolmate was the Duc de Chartres, son to the Duc d'Orléans, who after the Revolution of 1830 became Louis Philippe; the young duke, who was very correct in his bearing and manners, did not like the rowdy, untidy Alton-Shée, though he was a peer, but inclined toward the neat, polite, well-dressed little Alfred, and included him frequently in holiday invitations to the ducal château at Neuilly, and after the young duke left school he continued to write letters to Alfred. One letter tells of his going to the circus:

Mon cher ami,

If I have delayed so long in writing to you it was because I had really nothing to tell you. But to-day I have done a glorious deed and I must write you about it. [He then describes the circus performance.] After a great many acrobatic feats, the ring was left free to a gigantic elephant, who became the theater of my prowess. This intelligent beast performed all sorts of acts at the order of his keeper. Finally the keeper invited all the spectators that wished to come forward and mount the elephant's back. Nobody budged. Seeing that everybody held back, I felt it my duty to set an example, so I, my brother Joinville, and the keeper climbed up on the elephant's back! No other spectator cared to come along too. There, *mon cher ami,* you have heard the heroic deed that I felt I must inform you of, for I was sure you would appreciate it at its true value.

FERDINAND D'ORLÉANS.

The Prince and the poet followed paths that carried them far apart, but the boyhood bond was never forgotten. Alfred stayed at the Collège Henri IV till the summer of his seventeenth year. He was a good student and ambitious. When he graduated he distinguished himself. A prize was offered, open to students of all the colleges of the same standing, for a Latin dissertation on the origin of human feelings. Alfred's dissertation was the best both for thought and form; but, being weak on the religious side, it received only the second prize, which was awarded, however, with full academic pomp. In the great hall, richly decorated, before three thousand people, with the ducal family of Orléans in the first box, and the Grand Master of the University presiding, the little fair-haired blue-eyed boy walked up to receive a crown, so much too big for his head that it slipped over his ears on to his shoulders. The Grand Master smiled at the prize-winner's diminutive size and praised him; the ducal family shook him by the hand; while his mother in a retired seat shed tears of joy.

Alfred was still very slight physically, but intellectually he was far more mature than most American boys of his age. School over, he went to visit his cousin, the Marquis, whom he called uncle affectionately, at the old feudal manor-house at Cogners, a great building part medieval and part of the seventeenth century, where he and Paul had often been before, for the aged uncle and aunt, whose son had shot himself, were very fond of their nephews, the uncle preferring Alfred and the aunt Paul. From there Alfred, not yet seventeen, wrote to his school friend, Paul Foucher:

Château de Cogners, Sept. 23, 1827.

No, old man, I haven't forgotten you. Your misfortunes have not separated us; you will always find me full of sympathy, whether for weeping or laughter, according as you ask me to share your joy or sorrow. How could you imagine for an instant that your friendship bored me? My brother has gone back to Paris and I am left alone in this infernal château, with nobody to talk to but my uncle, who, to be sure, is wonderfully kind to me. But the thoughts of a white-haired man are not the thoughts of a flaxen head. He is extremely well read, and when I talk to him of ladies that I like or of poetry that has impressed me, he answers: "Wouldn't you rather read about that in some good historian? History is always more accurate and truthful."—You have read Shakespeare and know what effect the learned Polonius had upon Hamlet! And yet my uncle is a good upright man, and everybody loves him! He isn't one of those people for whom a brook is merely running water, or a wood merely so many hundred faggots. God bless such people! They are perhaps happier than you and me!

I am bored and melancholy, but I haven't the courage to go to work. What shall I do? Shall I try to be original, in spite of myself and my verses? But as I sit reading newspapers (it is my only pastime here) somehow all that seems to me pretty useless! I don't know whether it's the pettifogging commentators, or the idiocies of publishers, that disgust me, but I don't care to write unless to be a Shakespeare or a Schiller. So, I do nothing! I feel that the greatest misfortune that can come to a man capable of vigorous passions, is to have none. I am not in love; I do nothing. Nothing is worth anything to me here. I'd give my life for two cents in order to leave it, if I was not obliged to make my exit by the door of death.

Such are my melancholy reflections! But *j'ai l'esprit français,* I am a Frenchman at bottom. I know it. If a pretty woman comes along, I forget all the misanthropic philosophy I have accumulated during the month. If she shall drop me a sweet side glance, I will adore her for— well—for six months at least.

I shall ripen with age, I hope, for now I am only good to chuck into the water. I'd give twenty-five francs for a play of Shakespeare's in English. The newspapers are insipid, their criticism dull.—Lay down your precepts, Gentlemen, establish your systems. You are only working over the cold monuments of the past. Should a man of genius appear, he will topple your building over and laugh at your rules.—At times I feel a desire to take a pen and bedaub a few sheets of paper; but beginning repels me; an overpowering disgust makes me shut my eyes and yawn. I need a pretty little foot and a neat waist, I need to be in love. If I were in Paris at this minute, I should snuff out whatever better feelings are left in me with punch and beer, and I should feel better. Doctors put a sick man to sleep with opium, though they know the sleep will be fatal. I should do the same with my soul.

Probably some dogmatic, bewigged, old fellow would say to me: "All this is the consequence of your age, young man. I was like that when I was a lad. You need a little amusement, not too much; then you will enter a lawyer's office and study jurisprudence!" I'd like to strangle such people! A creature capable of feeling and loving, who banishes from his soul all that can embellish it, who calls *love* a pastime and jurisprudence important! Tell me, ye Anatomists who dissect triglochine valvulæ, if such a creature is not a polyp?

Good-by, old Boy, tout à toi.

He writes again in October, to Paul Foucher from Mans, where he is staying with his Uncle Desherbiers:

I am not in love; I am a thousand miles from it—but I feel that I am made for loving; it is silly to repeat this so often to you—but I am such an ass! I hate women in theory, I detest that French character that delights in thoughts that keep a man awake at night. But it's no use, I shall be caught. "Deceive me! Ye cruel Shes, deceive me! But it won't be to your credit."

You see, dear Boy, that I am seventeen years old, and I am happy because I am young. I put a little of the ideal into everything I see with my seventeen-year-old eyes. I am made so. Believe me, that is the road to happiness. If some young stranger lass passes me in the street and looks pretty I shall not turn round to look at her again to see that I was mistaken; on the contrary, I shall hurry on, taking an image, half true, half false, and beautifying it all I can with my imagination.

I play madly at billiards. I spend all my evenings at it. I need some excess. I don't know what to do; I don't know how to get rid of this need of emotion. I often cast my eyes on your beloved poetry, as you may guess. Ah! old Boy, poetry is like a pretty woman. Think, my dear fellow, perhaps I shall meet her this winter; you, too, will meet one! And then what else matters?

D—n! Do you know what I want to be! what my nature is and what I aspire to? I should like to be a favorite with the ladies, *je voudrais être un homme à bonnes fortunes.* Not in order to be happy but in order to torment all of them to death, stirring all the chords of my mind, but never touching my soul. I should like to be envied by men and loved by women. Oh, if I could find among them the woman that I seek, and who is waiting for me perhaps at the other end of the world, perhaps close by. I should stop and say, "My task is done." As for you, charm them with your poetry, for your soul needs to sing its sufferings, *Vous dont l'âme a besoin de chanter ce qu'elle souffre.* Men will say, "Too bad, he deserved to be loved." But for me they won't know if I can be loved, and if I am they will not believe it.

So Alfred entered upon his adolescent years, intelligent, ardent, equipped with some knowledge of English and Italian, a smattering of Greek and Latin, and before him glided a magical ideal of woman beckoning him on. Of the sort of discipline that in our system of education is intended to do what schoolmasters call training the character—the inculcation of self-control, of dominating the sexual passion, of subordinating self to social interests, by games, by membership in team or crew, by school spirit—Alfred received none. His father, disciple of Rousseau, believed in trusting to nature, and did little more than suggest a liberal profession. In accordance with this suggestion, Alfred essayed the law but found it dry; then he attended the École de Médicine but the operations in anatomy disgusted him (1827-28). Then he studied foreign languages, drawing and music. At his drawing lessons he made so much progress that his master declared that he could be a painter if he wished.

Thus encouraged he continued drawing in an atelier. But his true bent soon manifested itself. The family moved out to Auteuil, a suburb of Paris, to the west; and Alfred on his walk home from the atelier would go through the Bois de Boulogne. One day he carried a little volume of André Chénier's poetry, and under the excitement of its verse he wrote his first poem. From then on his interest in his music and his drawing receded into the background.

CHAPTER III

THE DÉBUT

AT THE time of Musset's adolescence and early manhood
the young generation was stirred and quickened by an
eager longing for new things. The old world that had
lingered on to near the end of the eighteenth century
had been rudely shaken down by the great Revolution,
and the uproarious forces, suddenly released, having
stormed through the world of political thought and act,
were now pushing and pulling at the fabric of art and
literature. The hot desire for new things swept up impetuous against old tradition. Influences from outside
troubled and excited the intellectual youth—influences
from England (Shakespeare, Byron and Walter Scott),
from Germany (*Götz von Berlichingen, Werther's
Leiden, Die Räuber*) joined and swelled the flood of fresh
ideas that came from Jean Jacques Rousseau and
Châteaubriand.

All the arts fluttered and shook. Poetry, more than
the others, manifested the new orientation of men's
minds. In the multitudinous waves of change, one current set stronger than the rest, one group of young men
were the richest in color, the most picturesque, the most
exultant and militant. Of these the acknowledged leader
was Victor Hugo. This brilliant young man was eight
years older than Musset, and had already unfurled a
standard to which all opponents of the conventional and
the accepted could repair. His preface to *Cromwell* fur-

33

nished them with a declaration of independence and *Hernani* was soon to be a battle-field. Alfred de Vigny, Théophile Gautier, Gérard de Nerval, Émile Deschamps, Alexandre Dumas, and others of lesser note, were ready to follow, and even Sainte-Beuve, also, at no great distance. They were for the magnification of self, for ruined abbeys and crumbling machicolations, for the contrary of all that the classically-minded admired, they were for heights and depths, for gloom and passion, for sensibility and the derision of common sense, and, as to form of literary expression, they proclaimed *rimes riches, enjambement* (that is carrying a sentence beyond the end of the line), a fluctuating cæsura, a more democratic employment of words—*à bas les mots seigneuriaux!*—and all set in scenes of mingled opposites, sublime and grotesque, beautiful and ugly, tragic and comic. And, the better to express the soul within, they were all for bearded faces and satin waistcoats.

The leading spirits of this ferment, most of them contributors to the same paper, formed a literary club, the *Cénacle,* which used to meet at Victor Hugo's house. Into this coterie Paul Foucher introduced his young friend, Alfred de Musset, and among them Musset soon made sure that his real bent was not for painting but for poetry.

The salon of Charles Nodier was another that Alfred frequented. Nodier was a man of letters, of the generation of Alfred's father, and librarian to the library lodged in the old Arsenal between the Bastille and the Seine. Monsieur Nodier's salon was extremely simple. The guests passed through a narrow antechamber into the

SAINTE-BEUVE AT FIFTY-TWO

CHARLES NODIER
From the portrait by Paulin Guérin

dining-room, which was lighted by a little lamp standing on the stove. The dining-room table was pushed back against the wall; on it the guests laid their cloaks, overcoats and hats; beside it they stacked their umbrellas and *sacques,* for few guests were extravagant enough to come in a fiacre. There was a looking-glass, it seems, at which last adjustments could be made. A little corridor led into the salon. Here the guest turned the handle for himself and opened the door. The lighting consisted of two lamps on the mantelpiece, and two candle brackets on each side of a portrait of Nodier, which with some old wood carvings painted white was the main decoration of the room.

At Nodier's artists and men of letters met young ladies, and there were dancing, flirtation, reading poetry and general mirth and pleasantness. One of the regular visitors was Félix Arvers, the author of the famous sonnet

Mon âme a son secret, ma vie a son mystère

addressed to Mademoiselle Marie Nodier, daughter, of the house, a charming girl, to whom Alfred also wrote sonnets. There, too, Alfred met the great Lamartine, enaureoled by *Les Méditations,* a man twice his age. After Musset's death, in one of his discourses on French literature, Lamartine describes the young poet's appearance at this time. "He was a handsome young man, with long hair waving to his neck, a brow distraught rather than pensive, eyes more dreamy than flashing (two stars rather than two flames), a very delicate white mouth that hesitated between melancholy and a smile, a tall lithe figure, that already seemed to bend under the gracious burden of his youth, who stood modestly silent in the noisy tumult of poets and chattering women." And Madame Louise Colet, whom we shall hear of again near the end of the book, a literary lady, records her memory of seeing him at Monsieur Nodier's: "He was of medium height, slender and dressed with extreme care; his redingote [a jacket somewhat like that which tailors now call a morning coat] was of a green-bronze color with metal buttons, his waistcoat of brown silk adorned with a gold chain, and his cambric shirt was buttoned with onyx studs; his cravat of black satin, swathed tight round his neck, set off the pallor of his complexion; he wore white gloves, and his blond locks were arranged with great care and shone in different lights with shifting hues." From another acquaintance we learn his street costume: "Smartly dressed but a little extravagantly, the collar of his jacket was of velvet and reached to his waist, his pantaloons were sky blue and tight-fitting." He was undoubtedly a very good-looking young man, of a beauty a little effeminate, but singularly attractive to women. His eyes were blue, his features regular, his beard was blond and silken, his nose well shaped and slightly aquiline, his mouth perhaps a little large and his lips a little full, but his forehead had a delicate molding, slightly bossed as if to give room to the several intellectual qualities of the brain within. And in early manhood he had a look, owing perhaps to an extreme sensitiveness of expression, of fragility like that of a lovely flower that has been picked

and has begun to fade. The best testimony to his charm
lies in the gay, jovial, debonair characters in his plays,
for he was almost always thinking of himself, Octave in
Les Caprices de Marianne, Fantasio, Valentine and their
fellows.

Musset was modest in his manners, especially in the
presence of the great Lamartine whom he admired almost
to the point of reverence, but he did not lack self-
confidence, and when he found it the custom for poets
to read their verses in these reunions on Sunday nights at
Monsieur Nodier's, it probably needed little persuasion to induce him to follow their example. So he read
the firstlings of his verse to a warmly-applauding
audience; these he afterward published in a provincial
newspaper (August, 1828). That same year, hoping perhaps to show his father that he could support himself
by literature, he translated De Quincey's *Confessions of
an Opium Eater,* or, at least the French title reads
L' Anglais Mangeur d'Opium, traduit de l'Anglais. Paul
de Musset's comment on this book is: "As the novel was
utterly worthless, the translation could not make it good."
Monsieur Clouard, a Mussettist student, says that
Alfred improved the English book, that, by suppressing
long tedious digressions, heavy discussions and so forth,
the translator in three lines gives a livelier and more
poetical picture than De Quincey did in three pages. *De
gustibus.* One of Musset's interpolations is interesting
as it obviously narrates a personal experience. He says
that while pursuing the course in anatomy at the École
de Médecine, he had frequent nightmares of one partic-

ular character: He found himself sitting in his room, at the corner of the hearth, and reading before a little table with one candle. There was a mirror above the chimney. As he read, he lifted his head from time to time and saw in the mirror a corpse reading the book over his shoulders. The corpse was that of a man some sixty years old, with a long, unkempt gray beard, and long gray hair that reached to his shoulder, and Alfred felt his horrid hairs brush against his face and throat. Alfred rested motionless, not daring to turn the page, with his eyes fixed on the apparition in the mirror. A cold sweat broke out on him. The phantom did not move. Then the door opened, and Alfred saw in the glass, a long procession of hideous skeletons, each carrying its head in one hand and a tall candle in the other. They walked around the room, which had become ice cold, and some stooped over the hearth, to warm their long livid fingers, and turning toward him said, "It is very cold." Here, perhaps, is the first appearance of those hallucinations that caused him so much dread in later years.

This anecdote, and the possibility that De Quincey's habit of shutting out an unbearable reality by the use of opiates may have encouraged Musset to seek the aid of alcohol in moments of depression, are the only interesting items in the book, which is in no reasonable sense a translation, rather a paraphrase, and, as a French critic justly says, *royalement infidèle*.

But this hack work was a mere penny-catching device; Alfred's real interest at this time was poetry; poetry, half for her own sake, and half for her sister's. *La poésie*, he says, *chez moi est sœur de l'amour;* and poetry's sister asserted her rights as early as poetry did hers. He long looked back upon his first experience in love as an *amère souffrance,* and speaks of it with bitterness. It seems that a lady apparently encouraged his affection, but merely used the lad as a screen to conceal an intrigue with an older man. As was usual with him he made use of this experience in his play *Le Chandelier* which he wrote six or seven years afterward. His grief, except as a voluntary memory, did not last long, for another woman "who had been following him with her eyes *s'empressa de le consoler.*" It is of no consequence who she was; the list of Alfred's *innamorate* is tediously long, and we shall have to become well acquainted with several. There is a letter to Sainte-Beuve in 1828 in which he says: "I don't go to see you, my Friend, because I can't. Oh, if you have ever suffered from this miserable malady of love, pity me. I had rather have both legs broken. It is two days since I have seen her, and who knows when I shall see her? She is well guarded. My brain is a jelly. Adieu. Be discreet. I am ashamed of it. *A vous de cœur.*" And another in 1829: "I have spent the evening with the most beautiful woman I have ever seen in my life. She is a kept lady and very nice." Alton-Shée said that Alfred was prouder of his *bonnes fortunes* than of his poetry. Paul was equally proud of them, and says that he can remember the day when Alfred came back, consoled, with a bolder look and a hat tipped farther down on his right ear. An intelligent young man who frequented the same houses as the two brothers, said to Paul:

"Your brother is destined to be a great poet, but when I mark his face light up at these gaieties, and his air of an escaped colt, and the way he looks at women and the way that they look back at him, I fear of his meeting with *Delilahs.*"

However Love—as Musset was accustomed to call his amatory emotions—brought with her her sister Poetry. He went one morning early to see Sainte-Beuve who had published some verses under the pseudonym Joseph Delorme, and cried out, laughing, "I, too, write poetry," and at once recited some of his compositions. Sainte-Beuve sat down and wrote to a friend, "We have a boy full of genius among us." Thus encouraged, Alfred accepted an invitation from Émile Deschamps, a much older man, to read a long poem, *Don Paez,* before an assembled company. In this poem there is midnight love-making, audacious descriptions, bravado, a rival, a duel, and a great deal of Byronic melodrama. Paul says the poem was received with great enthusiasm, and that the line,

Un dragon jaune et bleu qui dormait dans le foin

called forth loud applause. There is nothing so charming as the stormy enthusiasm of artistic French youth, and the fault is surely ours if we sit quiet at the image of a blue and yellow dragon. Some six years before at Trinity College, Cambridge, a clever young undergraduate had written a poem on the thesis:

A dragon's tail is flayed to warm
A headless maiden's heart,

which contained the lines,

It was a pretty monster, too,
With a crimson head, and a body blue
And wings of a warm and delicate hue.

But English youth are more phlegmatic, and the verses
were considered comic. Long years afterward Sainte-
Beuve wrote of this occasion: "I see him still as he entered into the literary world, first into the little circle
about Victor Hugo, then of Alfred de Vigny and then the
Deschamps brothers. What a début! How easy his
grace! And what surprise and delight at the first verses
that he recited, the *Andalouse, Don Paez, Juana.* In such
fashion comes the spring! A very springtime of poetry
burst into life before our eyes. He was not yet eighteen:
his forehead masculine and proud, the roses of boyhood
sat upon his cheek, his nostril quivered with the breath
of desire, his step rang firm, his eyes lifted high, as if
sure of victory and secure in the pride of life. No man,
at first sight, gave a better idea of adolescent genius."

CHAPTER IV

EARLY POETRY

RUMOR has, for the ordinary reader, assigned to Musset such an unheroic rôle in that singular episode, known in literary circles as "the moral outrage committed by George Sand Lovelace upon Clarissa de Musset," and has had so many tales to spread abroad concerning habits which hardly tarnish the gay livery of youth but give to that of manhood a very shabby aspect; that one must remember that in his resplendent youth Musset had no mean share of those delightful qualities, wit, humor, gaiety, that make Benedick, Gratiano, Mercutio nonpareil. Of this rare charm there is no better evidence than the quick friendship that sprang up between him and older men.

Ulric Guttinguer, a poet and man of letters old enough to be Alfred's father, who, having burned the candle at both ends, now combined piety and pleasure, *un sybarite catholique*, as he is described, conceived a great affection and admiration for this young poet and invited him to his country house near Havre. The *châlet* was in the midst of a forest and commanded a magnificent view of the estuary of the Seine and of the cliffs of la Hève beyond. When Alfred looked out here, he exclaimed, "Oh, what a beautiful spot to kill oneself!" Sainte-Beuve says that the literary youth of the time had but one desire, to write poetry and to die. Alfred's bread-and-butter letter was a sonnet that has procured his

host such immortality as enshrinement in Musset's
Œuvres complètes can accord:

Ulric, nul œuil des mers . . .

Ulric, no eye has visited the deeps
Of thy unfathomed soul . . . Ulric! I swear
Thou bearest in thy breast a soul that leaps
From heaven to hell, from hope to grim despair,
But suffer me to gaze compassionate
On one so deeply wounded, and relate
Thy ravishment by woman's kisses sweet.

Though the poet was but eighteen he sounds this adolescent note of sympathy with unplumbed sorrow, as from
friend to friend. Sainte-Beuve was six years older and
had already made a name for himself, but his appreciation, also, readily bridged the gap of time and made them
equals, as this letter from Musset to him shows:

Mans, September 18, 1829.

Dear Friend,
This is rotten weather for hunting. I don't know if
it is like this in Paris, but I suppose that something is
the matter with *le Bon Dieu.* Here ennui has me by the
throat. Send me some of your verses. My only resource
is the society of a jackass of Lamartine's school. I am
writing in haste and on a drawing pad. I am so lazy and
so busy that I don't know where my time goes. I have
done nothing but play billiards from morning to night.
My uncle beats me occasionally, which makes me very
angry. Pray for me, I am going hunting. The next

time you kiss Francine, give her one more for my sake.

Yours, A. de M.

The allegation of laziness is mere bravado. His father, in a moment of return to a bourgeois attitude toward life had put him in an office. Hoping to recapture liberty, Alfred took the poems that he had completed to a publisher, who said that it needed four hundred verses more to make it a suitable sized volume in octavo. Alfred obtained a three weeks' vacation from an indulgent employer, who possibly had formed no very glowing expectations of Alfred as a man of business, and spent them with his Uncle Desherbiers at Mans. There he wrote *Mardoche*, a poem of nearly six hundred lines. The letter to Sainte-Beuve must have been written in the intervals of busy composition. But before publication, Alfred wished to try the poems on a select audience, and invited his literary friends to his father's house, and among them he ventured to ask Alfred de Vigny, who had published *Cinq-Mars* and was over thirty, and a distinguished man. Vigny had already invited Musset that October to the first performance of his translation of *Othello*, saying, "Come, Valiant Heart."

December 17, 1829.

Mon cher Monsieur,

May I hope that you will be good enough to come to hear a few unfortunate poems that I mean to read aloud? You will find some of our friends and give us very great pleasure. I can but borrow the exhortation you gave me for *Othello*—not that there is danger, but I am in need of support, and yours especially I call upon, for you are my literary godfather.

Vigny came and then sent Alfred a volume of his own poems.

Supported by these older men, as well as by his young friends, Alfred brought out his first volume of verse, entitled *Contes d'Espagne et d'Italie*, in which he included. *Dans Venise la rouge* (the unbudging horses of the first edition were subsequently changed to unbudging boats), *La belle Andalouse, Don Paez, Marrons au feu, Portia, Ballade à la Lune,* and *Mardoche.* These poems show facility, youthful enthusiasm for Byron and sensuality. Conservative critics found fault, they picked out flamboyant passages, said that they were imitations of Byron, echoes of Hugo, tags of clinquant tinsel. Musset, as sensitive men will, pretended not to care. "Just criticism," he said, "spurs me onward; while unjust criticism is harmless. In any case, I have decided to go ahead and not answer a word." His father wrote to a friend: "My apprehensions over possible quarrels were happily not justified, and I am greatly surprised by the stoicism of our young philosopher. I know from Paul, the only confidant he has,—he only betrays him to me—that he profits by all the criticisms, and for the most part is giving up that extravagant manner. Paul says that I shall be surprised by the change. I am looking forward to it with satisfaction (April 2, 1830)." And six months later the father again writes: "Our Romantic poet *se dehrugotise,* is freeing himself from Hugo's influence entirely.''

In fact Musset adopted the romantic tone very much as he put on a gaudy waistcoat, and his natural instinct for moderation, for wit, melody, threnody, his sympathy for the traditions of the eighteenth century, reasserted themselves. Even in that first volume, one may well take the *Ballade à la Lune,* (which gave scandal to over-serious-minded critics by its comparison of the full moon above the church steeple to a dot on an *i*) as a parody. Musset was too individual, too much absorbed in his own emotions, to belong to any school of the extreme romanticists. ''Every one of us,'' he said, ''has a certain resonant instrument within which he can sound like a violin or a clarionet.'' He soon cut loose from the more extravagant dogmas of the militant school, although at heart he was profoundly romantic all his life. ''When in composing, I feel a certain beating of my heart, I am certain that the verse is the best that I can produce.''

But it is idle to trace the course of his Muse, now flying off into romantic Turnerian sunsets, and now returning to the soberer gaiety of the eighteenth century. His father, in full sympathy with his son's literary ambitions, consented to his giving up his clerkship, and Alfred felt it incumbent upon him to earn something. So, going to a novel of Walter Scott's, that the French editor calls *Redgnauntley*, he adapted the *Tale of Wandering Willy* and made a little play out of it, *La Quittance du diable.* This play was accepted by Théâtre des Nouveautés, but the Revolution of July, 1830, which dethroned Charles X and set up Louis Philippe, deranged the plan. Alfred then wrote another little play, *La Nuit Vénitienne*, which was accepted by the director of the Odéon, and produced on the night of December first. This play, too, is cast in a romantic mold, but has an eighteenth-century quality and is still pleasant to read. Unfortunately, as the heroine in white satin (like Tilburina in *The Critic*) bent over the balcony of her father's palace on the eve of her betrothal to the Prince d'Eisenach, to give ear to the love-making of a wild gallant, she did not notice the fresh green paint upon the trellis behind; she leaned against it, and then turned her back, green-barred, to the audience. According to Paul de Musset, "they were a handful of Bœotians." Loud laughter bespoke their unpoetic minds. The poor disappointed playwright protested that he could not have believed that such a yokel audience could have been found in Paris. The play fell, and in his discouragement he renounced the theater.

Failing to augment his pecuniary resources by the stage, he now tried journalism and wrote a series of articles for *Le Temps*, which appeared under the head of *Revue fantastique*; but journalism and regularity bored him, and after a few months he gave this up and betook himself back to poetry. By the end of 1832 he had the materials for a new volume; as two of the three poems were plays which he did not intend for the stage, he called this book *"Un Spectacle dans un fauteuil."* The three poems were *La Coupe et les Lèvres, À quoi rêvent les jeunes filles* and *Namouna*. As before, he invited his literary friends to hear him read the poems. There fell a killing frost. Just why, it is hard for foreigners to understand. Sainte-Beuve speaks of borrowings or hints from Shakespeare, Byron, Chénier, Merimée, Mathurin Régnier, Crébillon *fils*, and *Clarissa Harlow*, and blames the cynicism found in *La Coupe et les Lèvres* and *Namouna*; and he says that the poet embodies, with a vigor and dash that are frightening in so young a man, all that is blasé, shattered and uneven in that period, all that is contradictory, and desperate and mad with power run to waste. But the romantic generation of 1832 would hardly have found fault with poetry for any such qualities. Perhaps they perceived that Musset was breaking away from them in those niceties of form that meant so much to them, and escape our uncultivated attention. Their fastidious ears were not satisfied by his prosody. Too often the structure of his verse reverted to classical tradition, to the usages of the eighteenth century; too often his sentences ended with the verse; too often his meter suggested Corneille rather than Victor Hugo; and his rhymes were not of the rich kind that the romantic school cried up; Sainte-Beuve detected such reckless negligence as rhyming *Danaë* and *tombé, griser* and *levrier*. Whatever was the cause, the reception, at any rate, was icy cold. Only Merimée was friendly. He said, "You have made enormous progress; the little comedy pleased me particularly." Merimée was right. *A quoi rêvent les jeunes filles*, which one might translate, *The Maidens' May-day Dream*, is the first of Musset's writings that displays the particular qualities of grace, charm, wit and gaiety that are essentially his, and have made *Fantasio, Les Caprices de Marianne,* and their fellows, so famous and so popular. The plot is simple. Two girls are quixotically romantic, and as the suitor, chosen by their father for one of the two, proves to be modest, shy and unimaginative, the father resorts to fantastic devices to trick him out with the necessary romantic glamour. The verses trip melodiously, keeping time and rhythm with the hopes and sensibilities of the two enchanting maidens, Ninon and Ninette. In this *proverbe,* as the French call it, Musset reveals his best side at its best. He is tender, chivalric, gay, humorous, mocking and very much of a gentleman. Nobody, perhaps, has written anything that one can put into the same category with his plays, *Les Caprices de Marianne, Fantasio, On ne badine pas avec l'amour, A quoi rêvent les jeunes filles.* Other plays may have as much wit, as much vivacity, but his *proverbes* have a tenderness, a softness of touch, that lift Alfred de Musset, as a playwright, into so individual a place.

As to the two Byronic poems, perhaps they will be still acceptable to readers of Byron. *La Coupe et les Lèvres* is a tragedy in five acts, and very melodramatic. *Namouna* purports to be an Oriental tale, and is extremely clever. As to imitation and plagiarism, Alfred took a boyishly inconsistent attitude. At one time he declares that *Manfred* and *Lara* are the two masterpieces of human melancholy, admits imitation and asks what of it:

> *Byron, me disez-vous, m'a servi de modèle,*
> *Vous ne savez donc pas qu'il imitait Pulci?*
> . . . .
> *Rien n'appartient à rien, tout appartient à tout.*

And then he denies:

> *On m'a dit l'an passé que j'imitais Byron,*
> *Vous me connaissez, vous savez bien que non.*
> *Je hais comme la mort l'état de plagiare;*
> *Mon verre n'est pas grand, mais je bois dans*
>   *mon verre.*

> They say that Lord Byron last year was my
>   model,
> You know very well such was not in my noddle.
> Before plagiarizing let death come to pass!
> My glass is not large, but I drink in my glass.

But the point is a matter of indifference. In the poems
and plays that constitute the fabric on which Alfred de
Musset's renown stands, his genius is certainly individual
and may flout with scorn any charge of imitation or plagiarism.

CHAPTER V

BACHELOR DAYS

DURING these years Musset led the gay life of a young man about town. No blight of Puritan teaching had ever touched him, and woman was his oyster. His brother Paul was inordinately proud of the successes of this younger brother, "with clear, bold look, dilated nostrils and vermilion lips." He was delighted to be the confidant of Alfred's adventures of which he declares that "some were romantic, some worthy of Boccaccio, some verging on tragedy." In those happy days, as Paul says, in order to please the other sex, a young man did not need to be rich, it was enough at nineteen to have the prestige of talents and fame. Alfred would wake Paul up at midnight to consult him as to what he had better do in certain delicate circumstances. Paul can hardly forbear to break the seal of confidence, but contents himself with saying, "I assure you that more than one of these adventures would have made Bassompierre and Lauzun [the Don Juans of their day] jealous." And in another place he writes also, "I would hardly be believed if I were to tell the success which befell his self esteem, and how high aloft he was carried by the whirlwind of success." Paul, however, in his admiration of Alfred, did not always notice the line that separates truth from falsehood; and Alfred's conquests were by no means all in high social class. It seems quite certain, without adducing *Rolla* as evidence, that Alfred de Musset then, and all his life, frequented cabarets and women of the lowest class. One of the arguments that he employed in his supplications to hesitating ladies was that their love would rescue him from bad company.

I think I had better postulate at once this permanent background of debauchery, and my readers from now on may take it for granted. George Sand, Madame Allan-Despréaux, Madame Louise Colet, Princess Belgiojoso, all refer to this weakness, this depravity; Alton-Shée speaks of Musset's *habitude de se délasser des femmes dans les bras de Bacchus.* Ulric Guttinguer, himself no ascetic, warned him twenty times against drink. Félix Arvers, back in 1831, asks, "What's become of Musset, is he finally determined to go to the devil?" And toward the end of his life it was well recognized that the deafness that came upon him was due to *l'abus de la femme et du vin.* We may now turn our backs on these *laideurs,* and betake ourselves to the society of his male companions, the young dandies of the *Boulevard de Gand, les lions de la Bohême dorée.*

Among this group were Alton-Shée, Alfred Tattet, Roger de Beauvoir, Prince Belgiojoso and Major Frazer. Belgiojoso, an exile from Milan, was husband of the Princess Belgiojoso—they had parted, as one of the friends said, *dignement, noblement,* but these adverbs did not prevent her from writing that she should go to Paris *quand j'aurai appris la bienheureuse nouvelle du départ de Belgiojoso* (on receiving the blessed news of her husband's departure), nor him from speaking of *les petitesses et cochonneries de ma chère épouse* (the little nastinesses of my dear wife). Major Frazer was a soldier of fortune, half Scotch, half Portuguese. They were all rakes and pleasure-seekers; but all loved poetry. For instance, Frazer, when an officer in the Russian Army, was in love with one the Empress's maids of honor, and in his eagerness to read her Lamartine's *Méditations*, he climbed up a tree that grew close to her window, and, ensconced on the nearest branch, read them aloud to her. They were discovered. In the Russian Army under the imperial régime, neither love nor poetry was an excuse for breach of etiquette. Frazer was sent to the Caucasus for three years.

Another of these gay young men was Roger de Beauvoir, who had acquired celebrity through a novel, *l'Écolier de Cluny*. He was a very handsome fellow, dressed to the height of the mode, and no one could carry it off as well as he;—in his redingote with great velvet lapels, which he wore in fine style, he had a grand manner. His black beard, his carefully coiffered hair, his brilliant smile, his happy look—like one of the young swells in Paul Veronese's *Marriage at Cana*—made him very attractive to women. And his eccentric behavior, *sa vie tapageuse,* made him a demigod with the students of the Latin Quarter. He was a particular friend of Gérard de Nerval, and he was one, and not alone, into whose life *la Dame aux camélias* had come.

Of them all Alfred Tattet was the closest to Musset. Both loved horses and women, both liked arts and letters and the society of interesting literary men. Years afterward Musset analyzed their friendship: "He took me as an intellectual luxury; I was as necessary to his mind, to his idealism, as his mistresses and horses were to his dissipated habits. I liked him for his *laisser-aller,* for the free carelessness of his life and indifference to what people thought of him." Tattet was a clever lad and like Musset had a cultivated uncle who had encouraged and stimulated his literary tastes; he was rich and possessed horses and a little house in the country where he invited companions of both sexes for visits, altogether a valuable friend. A scrap of letter from Musset to Tattet, dated January 14, 1831, shows their intimacy: "I am spending my time with half a dozen painters. What good fellows artists are when they follow some art other than yours! Also, I write about what is going on in the little theatres for the *Temps*, and when in the mood I scribble bits of rhyme." Alton-Shée, descendant of an Irish family, was a peer by birth; after a wild youth he had a distinguished political career and at his death Gambetta delivered his funeral ovation.

These young men were careless jovial fellows, lovers of transitory pleasures, always sauntering from amusement to amusement. They would sometimes go off into the country to pay Tattet a visit; or one or another of them might go to Normandy to stay with Ulric Guttinguer, but they were not out of Paris for long at a time, and they liked best to be in the city; and of Paris they preferred a region between the Faubourg Montmartre and the spot now occupied by the Opera House, all much changed from what it was then. Alfred de Musset has described this region of their idle ways: "The space between the Grange-Batelière and that of the Chaussée d'Anfin is not a gun-shot in length. In winter the place is all muddy, in summer dusty. The chestnut trees that used to cast some shade were cut down at the time of the barricades. The only ornaments now are half a dozen saplings and as many lamp posts. Apart from that there is nothing to look at, and there is no more reason to sit there than in any other place on the boulevard. Nevertheless, this little spot, foul with mud and dust, is one of the pleasantest places in the world. It is one of the few points in the world where pleasure is concentrated. The Parisian lives there, the provincial hurries there; the foreigner who merely passes by remembers it as he does the Via di Toledo at Naples, or the Piazzetta at Venice. Restaurants, cafés, theatres, bathing establishments, gambling houses, are all gathered together there. Within a hundred paces you have a whole world. Beyond these limits, all is outer darkness. This odd region is called the Boulevard de Gand. No life stirs there before noon. The waiters treat anybody who comes to lunch before then with contempt. At noon the dandies arrive. They enter Tortoni's by the back door, because the places in front are occupied by barbarians, people from the Stock Exchange. The world of dandies, clean-shaven and well barbered, lunches there until two o'clock, making a great deal of noise, and then trips away in varnished boots. There may be a game of cards or a fencing bout, but no information of it gets abroad. At five o'clock there is an entire change; the restaurants empty and remain deserted until six. At that hour the *habitués* of each restaurant appear little by little, and betake themselves to their respective planetary systems. The retired *rentier,* elaborately dressed, strolls into the Café Anglais with a theatre ticket in his pocket; the well groomed politician, the semi-fashionable man, seat themselves in Hardy's: large English families get out of hired carriages and go into the Café de Paris, ignorant that fashion has left it; two or three parties, well-mannered, with merry faces, strangers to the place, enter private dining-rooms in the Café Douix. The Union Club is now all lighted up, and many carriages stop at its door; dandies strut about before going into the Jockey Club. At seven o'clock all is deserted again. A few journalists sip coffee while everybody else is at dinner. At half past eight there is smoke everywhere; a hundred stomachs are digesting, a hundred cigars are burning, carriages roll by, boots creak, canes are resplendent, hats tilt to one side, waistcoats puff themselves out, horses prance. . . . Then the world of dandies trips away again. The gentlemen go to the theatre, the ladies to a dance. The company becomes very inferior. Hawkers disturb the quiet, crying their evening papers. At half past eleven the theatres empty. There is a rush at Tortoni's for an ice before going to bed. On a summer night a thousand are swallowed down. At midnight some dandy, who is lost or strayed, appears for a moment. His day has exhausted him. He flings himself into a chair, stretches his legs, one foot over the other, yawns, gulps down a glass of lemonade, taps some one on the shoulder by way of saying good night, and is gone. All the lights are put out. Everybody goes away by moonlight, smoking. One hour later not a soul is stirring, only three or four fiacres wait patiently before the Café Anglais for late roisterers who won't go home till daybreak.''

This life was agreeable, if not edifying. But we must not exaggerate its wildness or extravagance, any more than we should dwell too long upon Musset's depraved habits; it is very easy to lay too much stress upon one out of many aspects of any character, and so do wrong to the general likeness. Musset was often ready for a frolic, but often he preferred to be alone. Sometimes he would crave a quiet time, and drop in to see a friend for a cigar and a chat; or he might stay at home and say that his own room was a most delightful spot, and there he might talk with Paul about women or poetry till three in the morning, or consider the best frame for an engraving which he had picked up at some booth along the Seine. At other times Alfred frequented the theater, or took a season ticket for the opera. Or, as I have said, he went to a party at Charles Nodier's. A letter to Paul, who was at Aix, supplements this information as to his doings at this period of his life, the pre-George Sand period:

August 4, 1831.

My dear Boy,

You ask me how I employ the time. I don't employ it, I spend it or I kill it; and that is jolly hard. However, I may say that I argue a great deal. I even believe that I lose too much time in talking, analyzing and criticizing. I met Eugène Delacroix one night on my way home from the play; we talked painting on the street from his door to mine and from my door to his, till two o'clock in the morning. We couldn't leave off. With good old Anthony Deschamps I argued from eight o'clock at night till eleven on the boulevard. And when I come out of Nodier's or Achille Deveria's, I argue with one of them up and down the street. Did either of us learn anything by it all? Will one single line in a poem be the better for it, or will there be a single better stroke in the painting? . . .

On Sunday, after dinner, I was yawning like an oyster in the mall of the Tuileries, when I saw the Misses X sitting beside one of the orange trees. I went up to them and sat down next the youngest. She had on a little white hat with green ribbons. Everything that she said was charmingly guileless. In her looks there was something fresh and tender that she did not suspect. She was no more aware of the love within her than a flower knows its own fragrance. A maiden's beauty has an indescribable charm. I stayed an hour by her side, and felt as if I had glided under the wings of her guardian angel. When I left them, for the Tuileries Gardens were closing, I went to the Café de Paris. There I met M. who offered to bet that he would smoke two cigars at once without taking them out of his mouth and without spitting. This bet affected me so disagreeably that I went away. . . .

Good by, *mon cher ami*. I know that there are many pretty ladies taking the baths at Aix, Mme de V, Mme d'A, etc., and that you are flirting with them. I give you permission to kiss them all for me.

Your brother and friend,
A. de M.

So he fleeted the time carelessly enough; youth at the prow and pleasure at the helm. But he had his serious side. As he drew near his twenty-first birthday, Paul came upon him one night, sitting with his head in his hands, and offered him a penny for his thoughts. "I am thinking," Alfred replied, "that I am soon coming of age. In two months I shall be twenty-one. That is well grown up. Do I need to see so much of men, and to listen to women talk so much, in order to know them? Haven't I seen enough things to have plenty to say, if I am capable of saying anything? Either one has nothing inside and these new sensations awake nothing in the imagination; or, one has the elements of everything within oneself, and then it is sufficient to see a little in order to imagine all. Nevertheless I feel that I still lack something. Is it a great love? Is it unhappiness? Perhaps both. On that I do not dare to be enlightened. Experience is only good on condition that it does not kill you."

The feeling that he had reached man's estate, and must assume the responsibilities of a man, was increased by his father's death (April, 1832) and the fear that the family would be in very straitened circumstances. He talked to Paul seriously: "If a man is not well off, he has no leisure, and without leisure, there can be no poetry. The time for playing the spoiled child and for toying with a vocation that will not bring a livelihood, is over. I must act and think like a man. The mere thought of being a burden to the best of mothers, of perhaps hurting the future of an adored sister, who should be married within

ten years, is revolting to me.   No, I shall not subject
the devotion of those I love best to any such test.''   And
he expounded to Paul his plan to try a second volume of
poetry, and, if that did not succeed, to enter a cavalry
regiment.   *"L'uniforme m'ira bien* [the uniform will be
becoming].''   That second volume was the *Spectacle dans
un fauteuil.*

CHAPTER VI

GEORGE SAND

IN THE year 1833, Musset was twenty-two, attractive, self-confident, his mind set on poetry and his heart on women. He was singularly self-centered, caring for little outside his own feelings; these he nursed and dandled as a mother nurses and dandles her first baby. To this self-centeredness, and not to strength of character, he owed his detachment and separation from the turbulent, Romantic movement. Fastidious by nature, shy and proud, he preferred to take his own way, rather than be one of a crowd; he was also influenced by the conservative taste of his cultivated Uncle Desherbiers, and perhaps a little annoyed by the triumphant exuberance of Victor Hugo and his followers, and now he was alienated by their lack of appreciation of his poems. He walked alone and reached about for his own best method of expression. As time went on his genius found two methods, or rather his two principal dispositions expressed themselves separately in admirable and appropriate ways. His passion of self-pity, the strongest emotion that he knew, issued forth in lyrical poetry, as natural and melodious as the song of a bird. And for the other, for his happy undisciplined boyishness, for the Mercutio in him, he chose the dramatic form of comedy, tragicomedy, *proverbe,* and he chose well. These two arts, as I say, correspond to the two dominant aspects of his character. When in love, he is passionate, capricious, unstable, tossing from desire to satiety, from satiety to desire, seeking pleasure on the edge of pain, hugging his grief; and, on the other hand, when conscious again that he is a member of society, he is happy in the spirit of *camaraderie,* he is gay, debonair, tender, and revels in the bright pattern of youthful life. Of these two arts, the former was brought to its perfection, was forced as in a hothouse, by the famous episode of companionship with George Sand which began in the summer of this year. The other had already reached its maturity during the prodigal period after coming of age and before that devastating experience, and continued after, and in spite of, that experience, as if in one soul two personalities were lodged, like Octave and Cœlio in *Les Caprices de Marianne.* But notwithstanding the predominance of these two talents, Musset possessed a third, the art of story-telling, or rather of narrating episodes of his own life in an imaginary setting, and this talent ultimately expressed itself in *Le Fils du Titian, Le Merle Blanc* and *Mimi Pinson.* But as yet he was feeling his way.

It was necessary for Alfred to do something. The family purse had proved to be not so lean as had at first been feared; nevertheless, in order not to be dependent upon his mother, he must earn some money. He had renounced the theater for he did not propose to be hissed a second time, he had been bored with journalism, and he had found that poetry was not remunerative. Chance opened a new door. At that time the *Revue des Deux Mondes* was in its early youth, and under the vigorous editorship of its founder, François Buloz. In this review, on January 15, 1833, Sainte-Beuve had written an article upon Alfred de Musset, in which among balanced criticism he said that the young poet was one of the most vigorous artists of the time, and that poets had entered the Academy for verses not equal to some of his. Sainte-Beuve's article drew Buloz's attention to Alfred de Musset, who became in consequence a regular contributor to the magazine. On April first, he published *André del Sarto* and on May fifteenth, *Les Caprices de Marianne.* He was writing *Rolla.* He was become a personage, an author of distinction, and of greater promise, he was handsome; a world of fame and women lay open before him. He received an invitation from Monsieur Buloz to dine at the Café Lointier to meet the more distinguished contributors to the *Revue des Deux Mondes.* He accepted, went, and was placed beside the only lady present, Madame Dudevant.

Amandine Aurore Lucile Dupin, Madame Dudevant, was six years and six months older than Musset. Her father, Maurice Dupin, was the son of Madame Dupin de Franceuil, illegitimate daughter of Maurice, Maréschal de Saxe, the hero of Fontenoy and an illegitimate son of a King of Poland. Her mother was a little dressmaker's assistant who during the early Napoleonic wars had accompanied some general over the Alps to Italy, where she abandoned the general for Maurice Dupin. The pair came back to Paris barely in time to be married before Aurore was born. Maurice died young. The mother and grandmother were too far apart in social breeding to be happy together; the mother went to Paris, Aurore stayed with her grandmother at Nohant. For her in-

struction she was put in a convent in Paris, for several
years. On her return to Nohant, Aurore read Voltaire
and Rousseau, adopted man's attire for riding, breeches,
blouse and boots, and rode about the country exciting the
amazement of the country folk. On her grandmother's
death she went to Paris to live with her mother. Her
mother assumed a galling authority, and for liberty's
sake Aurore married the Baron Casimir Dudevant and
went to Nohant to live. She had two children, a boy
and a girl; her husband was an odious person, rough, uncultivated, gross and inclined to brutality, a lout. At
Cauterets in the Pyrenees she met a charming high-bred
gentleman, Aurelian de Sèze, a lawyer of Bordeaux. For
years there was a very tender affection between them, so
much so that her less sympathetic critics have disbelieved
that it was platonic. At any rate, home with Dudevant
was impossible. She left him and her children, and went
to Paris for the sake of freedom and literature. She was
conscious of great talents. A young fellow, from her
part of the country, with nineteen years, an empty purse,
good taste, some literary capacity and an ambition to
write, by name Jules Sandeau, joined her. They lived
together and wrote together. She took to herself the first
half of her companion's name, and became George Sand.
It was soon easy to recognize which of the two possessed
the greater gifts. She wrote *Indiana*, and became famous.
One day on her return from a visit to her children, she
discovered a scene that might fittingly be in *Tom Jones*
and broke with Sandeau. She was always generous; she
gave him money and sent him off to Italy.

GEORGE SAND

From the portrait by Delacroix in the Louvre

FRANÇOIS BULOZ, FOUNDER OF THE "REVUE DES DEUX MONDES"
From a medallion made a short time before his death

She was then close upon thirty, and living alone and lonely, writing *Lélia,* and smoking cigarettes in her little apartment on the Quai Malaquais. She needed companionship, and took Prosper Merimée for a companion. The episode was extremely short lived, they had little or nothing in common. Prosper Merimée is said to have related (I borrow this anecdote from Henry James) that during this period he once opened his eyes, in a raw winter dawn, to see his companion, in a dressing-gown, on her knees before the hearth, a candlestick beside her and a red madras handkerchief round her head, making bravely, with her own hands, the fire that was to enable her to sit down betimes to her pen and paper. She wrote as other people walk, or talk, or breathe; she loved her children, she was attached to her lovers, but writing came by instinct, and the need of it was the most fundamental of all her instincts. After the week with Merimée, George Sand found herself more lonely than before, with disillusion and a touch of cynicism added to her loneliness. She consulted the kind and sympathetic Sainte-Beuve, who proposed to introduce Musset. She refused; she said that he was too much of a dandy for her taste—he so typically a *boulevardier,* she so Bohemian—and asked Sainte-Beuve to bring Alexandre Dumas. But she and Dumas were not interested in each other; so she continued unsettled, uncertain, lonely and prodigiously industrious. Her experience of life with Dudevant, Sandeau and Merimée had been harsh, for, explain it as one will, she needed sympathy as she did daily bread. But she was not ready to acknowledge it; or, possibly her waking consciousness was not aware of it. She wrote to Sainte-Beuve: "I feel that love is no more appropriate to me than roses on the brow of a woman of sixty, and for three months, the first three months that I have really lived, I have not felt the slightest temptation toward it." It was in this mood that she met Alfred de Musset at the dinner for contributors to the *Revue des Deux Mondes* at the Café Lointier.

Interested in the lady whom he had sat next, Musset went home, reread portions of *Indiana,* which is a very outspoken book, and sent her a poem concerning

Cette scène terrible où Noun, à demi nue,
Sur le lit d'Indiana s'enivre avec Raymond.

She replied that she would like to see a passage of *Rolla;* he sent it begging her please to see that her *petit caprice de curiosité* should not be shared with any one. Then he called upon her at the Quai Malaquais, and he wrote to her. The termination of his letters advanced from *Votre bien devoué* to *Tout à vous de cœur.* She then goes to call upon him, and sends him a copy of *Lélia.* He writes her a fervent eulogy of *Lélia;* he says, "There are scores of pages in it that go straight to the heart, and are quite as beautiful as any in *René* or *Lara.*" For her, a romantic, there could be no higher compliment. And then, having prepared the way, Alfred goes on in more personal fashion: "You know well enough to be sure that the ridiculous speech 'Are you willing, or are you not?' shall never pass my lips in speaking to you. In that respect a Baltic Sea lies between us. You can give nothing but platonic love (*l'amour moral*), and I give that to no woman (even supposing that you should not send me about my business at once, if I ventured to ask for it), but I can become, if you should think me worthy, not exactly a friend, even that is too platonic for me, but a sort of comrade of no importance and with no claims, and therefore without jealousy and without quarrels, a comrade, able to smoke your tobacco, and catch cold in discussing philosophy with you under any horse-chestnut trees in Europe. If, on that basis, whenever you have nothing to do, or when you wish to be foolish (polite of me!), you will let me pass an hour or an evening with you, why then, instead of a visit to a lady who writes books, I shall be calling on my dear Monsieur George Sand, who from now on is for me a man of genius. Excuse my bluntness, there is no occasion for falsehood.

>"*A vous de cœur,*
>
>"ALFRED DE MUSSET."

The next step was to make a sketch of her. He made several. In one she is represented as standing with her back turned, in a dress rather *décolleté,* and an open fan in her left hand. She is looking over her left shoulder. The sketch suggests that the artist has studied in a school where Ingres was held in honor. The big black eyes dominate the face, the eyebrows are finely penciled, the nose is slightly aquiline, the mouth small, the lower lip rather full, the chin rounded, the brow high, the dark hair parted on the left and hanging in two strands, each brought to the front over a shoulder. His other sketches of her confirm this likeness.

The two approached nearer and nearer to each other. *Alma Venus* led them on; each was blindfolded. He felt a mystical yearning for emotions beyond human reach, and asked her:

> *O George, n'est-ce pas la pâle fiancée*
> *Dont l'ange du désir est l'immortel amant?*
> *N'est-ce pas l'Idéal, cette amour insensée*
> *Qui sur tous les amours plane éternellement?*

> O George, is not our mad insensate love,
> That over other loves flies ever higher,
> The true Ideal—the pale Bride above,
> Whose lover is the Angel of Desire?

And she, lonely and yearning for tenderness and love, debated with herself, seeking to discover whether she was an *âme d'élite* charged with the performance of some holy task on earth, or the mere toy of romantic imagining; and a perception of her own passionate nature, spiritual, intellectual, physical, half frightened her. A suggestion of this is recorded in her *Journal*: "As to you who are always struggling against ill-quenched passion, you, who, far from snuffing out the last sparks of your desires, stir them up with childish solicitude, what will become of you when the chill of old age shall come, when God shall first have pity on you? Unless He shall send you wisdom and a stoical will to free you from your vain attachments, what will your life be when the heats of blood shall die down together with intellectual desire?" She questioned herself, for she knew how sensitive she was to emotions, to sudden quickenings of the heart, as well as to art, poetry and religion; she knew her own need of enthusiasm, her need of tears from the heart, and her power, at least so she thought, of consecrating herself to others. And as these thoughts danced, poor ineffectual supernumeraries, before her mind, *Alma Venus* led her on.

Then comes his letter: "Dear George, I have something very foolish to tell you. I should have said it on the return from our walk, but instead, like an ass, I merely write it. . . . I am in love with you and I have been ever since the first time I went to your house. . . . I know that you have already been in love, that you are kind, and I put my trust in you. . . . Adieu, George, I love you as if I were your child." She said afterward that this appeal to her as a child to its mother, overcame her. His trust was not misplaced, as a memorandum in his notebook under date of July twenty-ninth records. And on August first, he wrote a poem *To Love,* that contains these verses:

Jamais amant aimé mourant sur sa maîtresse
N'a dans deux yeux plus noirs bu la céleste ivresse,
Nul sur un plus beau front ne t'a jamais baisé.

Later she says: *"Je m'y suis rendue plus par amitié que par l'amour* [I surrendered for friendship's sake more than for love]," averring that it was his poetry that had won her. "You know that I love your poems passionately, it was they that called me to you, in spite of myself." To Sainte-Beuve she wrote, "Although I often speak contemptuously of love, I well know that it is the only noble and holy thing in the world."

Then the drama began. To her it was but one chapter in life, her stalwart spirit with its wide curiosity carried her lightly on; but for him it proved to be the crowning adventure of human experience, and, in a fashion, that perhaps no other experience could have done, attuned his muse to her melodious perfection. George Sand wrote to Sainte-Beuve: "I am in love, and this time most seriously, with Alfred de Musset. It is not another caprice, it is a union." Alfred went to live with her at 19 Quai Malaquais, and all proceeded merrily. She continued to wear man's apparel, sat on a cushion, smoked a narghile, and wrote and wrote. Her little daughter, Solange, aged four, was with them. The tutor, Boucoiran, made part of the family; and familiar friends, not all attractive to outsiders or to one another, commonly occupied the little salon. Paul de Musset says: "Conversation never lagged, everybody was wildly gay; I never saw so happy a group, so little concerned with the outer world." They talked, they had music, Alfred drew caricatures. One day they invited some of the contributors of the *Revue des Deux Mondes* to dinner, among them Monsieur Lerminier, a grave scholarly man, a professor of philosophy, and, without giving his name, the popular clown, *Pierrot des Funambules,* Debureau, whom Monsieur Sacha Guitry has made famous in our day. Debureau did not appear as a clown, but as a member of the British House of Commons sent on a secret diplomatic errand to Austria, and was dressed to suit the French idea of the part, long black coat, frilled shirt-front, stock, a much starched cravat, pumps and shiny gloves. He came late; as with the English time is money. He was presented to the company, bowed stiffly and stood before the hearth with his hands behind his back, disdainfully silent. They waited a few minutes for Alfred, but as he did not come, they sat down to dinner. The distinguished Englishman was placed in the seat of honor. A young peasant girl from Normandy waited on the table. She had a short skirt and ribbed stockings, a gold cross on her neck, and bare arms. The scholarly Lerminier was assigned to draw the Englishman out, and George Sand led the conversation on foreign politics, up to Sir Robert Peel, Lord Stanley and other eminent statesmen. The distinguished guest answered only *oui* and *non*. At last some one used the phrase "European equilibrium." At this, the guest, speaking excellent French, stretched out his hand, and said: "Do you wish me to indicate how I view the European equilibrium, under the present grave circumstances in which British foreign policy on the continent now stands? If so, I will try to make my idea clear." So saying, he picked up his plate and giving it a great spin tossed it into the air, caught it on the point of his knife and held it there, the plate still rotating in equilibrium, and said: "*Voilà!* There you have an example of European equilibrium. Outside of that there is no safety." Meanwhile the waitress had become more and more awkward, dropping this and that, handing forks prongs backward, offering a knife in place of a spoon, and doing worse and worse the more the hostess chided. And when the Englishman tossed up the spinning plate, she seized a carafe, and in her amazement at his dexterity, tipped the water over Lerminier's head. Then the hostess presented Monsieur Debureau and Monsieur Alfred de Musset.

But occasionally the two lovers were left to themselves and they read together, for instance, *Götz von Berlichingen*. In October the desire to be alone together, or perhaps the heat of Paris, sent them to Fontainebleau for a more romantic honeymoon—the more completely to enjoy what she calls, *"l'amour vrai, chaste et noble."* It was there that the tragic motif that runs through this passionate drama first sounds clearly. He tells of it in the *Confession d'un enfant du siècle;* she does also in *Elle et Lui,* and Paul also in *Lui et Elle.* They chanced to be in a wilder part of the forest when Alfred left her for a little, and had some sort of fit, some hallucination, in which he saw the specter of himself as a debauched old man. This phantom prophecy seized upon him like a nightmare, only worse, for there in front of him, beside him, round about and in among the horrible images of distorted fancy, was what he knew was real, the earth solid beneath his feet, leaves that rustled in the wind, branches that bent, and clouds scurrying above in a familiar sky. All combined to convince him that the hallucination was true. She found him, like a creature possessed of a devil, writhing upon the ground, as if wrestling with the evil spirit that had cast him down. The most distressful element in the dreadful experience was that, though far more terrible, it fitted in with unmistakable kinship to other psychical experiences of his—nightmares, dreams and waking uncertainties. The fit passed, but the memory of it had burned itself into each of them.

Before their liaison George Sand had entertained the prospect of a trip to Italy. Now she revived it. To the romantic school, Italy and Spain were fresh woods and pastures new where, like Childe Harold, jaded souls might find incentives for love and poetry. Musset had already been there in fancy, and he was eager to accompany his lady. One day early in December, after lunch, Paul saw him walking up and down with an air of indecision; then Alfred stopped, and confronting mother and brother, announced his resolution of going to Italy with George Sand; he added that it should be subject to his mother's approval. Madame de Musset spoke up promptly, "Never will I give my consent to this journey; I consider it dangerous, fatal. I know that my opposition is useless and that you will go, but it will be against my will and without my consent." Alfred, seeing that his mother was on the verge of tears, said: "Comfort yourself, Mama, I will not go. If some one must weep it shall not be you." And he countermanded his preparation.

That evening Madame de Musset was alone with her daughter, by the fire, when she was told that a carriage had stopped at the door, and that a lady in it asked to speak with her. Without knowing who the visitor might be, she took her maid and went down, and accepting the strange lady's invitation, got into the carriage. The lady employed all her eloquence to persuade Madame de Musset to entrust her son to her; she kept repeating that she would love him like a mother, and take better care of him than his own mother could. As Madame de Musset

said afterward. "The Siren wrung my consent from me."
But she wept as she gave it.

When George Sand returned triumphant with permission to take her poet away, she little thought that the day would come when she would accuse him of having "abducted her from her children, her friends, her work and her duties, to take her 300 leagues away."

CHAPTER VII

VENICE

ALFRED promised his mother to write regularly. On December twelfth, they left Paris on a foggy evening, and Paul, when long afterward he looked back with a malignant eye, remembered to have perceived all sorts of evil auguries. In spite of a slight accident at the start, however, the mail coach arrived safely at Lyons, where they embarked on a Rhone boat for Marseilles. Stendhal was on board, and did his best both to be agreeable and to enjoy himself. He was a stout man, and his face heavy, but his look was very clever; he was extremely witty, satirical and showed himself fond of mockery. George Sand found him very pleasant. His charming mind and originality compensated for the pose that he usually adopted. They dined with him and other travelers, at a village inn, during some delay; Stendhal was wildly gay, and reasonably tipsy, and, dancing around the table in his great furred boots, presented a grotesque and not a pretty figure. At Avignon he took them to see the chief church, and finding there a nude painted statue of Christ in wood he railed at it, said he would like to punch the repulsive image. This irreverence seemed in bad taste, and caused George Sand to say good-by to him without regret. The lovers left him at Marseilles and sailed for Genoa; Alfred was seasick; she sat on deck and smoked. At Genoa he was charmed by the pictures and the gardens, but she was not well. From Genoa they went to

75

Florence, where Musset discovered Varchi's *Chronicles of Florence,* read the chapters that told how a young Lorenzo de' Medici murdered his cousin the Grand Duke Alexander, sketched the plot of *Lorenzaccio* and then wandered about to study the palaces in order to have a fit setting for his drama. That accomplished, they tossed a coin to determine whether they should go to Rome or to Venice, heads or tails. Fate decided in favor of Venice. They arrived in a jolting vehicle at Mestre, toward ten o'clock at night. It was cold and gloomy. George Sand was sick and miserable. They groped their way into a gondola, and their luggage was slowly piled aboard. It seemed to her like getting into a coffin. They rowed across where the railway now runs, and skirting the town entered the Canale della Guidecca. As they came past the *dogana* into the mouth of the Grand Canal, Alfred pulled aside the curtains, and they saw the city glittering in all its lights. A red moon was rising behind San Marco, and the Torre and the roofs of the Libreria and the Palazzo Ducale showed their noble outlines against the sky. They rowed along the Riva degli Schiavoni, disembarked at the Hotel Danieli and lodged themselves in some rooms with a salon that looked out on the quay. Musset was delighted with this ancient palace and the view of the Grand Canal and *Santa Maria della Salute.* But George Sand was sick and miserable. Instead)of showing sympathy he showed vexation. "It's very disagreeable," he said, "to have a sick woman for one's companion." She went to bed, wrote and wrote, with her *"petites mains sans os, moelleuses, ouateuses, presque gélatineuses* [little boneless, soft, wadded, almost gelatinous hands]," as Dumas called them, while she could, for she depended on her literary earnings and the *Revue des Deux Mondes* was impatient for copy. Alfred went off to amuse himself. He strolled about the streets, according to Paul, picking up Venetian phrases, noting Venetian habits and customs, and talking to gondoliers; but beside these doings he frequented cabarets, gambling dens and brothels. That his companion's illness did not dampen his spirits is plain from his writing that delightful song that charmed Swinburne and haunted Gautier:

> *A Saint-Blaise, à la Zuecca,*
> *Dans les prés fleuris cueillir la vervaine,*
> *A Saint-Blaise, à la Zuecca,*
> *Vivre et mourir là!*

When he reappeared at the hotel, he and she quarreled. He said to her: "Oh, you are ennui personified, you are stupidly pious, lost in dreams," and so on. She lost her temper and retorted: "We don't love one another any more; we never loved one another." These little phrases are important, for according to the code among French lovers, when they have been said, each party is released from moral obligations to the other and may look for amusement or consolation elsewhere.

It had happened that, one day at the beginning of their stay, she was sitting on the balcony of their apartment. Her black hair was wound up with a red silk kerchief, making a sort of turban. She wore a white collar and a masculine cravat and was smoking cigarettes. Musset sat beside her. She made a striking figure and caught the eyes of two young Italians passing by. One of the two was a fair-haired, handsome, strongly built young man, about twenty-seven years old, by name Pietro Pagello; the other was a friend of his. Pagello was a young doctor. The next day the proprietor of the Hotel Danieli sent for Doctor Pagello to see a patient at the hotel. The doctor was ushered into the room of *la belle fumeuse*, as the two young men had nicknamed the lady on the balcony. She was sitting up, with her head leaning on her hand, and said that she had a bad headache. The doctor felt her pulse, and prescribed bloodletting. That was done and she felt better. She recovered sufficiently to go down into the casino of the hotel. She did not get much sympathy. Musset said: "George, I have been mistaken, I beg your pardon, but I don't love you." That night they shut the door between their bedrooms. She would have gone away then, she says, only she took to her bed the next day, and he had no money, and she, with a maternal feeling for him welling up, did not wish to leave him alone without a penny in a strange city, when he could not speak the language. Then she had a relapse; and on January twenty-ninth or thirtieth, he fell ill too. On February fourth she wrote to her friend Boucoiran, the tutor: "I have again been ill for five days with bad dysentery. My traveling companion is very ill, too. We are not proclaiming this because we have a crowd of enemies in Paris who would be delighted to be able to say, 'They went to Italy to enjoy themselves and they have the cholera! What fun! They are both ill!' Besides Madame de Musset would be in despair if she learned that her son was ill, so don't breathe a word. He is not in an alarming condition, but it is sad to see a person you love languish and suffer, especially one who is usually kind and gay. My heart is as much upset as my stomach." But the next day he was worse. She wrote to Boucoiran, "I am devoured by apprehension, overwhelmed with fatigue, sick and in despair. . . . But keep absolute secrecy about Alfred's illness on his mother's account, for she will hear of it and die of grief." She also wrote that same day to Buloz, telling him how matters stood and begging for money. The doctor said that the crisis would not come for two weeks, and Musset could not be moved for a month, and she had but sixty francs left. Her situation was indeed desperate. Alfred was delirious and in a horrid state of agitation, and snatching what minutes she could, it had taken her nine hours to write her letter of three pages.

The first doctor who had come to see Musset was more than eighty years old, and inspired George Sand with no confidence. So she wrote to the young doctor whom she had had:

Dear Doctor Pagello,

I beg of you to come to see us as soon as you can, with a good doctor, to hold a consultation on the condition of the sick Frenchman at the Hotel Danieli.

I must tell you beforehand that I am more alarmed about his sanity than his life. Since he has been ill, his head has been exceedingly weak, and he often has no more sense than a child. And yet he is a man of energetic character and powerful imagination. He is a poet, and much admired in France. But over-excitement from intellectual work, from wine, carouses, women and gaming, has fatigued him too much and frayed his nerves. At the least trifle he is as much agitated as over an important matter.

Once, three months ago, he acted like a crazy man, all night long, in consequence of a great alarm. He saw specters all about him, and cried aloud with fright and horror. At present he is agitated all the time and this morning he does not know what he does or what he says. He weeps, and complains of some evil, without name or cause. He misses his native land and says that he is going to die or become mad.

I don't know whether this is the result of fever or of over-excitement of his nerves, or the beginning of lunacy. I think blood-letting might relieve him.

I beg you to tell all this to the doctor, and not to let yourself be discouraged by the difficulties that attend a lack of docility in the patient. He is the person I love best in the world, and I am in great anguish to see him in this condition.

I trust that you will show all the friendliness to us that two foreigners can hope for.

Excuse the wretched Italian in which I write.

G. SAND.

Pagello went, and replaced the aged physician at Musset's bedside. He also brought a colleague in consultation, Doctor Zuanon, from the hospital of San Giovanni e Paolo. Their diagnosis was a nervous typhoid fever. Doctor Pagello was obliged to be there a great deal of the time. He and George Sand sat up all night long, night after night, watching over the patient. Once Musset's frenzy was so wild and fierce that in spite of the efforts of two strong men, he ran naked around the room. For eight days George Sand did not take off her clothes; she slept on the sofa, ready to get up at any moment. A period of exhaustion followed the fits of fury, and when the patient slept the nurse and doctor got to know each other. They talked together of literature, of the Italian poets, of Italian artists, of Venice, its history, its monuments, its customs. Every now and then, in the course of their conversation, she stopped and asked what he was thinking of. Pagello was embarrassed to be caught in inattention of the conversation, and blushed, and she said with an almost imperceptible smile and a subtle look: "Oh, Doctor, I bore you with my multitude of questions." To this Pagello had nothing to say. One evening the sick man asked them to go farther from his bed as he felt pretty comfortable and wanted to go to sleep. They withdrew a little to a table by the hearth. Pagello asked: "So you are going to write a novel about Venice?" "Perhaps," she answered, then took a sheet of paper and wrote like lightning. He looked at her in astonishment; then, in order not to disturb her, opened a volume of Victor Hugo that lay on the table, but could not fix his mind on it. She wrote for an hour, laid down the pen, and putting her head between her hands sat motionless for fifteen minutes. Then she looked at him, picked up the pages she had written, folded them, put them in an envelope, with no address, and handed it to him. He asked her whom he should give it to. She wrote on the envelope, "To the stupid Pagello." Then taking the candle she walked softly toward Alfred, who was asleep, and asked: "Do you think he will have a quiet night, Doctor?" Pagello answered, "Yes." "Then," she said, "you may go and come back to-morrow morning." He went home and read the manuscript. This is what he read in his own room while Alfred de Musset was lying asleep at the Hotel Danieli:

We were born under different climes, we have neither the same thoughts, nor the same language; are our hearts, at least, alike?

The warm, foggy climate from which I come has left me with sweet and melancholy moods! What passions has the generous sun, that has bronzed your face, bestowed upon you? I can love and suffer; and you, how do you love?

Your ardent looks, your rude embrace, your bold desires tempt me and frighten me. I can neither combat your passion, nor share it. Men do not love like that in France. Beside you I am like a pale statue, I look at you with amazement, with desire, with alarm.

I do not know whether you really love me. I never shall know. You can hardly speak a word of my language, and I don't know enough of yours to ask such subtle questions. Perhaps it will be impossible for me to make myself understood, even if I knew your language perfectly.

The differences of our environment, of our teachings, no doubt, are the reason that our ideas, our sentiments, our needs are inexplicable to one another. My weak nature and your burning temperament must engender very unlike thoughts. You would not understand, you might despise, the thousand little troubles that pain me, you would laugh at what makes me cry.

Perhaps you are not acquainted with tears? Shall you be my support or my master? Will you console me for the sorrows I suffered before we met? Will you understand why I am sad? Are you acquainted with pity, with patience, with friendship? Perhaps you have been brought up in the conviction that a woman has no soul? Are you neither Christian nor Moslem, neither civilized nor barbarian? Are you a man? What is there in that male chest, in that lionlike eye, in that haughty brow? Have you pure and noble thoughts, have you a dutiful, brotherly feeling? When you sleep do you dream that you are flying up to heaven? When men use you despitefully, do you trust in God?

Shall I be your companion or your slave? Do you desire me, or love me? When your passion shall be satisfied, will you know how to thank me? If I make you happy, will you know how to tell me so?

Do you know me? Or do you take pains not to know me? Am I something unknown that makes you dream and seek, or am I in your eyes merely such a woman as fatten in harems? Does your eye, in which methinks flashes a

light divine, merely express the desire that such women
satisfy? Do you comprehend what the soul's desire is,
that time cannot tame, that human caresses neither put
to sleep nor weary? When your mistress lies asleep in
your arms, shall you remain awake, looking at her, pray-
ing to God and weeping?

So, almost as long again, this unusual letter proceeds.
The last words are, "Hide your soul from me, so that I
may always believe it beautiful." Pagello said afterward that he could not deny that "he was surprised and
reduced to a pulp,—*que le génie de cette femme me sur-
prît et m'annihilât.*" He longed to throw himself at her
feet and vow an imperishable love, "*Mais il était tard.*"
It was late, and on rereading the letter the third time
something *d'indéfinissable et d'amer* [something strange
and bitter] went from his heart to his head. "*Sera-t-elle
la première ou la dernière des femmes* [was she the noblest or lowest of women]?" He remembered that he was
young, beginning to get a practise in Venice, that an
austere conduct was desirable; he also remembered that
Alfred de Musset, a foreigner, and very ill, trusted in his
friendship and his care; and, looking at his mother's
picture, he could hear her dead lips repeat, "If you meet
in life temptations that run counter to the moral principles
I have taught you, they will make you unhappy."

At ten o'clock the next morning, he went as usual to
visit his patient in the Hotel Danieli. Musset was much
better. The doctor sat on his bed and chatted with him,
wondering where George Sand was. Of a sudden the door

opened and the lady appeared, dressed with an elegance he had not seen before. Her gown was of a nut-brown color, her little bonnet was of plush, decked out with a nodding ostrich feather, her cashmere shawl gay with arabesques. Pagello was taken aback. She walked up to him *avec une grâce et une désinvolture enchantresse* and said: "Signor Pagello, I need your escort as I have little purchases to make, if it will not inconvenience you." They walked for three hours up and down the Piazza di San Marco, conjugating, he revealed afterward, the verb *amare*.

How much did Musset discover? The answer to that question has been hotly discussed.

But, O, what damned minutes tells he o'er,
Who dotes, yet doubts, suspects, yet strongly loves!

How great a claim he had to her constancy depends upon one's code. That he was guilty in Venice, while she was ill, of what the liberal-minded call *quelques passades sans importance,* can hardly be doubted. But for her, at his bedside, while he was ill, she his nurse, Pagello his physician—that is another matter. Clouds of angry dust still obscure the facts.

CHAPTER VIII

THE CUP OF TEA

THERE was one episode, or hallucination—for Alfred undoubtedly in hours of illness saw phantoms, frightful imaginings bodied forth in human guise—that lifts itself above the other happenings in the Hotel Danieli. Paul says that Alfred dictated the story to him in 1852; that is nearly twenty years after it happened. One night while Alfred was very ill, George Sand and Pagello were sitting near his bed. Alfred could see one of them only, but heard them both. At times their voices sounded distant and faint, at times the noise rumbled in his head insupportably. He felt a cold vapor wrap him round and penetrate to the marrow of his bones. He conceived the idea of calling to them, but the organs of speech were too far from the organs of thought. He began to fear that they might think him dead and bury him. He could not make a sign. Fortunately, a hand lifted a cold compress from his forehead and he felt a touch of warmth. He could hear the two consult about his condition; they hoped to save him. Pagello took his pulse. He dropped the sick man's arm as if it belonged to a corpse, and caused him horrible pain. Musset fainted. That day or the next, he did not know which, he saw a scene, which he would have believed an hallucination, if other proofs and avowals had not shown him that it was real. Opposite him he saw a woman seated on a man's knee. Her head was thrown back. He had not the strength to lift

86

his eyelid high enough to see the man's head. The bed curtain partly prevented his seeing also. Then the other head came into his range of vision. The lips kissed. At the instant the scene did not make a vivid impression. It took him a minute to understand what it meant; suddenly he understood and uttered a slight cry. He then tried to turn his head on his pillow and was surprised to find that he could turn it. This caused him such delight that he forgot indignation and horror, and wanted to shout out, ''Friends, I am alive!'' Then he thought that they would not share his joy, and he looked at them fixedly. Pagello came near, and said: ''He is better. If this continues, he is saved.''

That same evening, or the next day, Pagello was making ready to go, when George Sand bade him stay and have tea. Pagello accepted, sat down and talked gaily. Then they spoke in low tones, and Alfred heard that they proposed to dine at Murano together. He thought, ''When do they mean to dine at Murano? Apparently when I am buried.'' As he watched them take tea, he perceived that they drank, first one, then the other, out of the same cup. Then Pagello went; George Sand escorted him to the door; they passed behind a screen and he suspected that they kissed. She then took a candle and lighted the doctor to the stairway, where they stood talking. Musset contrived to lift himself and crawl on all fours on the bed, to where he could see the tea table clearly. There was but *one* cup. Under the French code, that meant that they were lovers. Nevertheless, the idea was so hideous that he still found a way to doubt—

cependant, je trouvai encore le moyen de douter.

This *moyen de douter* consisted in the likelihood of the scene being an hallucination; and such, apparently, he came to think it, but long afterward, when his love had turned to indifference, and indifference to aversion, he believed, or let Paul believe, it to have been real. On the other hand, George Sand treated the scene as an hallucination. If the scene was, indeed, a vision of Alfred's diseased imagination, she acted tenderly; if it was a glimpse of real doings, she adopted the attitude of incredulity with amazing skill, with what a misogynist might call diabolical feminine ingenuity. After Musset had gone back to Paris, acting under the combined urgency of her need for money and her need to write, she wrote for the *Revue des Deux Mondes* the *Lettres d'un Voyageur,* which, while living with Pagello, she dedicates affectionately to Musset. And this that follows is the labyrinthine manner in which she asserts to him and to the world (in case Alfred should forget himself and peach) that the scene was an hallucination. At the moment of writing she is in the beautiful upper valley of the Brenta that makes her think of the Garden of Gethsemane, and she apostrophizes to Alfred: *"Et toi aussi tu as été cloué sur une croix!* [You, too, have been nailed to a cross.] Have you to redeem some great sin, that stretches you as victim on the altar of pain?" And with a subtlety worthy of Duns Scotus she implies that he, the divine young genius, had misbehaved, that "his body, as fatigued and weakened as his heart, had succumbed, and, like a fair lily, bent down to die. God, irritated by your rebellion and your pride, laid his hand hot with anger on your brow, and in an instant your thoughts were confounded, your reason forsook you. The divine order, housed in the nerves of your brain, was overthrown. Memory, judgment, all the noble faculties of intelligence, so debonair in you, were troubled and swept away, like clouds before a gust of wind. You lifted yourself on your bed and cried, 'Where am I, O my friends! Why have you lowered me alive into the grave?' " And continuing, subtle as the smile of La Gioconda, she dwells with pity upon this strange mental state. She assumes his genius; she alludes to his debaucheries; she implies that he has contracted a debt of gratitude toward God—and that she, (as she had done with his human debts) will pay it. Then, sitting at her desk, she perceives that an odor of sweet sage clings to her and she says, *"Le parfum de l'âme, c'est le souvenir.* Fear not, O you who have left a fragrance on my path, never fear that I shall let it be lost." She is an immensely interesting woman. In 1835 Alfred wrote to Tattet: "Madame Sand is still the most womanly woman—*la femme la plus femme*—that I have ever known."

There is no doubt that a liaison existed between Pagello and George Sand, while Musset was ill in bed at the Hotel Danieli. There are admissions by her of unquestionable authenticity. Nine months later she wrote in her *Journal* (1834): "What is a crime indeed? Is love of life a crime? Suppose a man comes to a woman and says: 'You are abandoned, despised, driven away, trampled under foot. Perhaps you deserve to be. But

I know nothing of your guilt or conscience. I do not know you, but I see your grief, and I am sorry for you and I love you. I will devote myself to you, and to you alone, all my life. Be comforted, live. I will save you. I will help you to fulfill your duties beside a convalescent; you will tend him to the end, but you will not love him again and you will come back. I believe in you.'—Could I think that the man who said that to me was doing wrong? And suppose that man conceived the hope of persuading that woman, suppose he was swept away by his senses, or by the wish to win her faith before it was too late, and beset her with caresses and tears? Suppose he tries to stir her senses by a mixture of audacity and humility? Ah, men don't know what it is to be adored and persecuted, and implored for hours! There are men of another kind, who never do that, who never persist in tormenting a woman, more delicate-minded, more proud, they wish the surrender to come from her. That is the only kind of men I had met. But this Italian, O God! His first words wrung from me a shriek of horror! Oh, why did I yield, why, why?" And in a letter to Pagello she says: "Shall we have enough prudence and enough luck to hide our secret from him for a whole month? Lovers have no patience, they do not know how to conceal. . . . If he discovers the truth at present, what shall we do to quiet him? He will hate us for having deceived him." And she goes on, "*Ah! c'est que l'amour est une chose si grande et si belle! . . . L'amour, selon moi, c'est la vénération, c'est un culte*. . . . Is my heart as pure as gold, has it the right to ask for *un amour irréprochable?* Alas,

I have suffered so, I have hunted so for this perfection without ever meeting it!" Fortunately (for several months) Pagello is perfect. All she asks is to be happy for a year and die. Conversing with him she forgets her griefs. In her *Journal* she also writes, as if addressing Musset: "Alas, I certainly did more wrong than you at Venice when I consoled myself. . . . One can't love two men at the same time. Yet, I did it. I deceived you. I was there between two men, one who said: 'Come back to me, I will repair my wrongdoings, I will love you, I shall die without you!' And the other, who whispered in my other ear: 'Look out; you are mine, it is too late to go back. See, God will absolve you.' Nevertheless, it is always sad to lie."

The drama, however, is more subtle (more satisfactory to a Pirandello), than the mere fact of infidelity; it turns on Alfred's knowledge of that infidelity. In 1852, when (at least so Paul says) his indifference had turned into dislike and desire for revenge, he dictated to Paul a second scene in the drama. He says that he entered into explanation with George Sand, that she denied what he had heard and seen, and alleged that it was all a creation of his fever. During the night he spied a light through the crack of the door that separated their rooms. He put on his dressing-gown and went in. The rustle of paper informed him that she had hidden a letter in her bed; the ink was on the table beside her. He said, "You are writing to Pagello," for he suspected that she wished to let Pagello know what she had said, and he told her so. She became angry and said that he should never leave Venice. He asked her how she would prevent him. She answered, "By shutting you up in a lunatic asylum." She afterward denied any such speech or thought as a horrible calumny; nevertheless, long after he had left George Sand he said that a fear was always present in his nervous crises that he would be locked up in an asylum. At any rate, according to Paul's story, Alfred was frightened and went back into his room. He then heard her walk to her window, open it and shut it, and was convinced that she had torn up the letter and thrown the bits out of the window. He waited for daybreak, and then, in his dressing-gown, went down into the street. There she was, looking for something. He tapped her on the shoulder: "George, George! What are you doing here at this hour? You want to find the pieces of your letter. The wind has swept them away, but your presence here proves to me that you wrote to Pagello." (I am giving you Paul's story.)

She shouted that she would have him arrested at once, and ran off. He followed. At the Grand Canal she jumped into a gondola, crying, "To the Lido." He jumped in after her. She did not say a word. At the Lido she began to run again, jumping over the graves in the Jewish cemetery; he after her. Tired out she sat down on a tombstone and wept. He said: "If I were you, I should renounce an impossible enterprise. You will never succeed in joining Pagello without my help, you will never shut me up in an asylum. Confess that you are a——" "Well, yes, I am," she replied. "And a forlorn——" he added. Then they went back.

The story, especially in the latter part, sounds as if Paul, the *romancier,* had, to say the least, *embellished* it. For a man just out of a serious illness, early in March at daybreak, to leave his room in his *robe de chambre,* leap into a gondola, and run and leap among the Jewish graves, sounds incredible. It seems likely that the teller of the tale, whether Alfred or Paul, meant not the Lido, which is at least half an hour from the Grand Canal in a gondola, but the Giudecca; and yet why should she go there? However, there is an item of evidence to support the story. Ziem, the well-known painter of Venetian scenes, was in Venice that winter, and he, so it is said, reported that one day he happened to see a crowd gathered about a young man who had just been pulled out of the water. It was Alfred de Musset, who had flung himself into the canal in order to recover a letter that had been thrown in. Overcome by the cold, Musset had nearly been drowned.

There is also reference to a letter, over which they had quarreled, in their correspondence after his return to Paris. After saying chivalrously, "You never lie, and for that reason I love you," he adds, "I remember very well the night of the letter. But suppose that all my suspicions had been true, in what way were you false to me? [One must bear in mind the *code d'amour* that I referred to.] You were not saying to me that you loved me. Was I not forewarned? Had I any rights, beloved child? So long as you loved you were never false to me." George Sand refers to this letter also and asserts that it consisted of nine lines written on the back of a ballad sold in the streets, and was written in Italian to Pagello, and merely said: "He has been very ill to-night, poor old fellow. He thought he saw phantoms about his bed, and kept crying out, 'I'm mad—I'm going crazy.' I am greatly alarmed for his sanity. We had better find out from the gondolier if he didn't drink Cypriote wine in the gondola yesterday. If he was only drunk. . . . " She was writing on the first scrap of paper at hand in order not to awake him. He moved; she thrust the paper in her pocket. He noticed this and asked to see the paper. She refused. She also explained afterward that, in spite of precautions, he had sometimes succeeded in getting drink, under the pretext of a row in a gondola; each time he had a terrible attack, and it was impossible to tell the doctor in his presence, as he became furious at the revelation. She refused to show him the letter because of her reference to his cry that he was going mad.

During the whole episode she certainly showed extraordinary endurance, strength and will. That autumn she wrote in her *Journal:* "O, God, give me back *ma féroce vigueur de Venise,* give me back that rude love of life, that seized me like a fit of rage, in the midst of most fearful despair."

The story is sorrily befogged by his hallucinations on the one hand, and by her dissimulation on the other. Buloz, the editor of the *Revue des Deux Mondes,* who was intimate with both of them, noted down these two stories of the *tasse de thé* and *la lettre,* as he heard them:

In the morning, when he (Alfred) was getting up, he found in the next room a table with tea things still on

it, but only one cup. "So you had tea last night?"
"Yes," George said, "I had tea with the doctor." "Ah,
how does it happen that there is only one cup?" "They
must have taken away the other." "No, nothing has been
taken. You two drank out of the same cup!" "Suppose
we did; those things are none of your business." "It is
my business because I still am considered your lover.
You ought to show respect, at least, for me, and as I
am going away in three days, wait till I am gone to make
yourselves so much at home."

The evening of that episode, Alfred de Musset found
George Sand sitting up in bed, writing a letter. "What
are you doing there?" "Reading," and she blew out
the candle. "If you are reading, why do you put out
the candle?" "It went out itself; light it again." He
relit it. "Ah, you say you are reading but you have no
book. Confess, shameless woman, that you are writing
to your lover." George Sand betook herself to her usual
screams. She wanted to escape from the house. He
guessed it. "You think a terrible thought. You want
to go to your doctor and claim that I am mad and mean
to kill you. You shall not go out; I will stop that crime.
If you go out, I will write an epitaph on your tomb that
will blanch the cheeks of those who read it." He spoke
with dreadful determination. She trembled and wept.
"I don't love you any more," he said, and mocked her.
"Now is the time to take your poison or throw yourself
in the water!" She admitted to Alfred her secret as to
the doctor. *Rapprochement.* Alfred departs. Enthusiastic, tender letters from her.

The honeymoon had certainly proved a failure. Fortunately, Tattet arrived and spent a few days. He found George Sand completely tired out and tried to arouse her by taking her to the theater and so forth. Naturally enough, Tattet suspected that something was going on behind Alfred's back and intimated his suspicions to Alfred, who at once wanted to fight a duel. But after some intimate talks with George Sand, Tattet succeeded in soothing the excited invalid, and promised him never to mention "what happened in Italy." When Tattet left Venice, Musset was quite out of danger and George Sand had entirely recovered from the effects of her vigils. He wrote to Sainte-Beuve that Pagello was devoted, very capable, and took care of Alfred like a brother, and that as soon as Alfred should have regained his health, he and George Sand proposed to go to Rome, which Alfred was crazy to see.

George Sand, at her first opportunity—I write this from an ungenerous, and perhaps unjust, point of view— set to work to erect the elaborate artifice of her story, the story that ultimately was to be turned into the romance of *Elle et Lui;* or rather having begun by verbal persuasion of Musset that his eyes had not seen, nor his ears heard, she laid the second stone by a letter to Tattet. It was very important to have the visitor from Paris on her side. It was also important to have him and Pagello friends. She says that Alfred is nearly well again, she thanks Tattet for her only pleasant hours in Venice, says that she had opened her heart to him and was deeply grateful for his interest, and avers that they certainly have one thing in common, their affection and devotion for Alfred, who, she says, will march on to fame and fortune, while she will seek God in solitude. Then she adds in a tone that shows that she and Tattet had come to a friendly conclusion in their talks about Pagello: "*L'illustrissimo professore Pagello* sends you a multitude of compliments and salutations. I translated to him exactly that dark, mysterious passage in your letter which refers to him and Mademoiselle Antoinette, without adding the slightest question-mark, or trying to lift a veil that covers perhaps an abyss of iniquities. Doctor Pagello grunted, blushed, blanched; the colossal veins in his forehead swelled; he smoked three pipes; then he went to hear a new opera by Mercadante at the Fenice; when he came back and after drinking fifteen cups of tea, he heaved a great sigh, and uttered a memorable word which I transmit blindly for you to apply to any of your questions that you please: *Forse!* [Perhaps!]

"Next I told him you entertained a very high idea of him, and he replied that he thought at least as much of you, that he liked you *immensamente* and that he regretted very much that you had not broken your leg in Venice, so that he might have had the pleasure of setting it and of seeing you for a long time. I thought that was stretching friendship too far, but I shared his regret to have lost you so soon." (March 22, 1834.)

Certainly Pagello and Tattet remained good friends. On June seventh, Pagello writes him that he has executed his commission, that he is assured that the two cases of bottles are *en route* for France, and adds, "If you see

Alfred, kiss him for me. *Addio, Addio*, your sincere Pietro Pagello.''

Now—to return from George Sand's brilliant hypothesis of what had taken place, and from her preparation of materials to support that hypothesis—matters in Venice had reached the point where it was clear enough to the three actors in the tragicomedy that Alfred must go; but one last scene remained to be enacted, worthy of the ancient palace in which the lovers had lodged, worthy of the *Riva degli Schiavoni,* worthy of the Golden Book, and the flag of St. Mark's, worthy of George Sand at her best. The three actors in the drama were together, all in a very exalted state of mind. Alfred, his eye in a fine frenzy rolling, vaulted upon the Pegasus of his undisciplined imagination. Swept upward in a cloud of penitence for his treatment of George Sand, for his suspicions, for his general unworthiness of her, and inflamed by his gratitude to both for saving his life, he burst into a lyrical mood, carrying the other two with him, and, standing forth, as if in church before the altar, he gave, transferred and made over—as if a priest had asked, Who giveth this woman?—his former mistress to her new lover. Of this ceremony the evidence comes through casual remarks, dropped in subsequent inevitable moods of prose. George Sand wrote to Alfred: ''Farewell, then, to the beautiful poem of our holy friendship, farewell to the ideal tie that was wrought between us three, when there in Venice you wrung from him (Pagello) the avowal of his love for me, and he swore to you that he would make me happy. Oh, that enthusiastic night, when in spite of us, you joined our hands and said to us, 'You love one another, and you also love me too; you have saved me body and soul.' " And again she refers to Pagello as "the friend to whom you entrusted me"; again says, "you placed me in the hands of a creature whose affection and virtue are unchangeable as the Alps." And Alfred says, "Perhaps what I did was a very simple thing, but I *did* it, and my heart swells in spite of my tears . . . I have two dear friends and they are happy."

After this ceremony go he must. He made ready and attended to his passport, and wrote his mother that George Sand had been most devoted to him. George Sand, disturbed by the idea of his going all alone, secured a hair-dresser, a perruquier, Antonio, who desired to see the world, to go with him as valet.

CHAPTER IX

AN ODD CORRESPONDENCE

ON MARCH twenty-ninth, Musset left Venice. George Sand gave him a little note-book. On the first page was written, "To her good comrade, brother and friend, Alfred, from his mistress George," and on the last; "Pietro Pagello commends M. Alfred de Musset to Pietro Pirzio, Vincenzo Stefanelli, M. J. R. Aggiunta." He kept it and used it, noting down quotations from Seneca, Pindar, Marcus Aurelius, Homer, Byron, and so on. And on one page are the words: "We must remain friends and comfort one another sometimes, for we have suffered more than other people suffer."

But before he left Venice, letters began. He wrote, apparently while his perruquier-valet was making the last preparations for the journey:

Venice. March 29, 1834.

Adieu, mon enfant. I suppose that you will stay here. However much you may hate me, however indifferent you may be, and though the kiss of good-by that I gave you yesterday is the last one of my life, I must let you know that, at the first step I took away from you with the thought that I had lost you forever, I felt that I deserved to lose you, that nothing is too severe for me. If it means nothing to you whether I remember you or not, it is deeply important to me, now that your image is already vanishing from before me, to tell you that nothing impure shall rest in that furrow of my life where you have passed, and that he who did not know how to honor you when you were his, can still see the truth through his tears, and honor you in his heart, where your picture will live forever. *Adieu, mon enfant,*

A. de M.

This letter was carried to George Sand immediately. She scribbled her answer on the back of it and sent it to him as he was getting into his gondola by the Piazzetta:

"No, don't go like that. You are not well enough. I don't want you to go alone. Why do we quarrel? Oh, Lord! Am I not always George, your brother, your old friend?"

It seems that she hurried out, got into the gondola and accompanied him across the Lagoon to Fusina, by the mouth of the Brenta. His next letter seems to have been from Padua, where he stopped, instead of going on to Vicenza as she had expected him to do. "You bade me go, and I went. You bade me live, and I live. We stopped at Padua; it was eight at night and I was tired. Do not doubt of my courage. Write me a line to Milan, O my beloved Brother, my dearly loved George."

George Sand had recrossed the Lagoon and rejoined Pagello. But with her indomitable energy she was up at six o'clock the next morning. One conjectures that she must have experienced a vivifying sense of relief at getting rid of what one may call the second beau to her string. She wrote Musset that she was so ill on getting back to Venice that she was unable to go to Vicenza, as she longed to, in order to ascertain how he had passed his first night away from her. Nevertheless, in fact she had strength and health enough to accompany Pagello on the morrow to Treviso, getting up, as I say, at six o'clock, and it was still in the month of March. Some Venetian friends, Signor Rebizzo and his family, took her in for the night. Their hospitality is a symbol of a general acceptance of her change of sentimental orientation; she was recognized now as being, for the time at least, a quasi-naturalized Venetian, taking her status from her acknowledged lover. The Rebizzos were extremely kind and talked of Musset with so much interest that (I am repeating what she says) it did her a great deal of good. It may have been their thoughtful conversation that restored the physical strength which she had lost by Musset's departure, for ten lines later in her letter to him she bids him not worry as she is strong as a horse. One is convinced that she must have been in the pink of condition, so readily do her sentences flow from her nimble pen. She had longed to follow him (with Pagello) to Vicenza, to see how he had passed his lonely night, but feared that she should not have the courage to keep from going to kiss him in the morning, and also feared to reawaken in him all the sorrow of parting. And now she really must go to visit the hotel where he slept, and perhaps find a letter from the perruquier-valet, Antonio, giving her news of him.

Mon enfant,—

. . . Don't be worried about me. I am strong as a horse.

ALFRED DE MUSSET
By himself

A SKETCH OF GEORGE SAND
By Musset

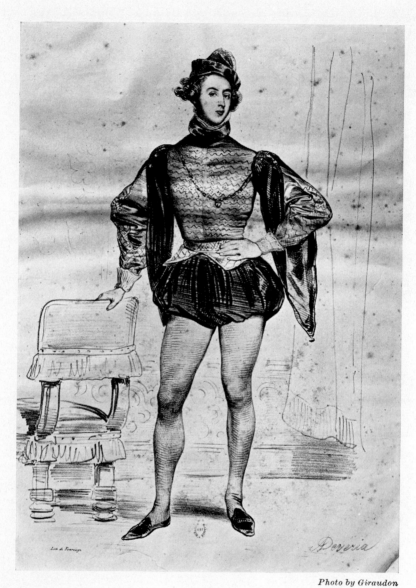

MUSSET IN THE COSTUME OF A PAGE

But don't ask me to feel easy and be gay. That will take time. *Pauvre ange,* what sort of a night did you have? Be sensible and prudent; as you promised me, and write me at every stop, or make Antonio if it bores you.

Good-by, *mon ange.* God Bless you and keep you and bring you back some day, if I am here. In any event, I shall be sure to see you in the holidays. How happy that will be! How dear we shall be to one another, shan't we, my little Brother, my child? Oh, who is going to take care of you, and whom shall I take care of? Who will need me, and whom shall I want to nurse? How shall I get on without the happiness and the unhappiness you have caused me? I hope you can forget the pain I caused you, and remember only the happy days! Most of all the last which leaves a balm on my heart and soothes its hurt. Good-by, *mon Petit Oiseau.* Never cease to love your poor old George.

I send no message from Pagello, except that he weeps for you almost as much as I, and when I gave him all your messages, he went off sobbing and angry.

Pagello may have been stupid, but it would have required a very quick comprehension to follow the moods of these two geniuses of the French race; besides he had had his own troubles at home. His Italian mistress, Arpalice, a lady of Titian hair and true Venetian coloring, having discovered his disloyalty, flashed up with a ferocious jealousy, and made him miserable. She asked George Sand to reconcile them, and George Sand tried to, though she felt doubtful whether she was doing them a good turn. Musset, however, continued to have the first place in her thoughts. His next letter to her was as follows:

Geneva, Friday, April 4.

Mon George chéri,

Write me at Paris. I left you very tired, exhausted by these two months of grief; besides you said that you had much to tell me. . . .

Poor George! Poor dear girl! You deceived yourself. You thought that you were my mistress, but you were only my mother! Heaven made us for one another. Our minds, high in their heaven, like two Alpine birds, flew to one another, but our embraces were too strong. We have committed incest.

Oh, my only love, . . . I made you suffer much, but thank God, though I might have caused still worse suffering, I did not. O my child, you are beautiful and young; you are walking under the most beautiful sky in the world, leaning upon a man, whose heart is worthy of you. Excellent fellow! Tell him how much I like him, and that when I think of him I cannot keep back my tears. I did not stand between you and blessedness! I did not push away from you the hand you needed to make you happy! Perhaps what I did was a very simple thing, but I *did* it, and my heart swells in spite of my tears . . . I am but a child . . . but I have two dear friends and they are happy.

When this letter arrived George Sand read it with emotion. Pagello leaned over and took it, read it and kissed it with his Italian *vivacité passionnée*. This letter crossed on the road one that George Sand wrote on April sixth to her friend Boucoiran about Alfred and herself: "He was still very delicate to undertake that long journey, and I am a little uncomfortable as to the way in which he will bear it. But it was worse for him to stay than to go, and every day of waiting for his restoration to health retarded it instead of hurrying it up. . . .

"The manner in which I was separated from Alfred has affected me greatly. It was very pleasant to see such a man, so frivolous, such an atheist in love, so unable (at least as I thought at first) to entertain a serious affection for me, become kind, affectionate and loyal more and more day by day. If I have suffered at times from the difference of our characters and especially of our ages, I have oftener had occasion to congratulate myself on the other aspects of the tie that bound us together. He has a store of tenderness, kindness and sincerity that must make everybody that knows him and does not judge by unimportant acts, adore him. . . .

"I doubt if we shall become lovers again. We have made no promises about that, but we shall always be friends, and the pleasantest moments of our lives will be those that we can pass together."

Madame Sand with every letter presents a new aspect. Here she says that at the beginning of their liaison she did not think Musset capable of a serious affection. In her eyes this incredulity on her part heightened the generosity of her surrender "for friendship's sake." Had it been for love, that was but as publicans do, and no merit in it. So she proceeds, having rejected marriage as an impossible solution of the problem of sex, seeking for a new ethical foundation on which, at least for the purposes of literature, a nobler edifice of passion, sacrifice and magnanimity might be built. Friendship of this unusual character wore a transfigured look in her eyes; but it was very difficult to maintain that glorious illumination at its maximum radiance, very difficult to persuade others—a Musset on the one hand, a Pagello on the other, not to speak of the world in general—that *friendship,* for which if need be the woman surrendered, was the road of human salvation, and the only road upon which she and her affinities could shine in transfigured glory, and, incidentally, provide the thoughts and emotions that could thereafter be embodied in more romances. But what (one asks) made her analyze her feelings for Musset to Boucoiran, who was nothing but a factotum, quite beyond the most extended paling of a "friendship"? Was it that at this period, and perhaps all her life, she, in her subconscious self, was more interested in her novel-writing than in her life, and that she uses her own experiences as so many courses of study in which to learn the subtler accomplishments of her metier? Or, was she preparing her coterie in Paris to accept her version of what she foresaw would become a disputed historic episode?

The poet reached Paris on April twelfth. He was nervous and irritable; "For goodness' sake," he said, "put me into some other room than mine. The mere thought of seeing that villainous green paper when I wake up, makes me believe that grief and misery have papered

the walls.'' But he sent for Buloz the next day and talked
to him about the publication of George Sand's novels;
she was finishing *André* and beginning *Jacques.* Alfred
was really miserable and looked ill, pale and thin; and
his hair was falling out. His sister says that he pulled
out handfuls of it, so that there were bare patches on
his head. That sounds like an exaggeration. Perhaps,
her memories are colored by Paul's views, or perhaps
Alfred assumes his own recovery before it was fully accomplished in the letter he wrote George Sand a few days
later.

Paris, April 19, 1834.

Mon Amie chérie,

[He tells her about his interview with Buloz, asks how
she is to pay for her proposed trip to Constantinople, and
bids her be careful.] ''For myself, . . . when I arrived,
I was almost perfectly well, except that sunburn on my
face and erysipelas on my legs made me look horribly
funny. Thank goodness, I am up to-day and quite recovered, except for a slow fever every night when I am
in bed; I say nothing to my mother about it, for only
time and rest can cure it. Apart from that, the moment
I am up I plunge headlong into my old ways of life.

How can I tell you what went on in my brain after
I left you? Well, in short, I suffered a great deal, and I
came home with the firm intention of amusing myself
and finding a new love. I haven't yet dined once with
my mother. Yesterday I had arranged for a *partie carrée*
with Alton-Shée. They put beside me a poor little opera

girl who was awfully stupid, but less stupid than I was.
I couldn't say a word to her, and went to bed at eight.
I have gone to all the *salons*, from which I have not been
excluded by my customary rudeness. What do you expect me to do? The more I go out the more fond of you
I become, and though very calm, I am devoured by grief
that never leaves me. . . .

Adieu, *ma sœur adorée*. Go to the Tyrol, to Venice,
to Constantinople; do what you please, laugh or cry, but
if the day comes when you are sad and alone, stretch
out your hand and remember that in a corner of the world
there is a creature for whom you are his first love and
his last. Good-by, *mon Amie, ma seule maîtresse,* write
to me, write to me.

A. de M.

A letter from George Sand to Musset crossed his; and
arouses again in me the ungenerous thought that the lady
is at work solidifying her hypothesis.

April 15, Venice.

At last your letter from Geneva has come. I am
deeply grateful, *mon Enfant.* I am always fearful lest
your affection makes you exaggerate your health. May
God prosper it, *Mon cher petit.* That is as necessary for
my life now as your friendship is. Without both I can
not hope for a single happy day.

Alfred, don't imagine that I could be happy if I thought
I had lost your heart. It makes little matter whether I

was your mistress or your mother, whether it was love or friendship, that I inspired in you, whether I was happy or unhappy with you; nothing of that affects my heart now. I know that I love you, and that is all. To watch over you, to keep you from all evil, from all annoyance, to encompass you with amusements and pleasures, that is what I miss and need since I lost you. . . .

It wasn't our fault. We followed our destiny. Our characters are more impetuous, more violent, than those of others, and prevented us from leading the life of ordinary lovers. But be sure that we were born to know one another and to love one another. Had it not been for your youth, and that your tears wrought weakness in me, we would have remained brother and sister. We knew that that was our true relation. . . . Well, what does it matter after all? We have walked a rough path, but we have reached the heights, where we can rest together. . . . You are right, our love was incestuous, but we did not know it. We rushed into one another's arms innocently. And, have we a single memory of our embraces that is not chaste and holy?

The reader must decide for him- or herself, whether in these letters George Sand is solidifying her hypothesis, or whether she really wrought herself up, when answering Alfred's letters, to a fine emotional frenzy, in which she felt herself mother, mistress and sister, in accordance with the passionate romantic fashion that made her novels so popular, or was her mood a mood of literature, and was there always present in her emotions, as they arose and swelled, an intuition that, ultimately when they should have cooled, they would be useful as copy? At any rate, as soon as she had posted a letter, she returned to her desk and wrote hard to give Buloz the last chapters of *André*, the first of *Jacques*, as well as the *Lettres d'un Voyageur*, stopping to smoke long pipes and drink many cups of tea and coffee.

By this time she had left the lodgings that she and Alfred had occupied after his convalescence began, and taken the lower story of a house, which she shared with Giulia, a natural sister of Pagello's, while Pagello and his brother Roberto, occupied the story above. They had one servant, a young girl, Catina, and she herself helped with the cooking. She made excellent sauces. She wrote six or eight hours on end every day, and while she wrote, a starling, which Pagello had given her, hopped about, dipping his beak in the ink, picking the tobacco out of her lighted pipe, sniffing the smoke, or perching on her knee or foot, or pecking the biscuit she was eating. In the evening Giulia usually sang, rolling her big blue eyes up toward the ceiling, while George Sand played her accompaniment on the piano, and Pagello dozed on the sofa, and the brother smoked and drank coffee, and Vespasiano, the cat, purred. Happily there was no jealousy between the brothers. Roberto did not understand his brother's infatuation for the pale French lady, whom he referred to as a *sardine*; he said in his Venetian dialect: "I don't see what beauty my brother finds in her; I like my Catina better." But peace is rarely perfect. One day Arpalice, Pagello's Italian mistress, not recognizing as George

Sand did that he was "an angel of virtue," rushed into his room, tore his best jacket and pulled his hair. There was the noise of thirty cats. George Sand heard the enraged Pagello cry out, "You rotten carcass, I'll kill you," and he would have, she says, had she not interposed.

But Arpalice seems to have received some pecuniary compensation and withdrew; and when the warm weather came there were excursions into the country and rows in a gondola by moonlight while Pagello sang Venetian love songs:

> *Ti xe bella, ti xe zovene,*
> *Ti xe fresca come un fior,*
> *Viene'l tempo de le lagrime,*
> *Ridi adesso e fa l'amor.*

> You are lovely, you are young,
> You are fresh as any flower,
> Tears will come to all hereafter,
> Make love and laugh, improve the hour.

In Paris, in the meantime, Alfred appeared to his family moody and suspicious, he accused them of this and that, and then, swinging about, reproached himself most extravagantly for doing so. He learned from Buloz that there was considerable gossip about the cause of his return alone from Italy. This disturbed him, and he wrote to Sainte-Beuve, who had expressed his sympathy, that he should feel very badly if anybody accused George Sand of the slightest misbehavior toward him, that he had the highest respect and esteem for her, and that he was particularly anxious though he did not care what anonymous fools said, that Sainte-Beuve should be set right about it. Inwardly, he was, at least at times, in a nervous and excited state, and he felt toward other objects in his room as he had once about the green wall paper. With Paul's help he had carried up his books into the attic, leaving in his room only his classics and best friends: Sophocles, Aristophanes, Horace, Shakespeare, Byron, Goethe, Dante, Petrarch, Ariosto and Tasso, the four Italian poets bound together as was the fashion in those days, Boccaccio, Rabelais, Mathurin Régnier, Montaigne, Amyot's translation of Plutarch, and André Chénier. He also put away his old engravings, and after a time replaced them with others after Michelangelo, Raphael, Giulio Romano, Titian and Rubens. He seemed to wish to get away from his past, nevertheless he saw his old friends, especially the lively, idle, debonair Tattet, and the equally frolicsome but more forceful Alton-Shée. His announcement that he had returned to "his old ways of life," frightened George Sand so that she wrote back: "I beg you on my knees, no wine yet, *pas encore de filles*, it's too soon. Don't abandon yourself to pleasure except when nature demands it imperiously, and never turn to it to dispel ennui or ill-humor, that is the worst thing of all." He replied that, though he has not forsaken his friends, he has renounced the kind of life he used to lead with them, and to reassure her about himself says: "I shall have other mistresses. The trees [it is at the end of April] are clothing themselves with green, and the odor of lilacs comes in great whiffs into my window; everything is born anew, and my heart in spite of myself leaps within me. I am still young, the first woman I shall take shall be young, too. I can not feel confidence in any mature woman.''

He returned to work with considerable spirit, although he rather resented the time not spent in coddling his grief. *Lorenzaccio* was published in the *Revue des Deux Mondes,* and then *On ne badine pas avec l'amour.* Both carried him away from his grief, and he missed its company. I repeat, he loved grief more than he grieved for love. In an autobiographical fragment he says: ''I abandoned myself to grief, like a desperate man; but little by little sorrow grew calm, my tears dried, my vigil ceased, I became acquainted with Melancholy and I loved her.'' The exalted mood of that Venetian day when he had put George Sand's hand into the hand of Pagello swept up over him again. He enjoyed the thought that he had done something noble; he would do the same again. He writes to her: ''I am going to write a novel. I want to write our story; it seems to me that that will cure me and elevate my heart. I want to erect an altar to you, even if it must be made out of my bones.'' The passion of magnanimity swells as he thinks of it. ''Tell Pagello,'' he adds, ''that I thank him for loving you, and watching over you as he does. Isn't that the most ridiculous statement in the world? I love that man almost as much as I do you; make of it what you like. He is the cause of my losing all the riches of my life, and I love him as if he had bestowed them upon me. I do not wish to see you together, and yet I am happy to think that you are together.''

Such a high-blown mood as this reaches out and seeks

to do good in commonalty spread. He will not only build an altar to George Sand, but that altar should be a beacon to warn all that wander in the perilous flood of such a love as his. "The world," he writes, "shall know my story. Perhaps it will save no one; but those that take the same road as I will see whither it leads; they that walk on the brink of the abyss will turn pale at the noise of my fall." But his thoughts concentrate themselves again on her. "I shall not die until I have written the book about you and me," he writes her, "especially about you. No, my beautiful, holy Bride, you shall not lie in the cold earth without its knowing whom it has borne. No, no! I swear by my youth and by my genius, nothing but spotless lilies shall grow on your grave. With my own hands I will write your epitaph in marble whiter than the statues of our ephemeral heroes. Posterity shall repeat our names like those of immortal lovers whose names are never said apart, like Romeo and Juliet, like Héloïse and Abélard. No man will mention one without the other. To speak of me shall be to speak of both. Ours shall be a marriage more sacred than those made by priests, the imperishable and chaste marriage of the mind. Future peoples will recognize in it the symbol of the only God they worship." He prophesies an Age of Enlightenment. "That age shall be a priest and bless us, that will lay us together in the grave as a mother puts her daughter to bed on her wedding night. She will write our monograms in the bark of the tree of life. Your story shall end with my hymn of love. I will appeal from the depths of a heart of twenty years to all the youth on earth; I will blow the trumpet that Christ left at the foot of his cross in the ears of this corrupt blasé, lewd, disbelieving generation. I shall make a grave for us that shall always be green; and, perhaps, future generations will repeat some of my words; perhaps some day they will bless those who have knocked on the door of freedom with the myrtle of love.''

He played on his sensitive nerves till his lyrical words ran to the borders of frenzy. One remembers Pagello's letter cautioning him against champagne, and George Sand's beseeching him to forego wine as well as women. But in between these lyrical moods, whether begotten by champagne, or by memories of his own magnanimity at Venice, there were intercalated periods, when, not at work on the altar or the perennially green grave, he served her in lesser ways. He received her manuscripts and took them to Buloz, and conferred with him about printings and payments, he did her errands, procuring articles that Venice could not supply, or could not supply at so economical a rate: a dozen pairs of shiny gloves, six yellow, six dark, two pairs of satin slippers, two more of black Morocco, note-paper, a box of patchouli, (six years later she was writing to Chopin to bring some patchouli from Paris to Nohant) and other little objects, cautioning him not to pay too much, and books, copies of *Valentine, Indiana,* and *Lélia,* his *Contes d'Espagne et d'Italie, Un Spectacle dans un fauteuil, Rolla* and the numbers of the *Revue des Deux Mondes,* with his plays, for she said that in Venice there was a great demand for Italian translations of their writings. Emotions were not only valuable as material for prose and poetry, but also for selling that prose and poetry when published.

In the meantime, for her part she was becoming a little weary of Pagello. "He is an angel of devotion, sweetness and kindness," but that was not enough day after day. "I am used to enthusiasm, and I feel the lack of that sometimes—*le brave Pagello* has never read *Lélia,* and I don't believe that he would understand it at all." And it further came over her that Pagello did not know what she was thinking of or feeling. "For the first time I live without passion [and this to Alfred about Pagello, to her old lover about her new] ... I need to suffer for some one; I need to put to use all the energy and sensitiveness that I have. I need to nourish my natural solicitude, which has become accustomed to watch over a weary, suffering creature.... Pagello does not suffer, he is neither weak nor suspicious, he has never known the bitterness that has devoured your heart, he has no need of my strength, he has his own calmness, his own virtue. He loves me tranquilly; he is happy, and there is no need for me to toil and suffer for his happiness. ... Oh, why was it not possible for me to live between you two, without belonging to either of you! ... It is true that I needed a father, but why could I not also keep my child near me?"

Moreover, or in consequence of this lack of call upon her energies, she found the air of Venice *coliqueux.* She did not feel well, and domestic tasks, sewing curtains, hammering tacks, covering chairs, even for the sake of *"notre petite maison"* began to pall. Out on the Lagoon, in the hush of evening, she would utter Musset's name, and Pagello, with a tinge of emotion that sounded sweet in her ears, would then say, "*Io l'amo,* I love him." But that was temporary solace. Besides, neither she nor he had any money. Pagello was obliged to pawn all that the pawnbrokers would accept.

George Sand was a woman out of the ordinary.

CHAPTER X

FLUTTERINGS

IT REQUIRED no prophet to foresee that these two must come together again. She writes to him that this new bond, *friendship* that had replaced love, was so beautiful, pure and sweet that for her it would never end. But she was not so sure of him. He, she felt, would get a new love, and the new love would oblige him to break his friendship with her. She bids him be happy; but to keep a little corner of his heart for her, and to visit there in sorrowful days for comfort and encouragement. Yet she writes, "Take a new love, Alfred, take her for life. Take a handsome young woman, who has never loved and never suffered. Deal gently with her and do not make her suffer. A woman's heart is a delicate thing." And she reminds him of his saying, "Nothing in the world is worth having except love." Then she returns to the thought of his new love. "Perhaps she will be happier and better loved." His answer consists in a wail for her: "All is crumbling about me. After passing the morning in crying, in kissing your picture, in talking mad nonsense to your phantom till I am beside myself, I take my hat, walk up and down, for I tell myself that this must end somehow. . . . If I go to see a friend, he suggests that we should go to a brothel. If I go into society, I am presented to Madame So and So who is quite ready to complete a little collection of God knows what. And when all that has set my ears ringing, and I feel sick at my stomach, I come back to solitude, and find it so deep and black, that I don't dare move here or there." He thinks it will do him good to go away. Both are restless. She decides to come to Paris, he to go to Aix. Perhaps they may meet at Geneva or Lyons. Long letters go rambling on.

Does the poet in his letters jot down the stream of his thoughts as they flow by, or is there a method in his selections? "I still have a fragment of life to give to pleasure and a heart to bestow in full upon love. I must hold a body in these empty arms, I must have a mistress unless I turn monk. . . . Don't say that with a mistress I shall have but a year or two to live. All right, one or two years! But with whom? And where? That is why I have longings to don my blue cotton blouse, take a bottle of rum and a little opium, and go lie on my back on the rocks at Fontainebleau. But the Spring forbids, the flowers, the verdure, call me to life. I feel that they are dragging me, but where? Six months ago the warmth of Spring acted on me like champagne; it led me, after dinner, to the first woman I met. So it was, two or three friends singing bawdy songs, a cigar, a sofa, and when I went home if I wept for an hour, I ascribed it to over-excitement, to ennui, to anything, and I went to sleep. That was my life when I met you. . . ." And then follows, incoherent, his old argument, in innuendo rather than in phrase, that only she can save him from vice.

Her letters are as wild and nearly as unintelligible as his. She says that she is indifferent as to any *cochon-neries* uttered against her, but that she can not bear to have any one say that she has accused him. And then as if to refute any such possible accusation, she bursts out: "And what is God himself, whom you call my Imagining and I my Eternity, but the love that I have hugged in your arms?" And so they rival each other. Like heron and hawk mounting, mounting higher and higher, each trying to outtop the other, they soar into the many-colored dome of rhetoric. He writes: "I have never been in so strange a mood . . . a strange instinct draws me on, I shiver, but I do not know whether with fear or pleasure. *Je vais aimer.* . . . All I want to meet is an elevated mind and a virgin heart. . . . *Two creatures who love on earth, make one angel in heaven.* I came upon this in a recent book the other day. Did you ever hear a more beautiful or sublime saying than that?"

It is hard to ascribe more than a temporary, wine-begotten, seriousness to this rhodomontade of hysterical passion. But one remembers Shelley's lines,

> On the brink of the night and the morning
> My coursers are wont to respire.

And they teach us that the thoughts of poets, however much they may owe to champagne, are not to be measured by our matter-of-fact yardsticks. The difference between him and George Sand consisted, I think, in this very seriousness of his rapturous moods. He transcribes his passing emotions; she is examining hers, not merely as they come, but as she voluntarily adjusts them under her vision, for the purposes of comparing and judging, as she might colors of ribbons to match a bonnet. Not that she does this consciously, but in a state of slight hypnosis, induced by the passes and counterpasses of her literary absorption. Musset expressed the difference between them a little crudely but not without truth: "I work all day long, and by night I have composed ten lines and drunk a bottle of brandy: She!—she has drunk two quarts of milk and written half a volume." The opposition, not merely in the liquid itself but in its mental and moral connotations, between brandy and milk, and in his seeking imaginative poetic truth, hard to be come at, and her pouring forth plausible and dramatic prose romance, is fair enough. So he goes on: "How I love you, Georgeot! What happiness there is in this sweet and elevated friendship which has remained between us two like the sweet perfume of your love!" His words become metaphysical, vague, maudlin perhaps, about this new life in himself. "I walk on the boulevards, to the opera, in the Bois de Boulogne, down the Champs-Élysées; isn't it strange and sweet, to walk still young in an old life? Tattet has come back. The dear boy says that *I present a new aspect to him*, those are his words. However, I drink as much champagne as before and that reassures him."

There are miserable details about money and material things; but they can not hinder for long these bursts of rhetorical emotion. His mind, owing possibly to champagne, is near the border of irrationability and therefore his letters are the more genuine; but with her, for she is perfectly sane, rhetoric has to play substitute to emotion, and for long it flows on like a spring freshet. She talks of temples, pedestals, eternal flames, crowns of thorns, tears of hope, hymns of happiness, mountain paths and God. Suddenly, in the midst of her fine rapture, she gives him excellent advice: "*Aime et écris c'est ta vocation, mon ami* [Love and write, that is your vocation, my friend]." But the reader is puzzled. Is Alfred, with his irrational emotion, merely obeying a subconscious desire to get her back? Is she, with her splendid easy flood of rhetoric, luring him on? She reminds him, after urging him to love again, that he has said that it was time for her to gather the fruit of a laborious life, and that a woman's last love is her best, and then she praises Pagello, but ends up, "Only tell me that you are happy and I shall be happy too." Is there method in her rhetoric? Is there method in his madness?

In the midst of this interplay of sentimental emotion, it is a diversion to come upon letters between the two young men: from Pagello to Alfred, and from Alfred to Pagello.

Venice, June 15, 1834.

Dear Alfred,

We have not written to one another yet, perhaps because neither of us wished to be the first. But that did not prevent that silent sympathy that shall always bind us together by ties which are sublime to us, though incomprehensible to others. I am so glad to hear that you are sound of body and strong in spirit. I have always prophesied favorably of your health, if you will only have the courage to resist those temptations to irregularities that are the consequence of your highly vi-

vacious nature. Whenever you are surrounded by a dozen
bottles of champagne, remember that jug of gum Arabic
water that I made you spew out at the Hotel Danieli, and
I am sure that you will have the fortitude to shun them.
Good-by, my dear Alfred, love me as I love you.

Your true friend, P. P.

Paris, July 11, 1834.

My dear Pietro Pagello,

It was very nice of you to write me a little note. I
say little, but it isn't little. And however small the
piece of paper that tells me of your friendship, it will
be most welcome at any hour of my life. Perhaps I can't
say the same about your recommendation about champagne, and I will not confess to the great "Pietro the
Saviour" how well founded a fit of remorse took hold
of me at that passage in your letter. And I promise you
that I shall never, never, drink again of that damnable
drink—without reproaching myself hugely.

George says that you are hesitating about coming with
her. You must come, *mon ami*, or not let her go. Three
hundred leagues are too long for a woman all alone. . . .
Come, and I promise to show you, if you would like to
see him, one of your best friends.

A. de M.

But Pagello had hindrances in his way: his father
deemed it imprudent to leave his practise and go to a
strange land, he blamed him for "living with a foreigner,
squandering his youth, ruining his career, publicly re-

nouncing the principles of Christian ethics that the best
of mothers had taught him," and so on; his old mistress
ranted; and he had no money. However, he got some
pictures that he hoped to sell for a good profit in Paris,
and he came. They went by the way of Milan. When she
could, George Sand, dressed as a man, got out of their
vehicle and walked. To her amazement, she met Antonio,
the perruquier, who had been sick in Paris and had come
back most of the way on foot, tattered and torn, but with
his hair so pomaded that she scented him from afar.
Antonio, as surprised as she, exclaimed "*Ah! par le sang
de Diane!*" In Switzerland they stopped for some mountain climbing. Then on again to Geneva. As the journey
proceeded poor Pagello found their relations becoming
cooler and more ceremonious. As he said afterward, she
was a little melancholy, and paid less and less attention
to him. "I perceived with sorrow that she was, under one
aspect, an actress well accustomed to these sorts of farce,
and the veil that had bandaged my eyes became transparent." The two arrived about the tenth of August.
She went to her apartment, 19 Quai Malaquais, he put up
at the Hôtel d'Orléans. Poor Pagello was at a disadvan-
tage. From the moment that he set foot in France, as
George Sand said, "he understood nothing." He did
not understand the language, he did not understand the
new friendship between George Sand and Musset, nor his
own relations to them. The curious gapers at notoriety
and scandal thought he was a strange wooer to have sup-
planted the poet. Connoisseurs turned up their noses at
his Italian pictures. Indeed *l'ami auquel tu m'as confiée,*

as she called him, "the angel of sweetness, goodness and devotion," began to molt his Venetian tranquillity and became suspicious, jealous and querulous.

George Sand and Alfred met, and it was plain that if the sublime pact of renunciation made in a moment of enthusiasm at Venice, was to be kept, Musset again must leave. He asked his mother for money and arranged to go to the Pyrenees; he admitted to George Sand that he had over-estimated his powers of self-restraint, but said that no one else should know why he was going away. He professed indifference to the judgment of *"Monsieur le Tout Puissant,"* but he writes her that though the effort will cost him dear, his own father from on high will not call him a coward when they meet. He would leave France and never return. Then self-pity swells up again: He writes, "I leave to-day forever; I go alone, without a companion, without a dog. I ask one hour of you and one last kiss. If you fear a moment's sorrow, if my demand displeases Pietro, do not hesitate to refuse. But if you have the courage, receive me alone, at your house, or elsewhere, as you like. . . . Let it not be a parting of an ordinary man and woman; rather a parting of two souls that have suffered, two suffering souls, two wounded eagles who meet in the sky and exchange a cry of pain before separating for ever. Our embrace shall be chaste as celestial love, deep as human sorrow. O my Bride, set softly on me the crown of thorns, and farewell. It will be a last remembrance of your child, who will be there no more for you to remember in your old age.

"ALFRED."

Another letter thanks her for saying yes, that she will grant his request. "You say I am mistaken in what I feel. No, I am not mistaken. I feel the only love of all my life. . . . I know it to be invincible, but invincible as it is, my will shall be invincible also. . . . *Ton enfant*, Alfred."

Pagello did not understand this behavior, he saw Musset very excited and he was disturbed. It was hard for him to grasp George Sand's theory that she regarded him as a sort of father and Alfred as their child. However, she explained it all to him, and he said he understood; and he consented that George and Alfred should meet alone for their parting. They passed two hours together: she left a kiss, as Alfred said, "as pure and chaste as her own fair soul" upon his forehead, and "their friendship was consecrated in the sight of God by the holy baptism of their tears," and it was to be "as immortal as God." As for him, his life was over, he was going to leave France for ever.

He went away on August twenty-fifth, not to the Pyrenees but to Baden. George Sand went to Nohant. Pagello stayed in Paris, poor, jealous and ill at ease. His Venetian ways, his gesticulations, his lively imagery, his habit of kissing men, matched badly his Parisian surroundings. He always used to speak to her of "our love for Alfred," but the very day that Alfred went away he read some words in Alfred's letter to her, or in hers to Alfred, and his thoughts ran riot, he imagined that she was complaining of him to Alfred, and so on. He did not understand that her grief when Alfred left was due, as she explained, not to parting from Alfred, but to the fear of losing her children, for her husband was bringing some legal proceeding to secure the right of possession of them. So Pagello became suspicious, unjust, acrimonious. George Sand, sending him an invitation, in which her husband joined, to pay them a visit at Nohant! Pagello did not accept. He turned for comfort to Alfred Tattet.

Paris, Sept. 6, 1834.

Mio caro Alfredo,

Your poor friend is in Paris. I asked for you at your house, but they told me that you were in the country. If I had had time I should have gone to give you a kiss, but as I am not going to stay long I send you this sheet. I don't know how many days I shall still remain in Paris. You know that I am constrained to obey my lean purse, and this has already ordered me to go. *Addio.* If I can see you in Paris I shall be fortunate; if I can't, send me back a kiss on a scrap of paper, Hôtel d'Orléans, No. 17, Rue des Petits-Augustins. *Addio*, my true, kind friend, *addio!*

Your affectionate friend,
Pietro Pagello.

Meanwhile Musset was fanning the flame of his passion. The company at Baden, men drinking and smoking, women dancing, the pleasant walks, the trees, the mountains on the horizon, all that cheered other visitors, was to him the abomination of desolation. He cursed the blue sky, he lost money at roulette, he sat in his room, drew her picture and set it on the table before him, and wrote her how his heart seethed and tossed and yearned for her.

Baden, September 1, 1834.

Ah, George! How I love you. . . . Don't you see, I am lost, drowned, sunk deep in love. I no longer know whether I live, eat, walk, breathe, speak; I know I love. O, I love you; you are my flesh, my blood! I am dying of love, of boundless love, I am lost in mad, desperate, nameless love! You are loved, adored, worshipped unto death! No, there is no remedy for me. None. I shall not try to live. . . .

O, my Bride, I ask one more request of you. Go out on a beautiful evening as the sun is setting, go into the country, sit down upon the grass under a green willow tree; look toward the west and think of your child who is going to die.

She wrote back in alarm: "You still love me too much, we must not see one another again. This is passion that you are uttering, but it is no longer the holy enthusiasm of your right-minded periods. It is no longer that un-alloyed friendship, which, as I thought, would gradually drift away from too lively expression. . . . My heart is turning to ice, and all I have just written you, all this wretchedness that I have disclosed, is so that, if we see one another again in Paris, you will not entertain any notion of our coming together again. We must part. . . . Farewell to the noble poem of our sacred friendship, farewell to the ideal tie formed between us three when you tore from him in Venice the confession of his love for me, and he swore to make me happy. Was all that then a romance? Nought but a dream, and I, poor silly child that I am, went on in belief and security! And you expect me, after this awakening, when I see that one of you *desires* me, and the other abandons me with vilification, still to believe in *sublime love!* Farewell, my poor child. Were it not for my children I should joyfully throw myself into the river!

G. S.

Baden, September 15, 1834.

George,

I think that I shall make a short visit to Paris. Write to me there if you write. [She it at Nohant.] But why? . . .

My going to Paris will be a shock to you perhaps, and to *him*, too. I confess I have finished handling people with gloves. If he suffers, let him suffer, this Venetian, who has taught me to suffer! I'll return his lesson! He gave me a masterly one. . . . By heaven, as I seal this letter, it seems that I seal my heart. I feel it crushed and turned to stone. Farewell!

A. de M.

CHAPTER XI

FIRES AND ASHES

On October 13, 1834, Musset was in Paris again; a few days later George Sand also went to Paris, and together they lived at her apartment, 19 Quai Malaquais. Poor Pagello slunk back to Venice, October twenty-eighth.

To Monsieur Alfred Tattet
13, Rue Grange Batalière, Paris

Paris, Oct. 23, 1834.

My dear Friend,

Before going, I send you another kiss. I entreat you never to say a word about my affair with George, I don't want a Vendetta. I go away feeling confident that I have behaved like a gentleman. That makes me forget my suffering and poverty. *Addio, mio angelo.* I will write you from Venice. *Addio, addio.*

Pietro Pagello.

However, Pagello had not wholly lost his time. George Sand had begged him, "no mother could have spoken with more affectionate good sense," to work at his profession. She introduced him to Buloz, who introduced him to doctors and procured him entrée into the Parisian hospitals. She sold his four pictures by Zuccarelli for twenty-five hundred francs, or said she had. He bought a box of surgical instruments and some medical books, paid his bills and went. But Pagello's fate was the most fortunate of the three. Musset's lyrical passion had depended on absence of possession, and the spoiled child of genius, undisciplined, unrestrained, beggared for the time of his nobler traits by his debauched habits, "mad in pursuit and in possession so," he turned the rose petals of his winged speech to thorns and nettles. The very day after the *bonheur rêvé et promis,* he accused her as of a crime for what had taken place in Venice. "Have we come to this?" she cried. "Oh, let me go. I wanted to go yesterday, my spirit had resolved upon an eternal farewell. Remember your desperation and all you said to make me believe that I was necessary to you, that without me you were lost; and so, once again, I was mad enough to wish to save you. But you are lost worse than before, for no sooner satisfied, than you turn your anger and despair against me. O God, what shall I do? Ah, I have had enough of life! What is it that you want, what do you ask? Already questionings, suspicions, recriminations, yes, already! Why ask me about Pietro, when I had forbidden you ever to speak to me of him? What right have you to cross-question me about Venice? Did I belong to you—*étais-je à toi*—in Venice? On the very first day, when you saw me sick, you were out of humour and said it was very vexatious to have a sick woman with you. And did not the breach between us date from that first day?"

So they wrangled. He, moody, suspicious, gross, fuddled perhaps by wine, was in the claws of green-eyed jealousy. He never had learned, he never had tried, to restrain his impulses, and he could not hold his savage, at times brutal, tongue. She, perhaps in part from pride and self-respect, in part because she saw that his outrageous questioning gave her the right to refuse to lift the veil, answered back with spirit. "At Venice I never allowed you to ask me the least detail, whether he and I had kissed, on such and such a day, upon the eyes or forehead; and I forbid you to enter into a phase of my life, over which I have the right to draw the curtain of modesty so far as you are concerned. The period in which we had become brother and sister was as chaste as if it had been a real relationship, and now that I have become your mistress again, you have no right to tear down the veil round Pietro and me; it is my duty to keep it up. Do you think that if Pietro had asked me for the secrets of our pillow, I would have told him? . . . Alas! Alas! Why did you not understand my repugnance to take up this fatal bond? Did I not foretell what would happen? Did I not foresee that you would suffer from this past, which went to your head like a beautiful poem when I refused myself to you, and now, that you have seized me again as if I were your prey, is become a nightmare to you? Let me go. We are fated to be more unhappy than ever. If I am as loose-lived, as perfidious, as you seem to say, why do you rage so to take me and keep me?"

And he, poor plaything of his passions, ranted with jealousy and then burst into self-reproaches and cries of devotion: "O my child! O my soul! I have laid burdens on you, I have wearied you, when I ought to pass my days and nights at your feet, waiting for a tear to drop from your beautiful eyes, to drink it, when I ought to look at you without a word, when I ought to rock your grief gently like a darling child. . . . I love you as no man ever loved . . . O God, if I were to lose you! My poor wits are going. Punish me, my child, I deserve your anger, banish me from your presence for a time. . . . Forgive, forgive, O my Life, my Supreme Good, I ask it on my knees.''

So they turned from each other with revilings, and again they threw their arms around each other's necks. At times Alfred is half delirious: ''Happiness! Happiness! then death, or death and happiness together! You forgive me, O my Soul, you shall be happy. Yes, before God, happy with me. . . . To-night. To-night!'' And that same day, unable to settle her thoughts, she writes him a long letter of love, of doubts, of apprehensions, and ends, ''do you want me to come at ten o'clock?'' Passion and satiety, endearments and quarrels, talks of separation, cries of despair. He fell ill of a fever. George Sand dressed as a servant, with cap and apron, and went to the Musset apartment and watched over him again like a mother. Once more passion flamed into white heat and died down exhausted. His discontent in her company became worse and worse, aversion, outbursts of anger, of cold and contemptuous raillery, and then the revulsion of tears, of behavior and protestations of love. But the breach came.

Poor woman, in spite of her rhetoric, in spite of her habitual subordination of emotion to literature, at last, and perhaps for the first time, certainly more than ever before, she was deep in love. She cut off her long black hair, her woman's glory, and sent it to him. With no one to confide in, she wrote her thoughts in her diary: "You love me no more, no more. That is easy to see. Last night when you left me, I was really sick. You knew it, and yet you went away. That was right. You were tired. But to-day not a word. You have not even sent to ask about me and I have hoped for you and waited minute by minute from eleven o'clock in the morning till midnight. What a day! Every ring of the bell made me leap. Thank God, my heart is physically weak. Oh, if I could only die. You still love me with your senses, more than ever so; I, too. I had never loved you, nor any man, like that. But I love you, too, with all my soul; but you, you have not even friendship for me. I wrote a note to you to-night. You haven't answered. They said that you had gone out; but you must have gone home very late; Goodness! where were you! Alas, it is at an end; you don't love me at all. If I stay here you will think me abject and odious. Besides you want me to go. You said the other night with an air of incredulity, 'Bah, you won't go.' You are in a hurry to have me go. Be easy, I shall go within a few days, and we shall never meet again. Forgive me for having made you suffer. Nobody in the world is more unhappy than I."

Just what happened, one can only guess.

On November twelfth, Musset wrote to Alfred Tattet:

"*Mon cher ami,* All is over.... *A vous de cœur,*" and to Sainte-Beuve: "I am very grateful for the interest you

take in me and the person of whom we spoke to-day, under
these sad circumstances. It is impossible for me, under
any pretext whatever, to maintain any relations with her,
whether by writing or otherwise. I hope that her friends
will not imagine they see in this resolution any intentional
rudeness to her, nor any design to find any fault with
her whatever. If any one is to be blamed in this matter,
it is I, who in a most illogical weakness consented to inter-
views that as you said yourself were very dangerous.
Madame Sand is informed of my intention and if it was
she who asked you to tell me not to see her again, I confess I do not understand her motive for doing so very
well, since I refused positively last night to let her in my
house. . . . *A vous de cœur,* A. de M.''

George Sand sought distraction at the opera. People
about her recognized her, and she could hear their remarks. ''There's George Sand! You don't say! Where?''
One old lady said, ''Well, well, in spite of her get-up
she has a quite respectable air!'' A gentleman, waist-
coated like a diplomat, examined her through his eye-
glasses. ''Why, she's really pretty!'' In a seat near by,
Buloz, the editor of the *Revue des Deux Mondes*, dozed.
People trod on his overcoat, on his hat, at last on his feet;
he woke; ''*Sacré nom de Dieu,*'' and dozed off again. In
the daytime she sat to Delacroix for her portrait, she
smoked cigarettes and they chatted. Delacroix showed
her his collection of Goyas, talked of Musset, and he
said that Musset would have made a great painter if
he had wanted to and he asked leave to copy sketches

in Musset's sketch book. She confided her sorrows to him. He bade her not fight against them. "Let yourself go," he said. "When I am so, I do not pretend to be proud, I wasn't born a Roman, I just give way to my despair." This seemed to her good advice and she poured her heart out in her *Journal*. Should she go to his house and pull his bell rope till he opened the door? Or should she lie on his threshold? Should she fling her arms round his neck and say, "You feel love for me still, you suffer from it, you are ashamed of it, but you are too sorry for me not to love me. You see that I love you, that I can love nobody but you. Kiss me . . . say some sweet words." And so her thoughts kept on revolving about her passion, which had been kindled afresh by loss and quickened by vanity, and she found relief by writing them down in her *Journal*, as if she were composing a novel. She felt the need of a strong arm, of an unselfish heart, to protect and comfort her.

Musset, the poet, the beautiful flower, that sweet fragrance that had intoxicated her, was gone, but there were other men. The charming and gifted Franz Liszt, in the freshness of youth and early triumph, she saw familiarly. They used to talk together. Liszt was very religious-minded, and told her that God alone deserved to be loved. She replied, "That may be so, but it is very difficult to love God when once you have loved a man." Liszt seems to have been a little embarrassed, for he added that he had never felt a very keen sympathy for anybody but for Lamennais, the religious reformer, and that he should never entertain an earthly love. Heinrich Heine, also

one of the coterie, was of quite a different way of thinking—she talked of love with him too—he said that love
was a thing of the head and of the senses and had little
to do with the heart. But Heine had married a little shop-
girl and loved her dearly. Not getting much help from
them she turned to her own sex. Madame Allart said that
a woman had to be sly with men and pretend to be angry
in order to win them back. But as usual Sainte-Beuve
was the most sympathetic of all. On November twenty-
fifth, the same day as the entry in her *Journal* she writes
a desperate letter to Sainte-Beuve: "I go out, I try to
distract my attention, I shake myself, but when I come
back into my room, I am crazy again. Yesterday, in spite
of myself, my legs carried me to his house. Luckily he
was not at home. I know that he is angry and hard when
he speaks of me. I don't know what he accuses me of, nor
with whom. This injustice eats out my heart. It is terrible to part for such reasons. . . . Oh, oh, *mon Dieu*, bid
me kill myself; there is nothing else left to do." She
asked Sainte-Beuve what love was, and he answered, "It
is made up of tears; if you weep, you love," and advised her to devote herself to seek distraction. But at the
theater, in man's dress, with her hair cut off, her cheeks
lean and her eyes hollow, she was filled with jealousy at
the pretty girls she saw. She seems to have caught from
Musset the poignant pleasure of torturing her nerves with
regrets and imaginings, and then she learned that Musset
may have coupled her name and Liszt's. Buloz advised
her to refuse to see Liszt; but the notion merely made her
write down in her *Journal* that "M. Liszt only thinks of

the Virgin Mary, who is not at all like me." Mind and body struggle in passionate remonstrance against her fate. She might be Phèdre speaking: "Spirits of celestial wrath, what fever have you poured into my veins? What harm have I done to the angels in heaven that they descend upon me and instil in me for punishment a she lion's love? Why has my blood turned to fire, and why, at the door of death, have I felt embraces more ravishing than men's? . . . What shall become of me, far from you, if this flame continues to scorch me? If I can not spend a night without crying for you and twisting on my bed, what shall I do when I have lost you for ever?" The heat of her mood carries her along like Mazeppa's horse; in the *Journal* you can hear the gallop of his hoofs, and her poor, naked body beating the ground. Even before she met Musset she had written: "To desire with no hope is a torture that outweighs all the bitterness that the disasters of life can bring." She was then meditating upon the disloyalty of Sandeau, and now her passion was a hundredfold increased. But the stormiest seas die down, and the memory of the most violent tempest is lost upon the level brine. She dropped in upon a friend and there she met Jules Sandeau. He came toward her simply, naturally, respectfully and quite unembarrassed. They entered into explanations. She referred to what he was reported to have said against her, that she had been angry, but believed the stories exaggerated and probably some of his strictures had been justified. He denied ever having said a word against her. He also asserted that he had not joined certain persons who had attacked her,

PORTRAIT OF MADAME EDMÉE DE MUSSET
From the drawing by Alfred de Musset

PAUL DE MUSSET

and gave proof of this. So they smoked cigarettes, talked of other things, while she warmed her toes and their host made puns. They parted in friendly fashion. She told him that it was impossible to see each other for fear of gossip, but should they meet she begged him to come up and give her a friendly how-do-you-do. She recorded in her *Journal*: "I am glad that I met Sandeau. It is dreadful to quarrel after one has been lovers. Dear me, what is love that changes its nature so much and takes on so divine a form in a new object? Perhaps there is only one true love in all this. Which was it in my life? Was it Aurelien? He is the fairest in my heart. But love, without corporeal union, is mystic and incomplete. Ah, yes, the first is the noblest and purest, the last the most involuntary, the most unhealable. It is the last one that is killing me. Ah, must I die so young? If I could but love Jesus as nuns do!"

But on both sides the violence of their emotions had been too great to subside wholly. In December Musset wrote her *une petite lettre assez affecteuese*. On January 13, 1835, she wrote to Tattet that they had become lovers again, and took the blame of their separation upon herself. But the fundamental differences between the two broke out again. Her *Journal*, quite different from many of her letters, bears the note of truth. She writes in it: "Let no one speak to me. I wish to kiss the earth and weep. I don't love you, but I adore you always. I don't want you any more, but I can't get on without you. . . . Farewell; stay, go, only never say that I do not suffer. Only that could make me suffer more, my only Love, my

Life, my Bowels, my Brother, my Blood, go, go, but kill me first." All was vain. Parting was inevitable. She feared a scene, and stole away on March 6, 1835, leaving a letter for him.

"No, no, enough, enough! Poor, unhappy fellow. I have loved you like a son. Mine is a mother's love; and I am still bleeding for it. I am sorry for you, I forgive all, but we must part. I do not know how to engage in strife. God made me gentle and yet proud. My pride is now broken, and my love is become pity. I tell you, we must get over this. Sainte-Beuve is right. Your behaviour is deplorable, impossible. O God, to what sort of a life am I leaving you? Drunkenness, wine, harlots, again and so on always. But since I can do nothing to save you from them, must I prolong this torture for you and shame for me? My tears irritate you. And in the midst of it all comes your mad jealousy, starting at a straw. The less right you have to be jealous, the more jealous you become! It seems like God's punishment on your poor head." So they parted; and from then on, unless the *Nuit d'Octobre*, or the *Merle Blanc* may be deemed exceptions, no angry words were spoken, no bitter accusations, no casting the blame from self to the other, no rancor, no controversy, troubled the memory of the past. The vulgar series of attacks and counter-attacks came after Musset's death. For a time they wrote occasionally to each other, friendly letters. In 1837 they spent several hours together in "fraternal intimacy," and in 1840 they correspond again as to what should be done with their love-letters. Passion, love, friendship, were

gone; but without a knowledge of George Sand, without
an understanding of their episode that dominated his
emotional and intellectual life, it is impossible to know
Alfred de Musset.

CHAPTER XII

Rouée, rusée, calculatrice, as a French critic calls her, George Sand retires to a remote background of our stage, where she writes multitudinous novels and encounters many new amorous adventures. Alfred de Musset went back to his old life, in which no doubt *le vin et les filles* were always at hand. But for the time being not to excess. A change had taken place within him. Under the heat of passion and grief, the seeds of his poetical genius had ripened and germinated. The products of his pen during the year are satisfactory evidence that he must have given more time to work and less to dissipation than in any other year. At the same time he became more and more self-centered, more and more indifferent, to the outer word, to politics, to Balzac's novels, to Victor Hugo's dramas and romances, to what Merimée or Gautier was writing. He frequented his friends but with less *brio*; Alton-Shée, Major Frazer and others wished to get him elected into the Jockey Club, but finding that there would be opposition did not nominate him. Musset did not care; he did not care for anything except his grief and his work. The Romantic movement bored him. He describes his opinion about it: Madame de Staël introduced the masterpieces of German literature to France, and the French world of letters divided into two and went to buffets; the old men, conservative, had continued in old ways and had no vigor except for quarrel-

142

ing, while the young men were hot to raise France to her ancient place among the literatures of Europe; fatigue succeeded to the violence of the combat; the two parties no longer fought over ideas, but over words; they wrangled about books, then over pages, paragraphs, sentences, then over the punctuation of the cæsura. How bored the thought of it all made him now. He kept to himself. His friend Tattet asked him what this seclusion and meditation were going to produce, and Alfred explained himself. A memory, he said, had been blinding him, and he had striven to shake it off. He had asked of grief all the questions that grief could answer, he had drunk his own salt tears, and now he felt himself stronger than grief, and had slipped his neck out of the yoke of the past. "This very day," he said, "with my own hands, I have nailed my youth, my idleness and my vanity, in their coffin. I feel that my thought, like a plant watered and tended, has drawn enough sap from the earth to spread its flowers in the sun. I think that I shall soon speak, for there is something in my soul that asks to come forth."

A great deal did come forth; the harvest was rich: *La Confession d'un enfant du siècle, Barberine, Le Chandelier, A Lucie, A Madame X (Belle Emilie), La Nuit de Mai, La Loi sur la Presse, La Nuit de Décembre.* Was it due directly to his grief, or, indirectly, in that grief kept him from company and dissipation and gave him time to work? *La Confession* had the special merit of compelling him to dwell upon himself, upon his memory of George Sand, upon his grief, and upon that glorious mood of magnanimity which had flared up, if not for long, at least with so much brilliance, the mood that gave him strength to be faithful to his promise that he would erect an altar to her memory, and he performed that promise. He depicted her, Brigitte Pierson, the heroine of his story, as charming, kind, tender, modest, and altogether in the right in her unhappy relations with her stormy lover, Octave, even at the end when she transfers her affection to Smith, who represents Pietro Pagello. The interest in the plot lies in this: that, although the setting is pure fiction, Alfred has tried to keep the moral values true; Sainte-Beuve analyzed the plot as follows:

Octave, born in 1810, is nineteen years old when the story begins and twenty-one when it ends. He belonged to the generation that came too late for the Empire, too late for the Restoration, and spent its adolescence amid the universal conflict of ideas, and the fragments of all beliefs. Octave is in love. He accepts love with naif trust and adoration, and so far he is like lovers of all generations. But at the rosiest of his dream, sitting opposite his mistress at supper, his fork happened to drop. He stooped to pick it up and saw—what? His mistress's foot resting on the foot of his best friend.

The awakening was frightful. Octave immediately catches the *maladie du siècle,* as one used to catch the smallpox. He quits his mistress, fights a duel with his friend and is wounded. When recovered, he flings himself into debauchery until his father's death pulls him out of it. Residing in the country, he sees there a sweet simple lady, older than himself, but still lovely, rather pious and distinctly mysterious, Madame Brigitte Pierson. He falls in love with her; she with him. Then follow a thousand charming details, walks in the wood, first with innocence, then with passion. He seemed cured of his old ways, happy and settled; but the old wound of debauch opens again, bleeds in the breast of happiness and corrupts him. The singular fashion, capricious and cruel, by which he destroys his own dream of happiness, and hers, is admirably depicted.

After many painful scenes, when a permanent reconciliation seems sealed for ever, and Brigitte Pierson consents to forget everything, to cut loose from the past, and travel far away with him for a long time, a third person appears, the virtuous Smith, who involuntarily falls in love with Brigitte and makes her love him. Octave notices this, questions them, discovers Brigitte's great unhappiness, realizes that his repeated blows of unkindness have killed her love, and that she has only a sense of duty left. He hesitates; he nearly stabs her but kindly feelings prevail. He withdraws and effaces himself with self-abnegation.

Such a novel, as Musset himself says, is not satisfactory; it is not true enough for memoirs, nor false enough for fiction, and the reader can not expect to find a literal revelation of the tragicomedy of the two passionate lovers, but he does find, rather to his surprise, that Musset has behaved like a gentleman, that he has taken all the blame upon himself and held his lady up to admiration. The book opens with a long passage of brilliant prose that describes the *mal du siècle;* but apart from that the modern reader is likely to find the story tedious. As for Al-

fred, himself, the book had a beneficial effect, it contrib-
uted to his peace of mind by his consciousness that he was
playing a magnanimous rôle such as he delighted to see
himself in, and through his peace of mind it brought him
to his first great achievement, the poem *La Nuit de Mai.*

His passion for George Sand had ebbed away completely, there was peace after war, port after stormy seas,
the poet felt his health of mind and body restored, he
counted his years, the number of them was but twenty-
four, he opened his throat and sang as the bird sings.
*"Il me semble que je vais bientôt parler et que j'ai quel-
que chose dans l'âme qui demande à sortir."* Paul tells
how the poem came to him. In the very beautiful month
of May, while the air was soft and the flowers opening
their tender eyes, the young poet was strolling in the
Tuileries Gardens under the wide-spreading chestnut
trees, and there, as he sauntered along, strophes of a dialogue between his Muse and himself came into his mind.
The next day he kept leaving the family circle to write
a few verses; that night he shut himself in his room, and
had his supper served there, as if he had a rendezvous
with his Muse, and he lighted a dozen candles in her honor.
No one was allowed to come in:

> Peace, ho!—the moon sleeps with Endymion,
> And would not be awaked.

By the morning he had finished; he blew out the candles
and went to bed. On reading it over, he found nothing
that he wished to alter.

THE MUSE SPEAKS

Poète, prends ton luth, et me donne un baiser;
La fleur de l'églantier sent ses bourgeons éclore.
Le printemps naît ce soir; les vents vont s'embraser,
Et la bergeronnette, en attendant l'aurore,
Aux premiers buissons verts commence à se poser..
Poète, prends ton luth, et me donne un baiser.

Poet, take your lute and give a kiss to me;
The eglantine's flower feels its blossoms unfold,
To-night the Spring is born; the breezes take fire,
And the early bird, while waiting for the dawn,
Upon the first green bush is hovering to alight.
Poet, take your lute and give a kiss to me.

The poet becomes aware of a veiled presence, whose foot
glides over the grass with flowers pied. The Muse speaks
again:

Ecoute! tout se tait; songe à la bien aimée.
Ce soir, tout va fleurir; l'immortelle nature
Se remplit de parfums, d'amour et de murmure,

Listen, all is still: dream of your best beloved:
To-night, all buds are burst; immortal nature
Fills herself full of fragrance, of whisperings and love.

Again the Poet asks himself why his heart beats so fast,
and yet he perceives no one. The Muse speaks again:

Poète, prends ton luth; le vin de la jeunesse
Fermente cette nuit dans les veines de Dieu.
Mon sein est inquiet; la volupté l'oppresse.

Poet, take your lute, to-night the wine of youth
Seethes in the veins of God. My heart,
Under the burden of desire, beats restlessly.

Ah! je t'ai consolé d'une amère souffrance!
Hélas! bien jeune encore, tu te mourais d'amour.

Ah, I have eased you of a bitter pain,
Alas, still far too young you nearly died for love.

Then the Poet perceives the vision is his Muse. She saw
that he suffers and she has come to weep with him,

Quelque amour t'est venu, comme on en voit sur terre,
Une ombre de plaisir, un semblant de bonheur,

A love has come to you, such as loves are on earth,
A shadow of a joy, a phantom of delight.

She is come to pluck him from idleness, and urges him to
come with her to some land of high romance and write
poetry. She knows the sacred wound he suffers from,

Rien ne nous rend si grands qu'une grande douleur,

Nothing makes man so great of heart as a great grief,
and the most beautiful songs are those born of deep despair, sobbed into immortality:

Les plus désespérés sont les chants les plus beaux,
Et j'en sais d'immortels qui sont de purs sanglots.

Then she recites the legend of the pelican feeding its
young from blood of its own breast; that, she says, is
what the great poets do,

Poète, c'est ainsi que font les grands poètes.

But he tells her that she asks him too soon, that he has suffered so, that if he essayed to sing his sorrow would break his lute.

In this poem Musset has found himself. The deep emotions that he had passed through have changed him, as he said to George Sand, from a boy to a man, they have lifted the clever apprentice, the brilliant versifier, the disciple of Byron, to the top of Mt. Helicon, and crowned him with the laurel crown. He has discovered that the notes in his compass are best suited for his own old emotions, or, perhaps the discovery should be stated inversely, that his own old emotions offered the best material for his talents. Such a discovery implied that those memories were cool enough to be handled without pain. He brooded over them and then sang, like the bard in *Wilhelm Meister,*

> *Ich singe, wie der Vogel singt,*

and like him Musset found that

> *Das Lied, das aus der Kehle dringt*
> *Ist Lohn, der reichlich lohnet.*

And so, to obtain such reward of his singing, he sang. That same spring he wrote the elegy, *Lucie*, which contains the lines that after his death were carved on his tomb and caused his admirers to plant a weeping willow beside it:

> *Mes chers amis, quand je mourrai,*
> *Plantez un saule au cimetière,*

J'aime son feuillage éploré,
La pâleur m'en est douce et chère,
Et son ombre sera légère
A la terre où je dormirai.

O my dear Friends, when I shall die,
Pray plant a willow by my grave,
  I love its drooping leaves that weep,
Its sweet and tender pallid hue;
Its shadow there will lightly lie
  Upon the earth where I shall sleep.

The furious emotions that he had been through, as I say, had been succeeded by a calm favorable for work, and he found work pleasant, quite apart from the need of making money. His poems were dependent upon his moods, but his stories and his little plays, comedies or proverbs, were part of the business of a professional writer, and with Buloz jogging his elbow he was regular and laborious. He wrote *La Quenouille de Barberine* and the *Chandelier*, two comedies. Whatever Musset wrote as a work of art he gave to it a shape, a grace, a courtesy that only he could give. The French admire the *Chandelier*, which is supposed to refer to an experience of the poet, but simple folk acquainted with the parson of their parish, who live within the ringing of the church bell, usually subordinate their esthetic sensibilities to an ethical judgment; for while the author condemns adultery with a popinjay of an officer, because he is a popinjay, he approves it with a mawkishly sentimental apprentice, because of the mawkish sentimentality. What has the Seventh Commandment to do with a work of art? Nothing. Nevertheless, when the play was put upon the stage, the Minister of the Interior suppressed it. *La Quenouille de Barberine*, on the contrary, is most correct; it shows a wooer caught in his own snare. In both plays there is an April-day charm that enables the English reader to understand what French writers mean when they call Musset "a child of Shakespeare," for one can hear, faint and of no great range, yet delicate and clear, the "native woodnotes wild."

That summer, also, the poet, contrary to his custom of complete indifference to political doings, was stirred by a severe law curtailing the freedom of the press, and wrote the poem, *La Loi sur la Presse*. I think there is little interest in it, other than the refreshment of finding him moved by an emotion in no wise erotic. It also affords good evidence that the storm of his companionship with George Sand had subsided.

In fact there are many proofs that that mouth-filling passion, that seemed to border upon delirium, and expressed itself as Manfred or Lara might be supposed to express themselves in French, had wholly passed into a quiet limbo or mental garret, where, when needed for literary purposes, it might readily be found. And I may as well submit some more of these proofs now. For instance: his friend Tattet was in Baden, as he had been, and like him sick for love of a lady:

July 21, 1835

My dear Alfred

. . . As to your question about Mme. X. I think that the best thing I can say to you, is that about eight or nine

months ago, I was in the very situation that you are,
going about all day cursing the bluest sky in the world and
all good things. I was drawing from memory the picture
of my faultless lady, I lived upon discontent, cigars and
money lost at roulette. I believed that all was over for
me forever, that I should never recover from it. Alas!
Alas! How completely I have recovered! My hair has
grown again upon my head, courage again fills my liver,
indifference lies in my heart. . . . The same will happen
to you, old Boy. And when you are cured, be sure that
you will not be sorry. . . *Je suis à vous*

A. de M.

The *"Sainte blessure* made by the black Seraphim"
has certainly ceased to smart. Another proof is offered
by the vision, brief but charming, of Suzon, a girl to whom
he wrote a song about this date, as we may infer from the
fact that it refers to his travels in Italy:

> *Bonjour, Suzon, ma fleur des bois!*
> *Es-tu toujours la plus jolie?*
> *Je reviens, tel que tu me vois,*
> *D'un grand voyage en Italie.*
> *Du paradis j'ai fait le tour;*
> *J'ai fait des vers, j'ai fait l'amour.*
>   *Mais que t'importe?*
> *Je passe devant ta maison:*
>   *Ouvre ta porte*
>   *Bonjour, Suzon!*

Good morrow, my wild flower, Sue,
The loveliest is always you.
I have come home, such as you see,
From traveling far in Italy.

I've made the tour of Heaven above,
I have made poems, I have made love.
    What's that to you?
And now I pass your house before,
    Open the door;
    Good morrow, Sue.

To Suzon, too, there is a second poem:

Que notre amour, si tu m'oublies,
Suzon, dure encore un moment;
Comme un bouquet de fleurs pâlies,
Cache-le dans ton sein charmant.

Ah, let our love, though you forget,
Suzon, persist a moment yet;
Like fading flowers laid to rest,
Hide them on your charming breast.

The story of Suzon is this. The poet went into the country to stay with some friends of Uncle Desherbiers. He was in the glamour of his young renown, he was charming and he charmed, and lightly made verses to lovely ladies, and charged them with expressions of more permanence than the love that they expressed. He flirted too easily. One young girl was so drawn toward him, that she went by night to his room, all in white, with a full blown rose in her fair hair. She held out her lips, nature leading her by the hand. The poet fell upon his knees before her, he praised her fair hair, but did not touch it, he smelled the rose petals but did not scatter them. He took her hand, spoke wise words to her soul and yet for a week (so the story runs), night after night, she came back; but his chivalry held firm,

Adieu, le bonheur reste au gîte . . .

Suzon was not the only feminine evidence that Musset's
heart was not in mourning.   Ninon, another vision, appears by the poet's side for a time, more corporeal than
Suzon, but also veiled in the charm of the half-seen.   Paul
is our authority; but Paul was not only a *romancier* with
a romantic pride in Alfred's *affaires de cœur,* he was like-
wise advocate with a brief for *Lui,* in the *cause célèbre* of
Elle contre Lui, that arose after Alfred's death, and he
also had what the prejudiced Anglo-Saxon regards as the
Latin indifference to truth.   But Paul is positive in his
statements; and Alfred's story of *Emmeline* is confirma-
tion enough.   Here is the story.   A lady spoke some ambiguous words to Alfred, and accompanied them with a less
ambiguous smile.   The suspicious poet, *"brouillé avec
l'amour,"* imagined that the lady was trying to use him
as a screen to conceal a more solid inclination, or as he
put it, that she and another were conspiring against his
peace of mind.   He complained.   The lady exculpated
herself: she said that she had not sought to inspire love,
but avowed this in such a way that she disclosed that
she felt it.   This put Alfred "in an embarrassing position."   However, he accepted the situation bravely; and
one morning while strolling down the Rue de Buci—these
are details that Paul puts in to convey an assurance of
fact—he suddenly exclaimed aloud, so that passers-by
heard him: *"Si je vous le disais pourtant que je vous
aime* [And yet, suppose I said that I love you]?"   And on
his return home, using this as the first line, he wrote the

charming poem *A Ninon*. He handed the verses to the lady with theatrical circumstance. *Aveux complets* soon followed. The lover's happiness, *le bonheur de l'amoureux*, lasted three weeks. Then, as Paul says, the poison that Alfred had drunk at Venice the year before, rose to his lips. "After a stormy week there was a rupture." Paul hints, rather than declares, that the fault was the woman's because of her lack of necessary sweetness and patience; but ardent advocates sometimes make too great claims for their clients. Letters, little gifts, faded flowers, were returned to their respective senders. Alfred, who took somewhat the same view of the way a woman should behave to him that Paul did, asked, "by what fatality he had encountered the only woman in the world capable of such hard cruelty?" But after a time the two agreed to be friends, nothing more. Alfred was enraged that the lady adhered to the agreement. Then, knowing her weakness for poetry, he wrote a second poem, *A Ninon,* and sent it by post—another of Paul's details to secure credence. The lady, fatally accessible to the charm of poetry, sent back the picture of a dial with its hands pointing to three o'clock. But before the end of two more weeks some gentleman with rights to jealousy had discovered the secret. Alfred learned that he was not only making this man *malheureux*, but that he would also cause *un catastrophe inévitable* and, therefore, at the lady's wish, he withdrew, and then, rigging it out in decent disguise, he told the tale in his story of *Emmeline*, which was duly published a little later in the *Revue des Deux Mondes*. The whole episode sounds a little like an echo of the earlier and greater tragicomedy; in this, as in that, Alfred is for a time sustained by the *grandeur de son sacrifice*, but though at first he was content with giving "an example of suffering nobly borne," he soon relapsed into querulousness, and asked what reason he had to live. Paul describes the scene: "I saw him dreaming of all he had lost, humouring himself with his grief. He plunged in it as deep as he could, for he preferred suffering to ennui. I represented to him that he was in danger of making his ill incurable. He answered: 'It is incurable.'"

On the first of December of that year Alfred de Musset also published the second of the *Nuits, La Nuit de Décembre,* another beautiful poem in which a *faible femme, orgueilleuse, insensée*, who has forgotten her eternal vows of constancy, is apostrophized as

> *Ah! pauvre enfant, qui voulez être belle,*
> *Et ne savez pas pardonner!*

The ordinary reader of the *Nuits,* furnished with some knowledge of the George Sand episode, would assume that the poet refers to her, and most of the commentators assert that he does, but Paul states most positively that Alfred refers to the Ninon of the poems, the Emmeline of the story, and not to George Sand. The other commentators regard this statement of Paul as convincing proof of his mendacity. There seems to be fair grounds for disagreeing with both views. The grievance of being abandoned by a faithless love was very dear to Musset; he clung to all his emotions of self-pity, whatever the episode that had engendered them, stored them indiscriminately as they came in a heap together in his heart, ready for use in plays, poems or stories. He was one of the most subjective of men-of-letters, and was far more absorbed in the effect produced upon him by broken faith, than in the individuality of the troth-breaker. George Sand was not the only one of these offenders, nor the first. There was an earlier treacherous leman, to whom he refers several times, as in the *Nuit de Mai*, for instance, and at great length in *La Confession d'un enfant du siècle*. Who this sinner was is uncertain, but a man of letters, himself a member of the *Académie Française* in due course, a man a dozen years younger than Musset, Maxime du Camp, saw such a woman many years afterward, and characterized her as the woman who first started Alfred de Musset on the path of debauchery—the Monna Belcolor (the seductrice in *La Coupe et les Lèvres*) who said to him, *"Monte à cheval et viens souper chez moi."* I quote his words: "I knew that person, already aged but always beautiful, proud of her title and of her big lackeys, white, sinuous in spite of her heavy figure, contemplating her own little hand, of which she was in love, a fallen divinity, a sort of shameless Cybele, her laughter spreading wide over her red lips—it was difficult to endure the boldness of her expression when she looked at you with her great black eyes, which are black with the blackness of hell."

The pains these famous ladies inflicted upon the poet were of very much the same character; and I repeat, when he came to put these preserved painful emotions to literary uses, it was no matter which particular woman had caused them. What he cared for was to recall the pain again in all its original intensity. Moreover any attack on George Sand, in December, 1835, was quite inconsistent with the building of an altar to her, upon which he was engaged at that very time; and the words I have cited do not, in any justice, apply to her, for just before the final separation in March, 1835, she says to him, *"je te pardonne tout"* and *"mon orgueil est brisé à present."* With a man like Musset, whose unstable emotions were often quickened by drink, it is idle to search too nicely for the *causa causans* of any particular emotion, or of the words in which it is expressed; the emotional disturbance within him seeks relief by the first outlet at hand, and like a flood of lava seething up in old craters broken open a hundred years before, it pours out into familiar channels of self-pity, regardless of the times or causes that originally engendered it.

CHAPTER XIII

Among the great poetical figures in France, from 1830 to 1840, time has decreed the first place to Victor Hugo, for his puissance, his vast variety, his eloquence and mastery of words; the second place to Lamartine; but at the time many set Lamartine the higher, and one of these was Alfred de Musset. The delicate beauty of Lamartine's poems, *Les Méditations,* which center about a very profound emotion for a lost love, called forth the best that was in him; Lamartine's passion, purified from all that is earthly by its religious effulgence and saved from tenuity by its intensity, caught his imagination; and the young poet said to himself, my love for her would have been like that, had she but been more worthy.

In the month of February, 1836, he reread the *Méditations,* and, under the influence of his reading, he composed the *Lettre à Lamartine,* which all agree is one of his master poems. This poetical epistle begins by reminding Lamartine that in his youth he had written a poem to Byron, *le prince des proscrits,* and he modestly suggests this as a precedent that justified his writing to Lamartine. Then he proceeds to tell the reason for his writing: he needs sympathy, he must speak out his woe, and therefore turns to one who knows the glory, the sacredness and sorrow of love. He will tell Lamartine, the lover of Elvire, the singer of sorrow, that he, too, has suffered the same glorious pain. He refers to his love and happiness,

159

to his pain and misery, and then preludes the tale of
the "*jour fatal*" by a famous comparison of the laborer
who comes home to find his house burned down and his
wife dead:

> *Lorsque le laboureur, regagnant sa chaumière . . .*

with that he recounts his own experience:

> *Lorsque abandonné d'une infidèle amante,*
> *Pour la première fois j'ai connu la douleur,*
>   *. . . . .*
> *O mon unique amour! que vous avais-je fait?*
> *Vous m'aviez pu quitter, vous qui juriez la veille*
> *Que vous étiez ma vie et que Dieu le savait?*
>   *. . . . .*
> *O toi qui sais aimer, réponds, amant d'Elvire,*
> *Comprends-tu que l'on parte et qu'on se dise adieu?*
> *Comprends-tu que ce mot, la main puisses l'écrire,*
> *Et le cœur le signer, et les lèvres le dire,*
> *Les lèvres, qu'un baiser vient d'unir devant Dieu?*

What has he done that his Love should forsake him, and
the very day after she has sworn to be true? Can Lamartine, who knows what love is, can he understand how a
hand could write, a heart seal, and lips—lips united in
the sight of God—utter such false words?

This passage is always assumed by the commentation
to refer to George Sand. But, I repeat Musset's emotions
are more complex than that. His senses had been so often
excited, so often satiated, so often glutted, that they demanded ever sharper stimulants; simple pleasure was

no longer enough, it must be fortified with pain. The more poignant his sorrow, the more he hugged it, as a madman might love the Iron Maiden whose breast is armed with spikes. No doubt George Sand was the chief woman of his experience, she was indeed the most remarkable woman of her time; she had come to him in the May-day of his youth, when body, mind and soul demanded their shares in love. But, I repeat, the fountain of his emotions was fed by many springs. There had been the first lady who had used him as a screen, there had been the mysterious *Monna Belcolor* to whom Maxime du Camp refers, there had recently been Ninon. No, Alfred was not really mourning over the loss of George Sand; he was indulging himself in the poignant pleasure of whipping his emotions, like recumbent beasts, into active fury. He had indeed suffered, he had greatly suffered; but nature had endowed him with the power of forgetting, with the lotus flower of indifferency, with a kind of tortoise-shell callousness, toward the heroines who had made their exits from his stage. They bow and go; but he always remains at the center, the cynosure of his own eyes, and as he can play but one rôle, and needs a mistress to kneel to, he immediately takes Sorrow for the part, Sorrow enhanced by champagne and decked out in all sorts of screen-lady—Monna Belcolor—Ninon—George Sand—attributes. The proof that this grief of his, depicted so eloquently in the *Lettre à Lamartine* is, if not wholly, at least in great part, wilful, hallucinatory and literary, lies close at hand. In this very month of February, while he is brooding over the amorous wrongs done

him, he finds time and occasion for what one may call
"taking a recess" from sorrow:

February, 1836.

To Madame Olympe Chodsko,

My friend, Alf. Tattet is dining to-day with the Mar-
quise. Are you woman enough to come with them and
me? This is a real carnival invitation, or worse still, a
day-after-carnival invitation. *Des vins discrets et des
sonnets bavards.*—If you have the courage, come! I need
a great deal myself to write point-blank to you like this.
Just say one word! And if it is yes, I will fly to your feet,
that is to say, I will take a fiacre and go to fetch you.

A thousand compliments, excuses and *amitiés,*

ALFRED DE MUSSET.

He may have just laid down his pen from the picture of
himself that he is drawing for Lamartine:

*Les deux mains sur mon cœur, et serrant ma blessure,
Et sentant y saigner un invincible amour,*

his hands clasping his bleeding heart while his unconquer-
able love is bleeding there. It seems that Madame Olympe
Chodsko accepted the invitation, that the party was a
success, and that the ice of formality was admirably
broken, for a second note to her followed a little later:

February, 1836

Pichrocholine [Little Olive-pit (?)]

Did you sleep well? How did you digest your supper?

Oh! How charming you were in your mask! You are divine in a mask; you are like the holy wafer which it is our Christian duty to eat, and you will certainly be eaten.

A. de M.

In hours of satiety, dejection or weariness when pleasure seemed futile and work a vain thing, he would remember all the wrongs women had done him and brood over his lost love, his bleeding heart, the horror of feminine infidelity (like his school friend, Paul Foucher, *dont l'âme avait besoin de chanter ce qu'elle souffre*), until emotion flooding up burst into divine song, most musical, most melancholy; but when the song had been written, when the candles lighted for the tête-à-tête with his Muse had been blown out, he summoned Tattet and arranged for a little *partie carrée* with pleasant ladies, discreet wines and babbling sonnets. Surely he was Octave and Cœlio in one, as George Sand had said.

Qu'est-ce donc qu'oublier, si ce n'est pas mourir?
Ah! c'est plus que mourir; c'est survivre à soi-même.
L'âme remonte au ciel quand on perd ce qu'on aime.
Il ne reste de nous qu'un cadavre vivant;
Le désespoir l'habite, et le néant l'attend.

What is it to forget, unless it be to die?
Oh, it is more than death—a survival of self!
The soul to heaven flies when it has lost its love.
Nothing of us is left except a living corpse,
Waiting for nothingness, housing despair.

But the admirer of *Pichrocholine* (so charming in her mask) seems to belie this description.

I said that all the commentators assume that the faithless woman of the *Lettre à Lamartine* is George Sand. Paul de Musset denies this, and asserts that it is the same she who is the heroine of the poems to *Ninon*, of the story of *Emmeline,* and of the episode that included the drawing of the clock with the dial hands pointing to three. This is the same position that he had taken with regard to the *Nuit de Décembre*. The commentators again think that Paul has prevaricated. Paul says that soon after the *Lettre* was published Ninon-Emmeline wrote Alfred a letter, in which she complains of his saying that her feeling had been a *caprice de femme*. "It was true love," she writes, "and no caprice that caused our suffering. Never do me the wrong to doubt that. Know that at this minute, if I thought of nobody but myself, I should again be ready to dry the tears that are blinding my eyes, and leave all, and ruin myself for you. One word from your lips would be enough. I am not afraid to say this to you now. It is because you love me that you leave me to my tears." It comforted Alfred to know that his grief was shared, and flattered his vanity. Twenty times he said: "I need but say one word to make her leave all; but I will never speak the word that would ruin her." That Paul is not truthful here, I agree; Ninon-Emmeline may have written such a letter, but not because she was heroine of the *Lettre à Lamartine*, and I am the more confirmed in my theory that Alfred's emotions in this poem do not concern one woman only but are a blended memory cast in an imaginary setting.

Paul then shifts the subject and says: "Fate owed

Alfred de Musset compensation for such great sacrifices,"
to wit, for not speaking the word that would ruin this
lady, and, I presume, as his word *sacrifices* is in the plural,
for respecting Suzon's maidenhood. Whether Alfred deserved to be rewarded or not for those sacrifices, he probably thought he did. At any rate, the friendship, to which
Paul refers, as the compensation in question, and which
was a great boon for years, had already existed for over
a twelvemonth.

Caroline d'Alton-Shée, a gay, vivacious, quickwitted,
laughing spirit lodged in the tiniest of human bodies, was
some six years older than her brother, Alton-Shée, Musset's friend. The brother stood but a palm's breadth
above four feet and she, standing on a footstool, merely
came up to his shoulder. Her foot was like a doll's, and
her hand no bigger than a great rose petal. At the age
of fifteen she was married to a magistrate of distinction,
Monsieur Maxime Jaubert, aged thirty-nine: "You will
take my father's place," she told him. By the summer
of 1835, three or four months after the final rupture with
George Sand, she and Alfred were already on familiar
terms, as this letter shows:

To Madame Jaubert

Paris, August 11, 1835

Glory be to God! Your letter is absurd! You, too,
Madame, have your lucky moments, its seems, like the
rest of us. Yes, I call Heaven to witness, when you
wrote, your window was wide open, your rose bushes were
swaying in the breeze—your hair was hanging down, or

else but half put up—and a bat, which, whatever the savants may say, is creation's masterpiece, had been hovering round you, and there must have been mites dancing in the sun's rays beside you. (By the way! these ephemeræ are the happiest creatures in the world, they live but a day and they pass it waltzing.)

Your letter is absurd, and therefore charming. You will not catch me laying my clumsy verses over your fancies that are as fresh as roses. So help me, my Muse, I shall not put into doggerel your charming thoughts of evening and dawn. But! ! ! I must find some comparison for you, to tell you once for all that nobody has one quarter of your wit, quite apart from your being as pretty as an angel. Let me see. I compare you to a delicate pearl —(How the wind blows! It's intolerable; my lamp has gone crazy.) There is much in common between you and the pearl. Pearls are tears turned to joy, true symbols of poetry. But I do you wrong to compare you to poetry. Your worth is greater than the Muses. . . . Well! I will compare you to Titania, Queen of the fairies in *Midsummer Night's Dream.*

> So, good night, with lullaby!
> Lulla, lulla, lullaby! (*descrescendo*)

Are you having a good time? I come from Montmorency [Tattet's country place], I lost my gloves in lake Enghien and my handkerchief at Andilly.—(The cats are making a fearful row in the court yard).—Farewell, Madame. I am writing without being certain that my letter will reach you; I am not sure of your address. The first time that you feel a littly fancy ready to open under your lilac bonnet, write it to me, I do beseech you.

Your devoted servitor

ALFRED DE MUSSET.

They became great friends. She nicknamed him *Prince Café*, because, as she said, there was a stimulant in his way of listening, of understanding, of quickening one's wits, like coffee, and also *Prince Phosphore de cœur volant*; and he, in turn, because she had christened him in this fashion, called her his godmother, *marraine*. They corresponded freely with each other, and she introduced him to her circle of friends. Of these the most distinguished was Pierre Antoine Berryer, a man of note in his time, an eminent lawyer, an eloquent orator, for a time the leader of the legitimists in the Chamber of Deputies. Berryer had a fine country estate at Augerville, beyond Fontainebleau, where after the labors of political and professional life, he liked to collect his friends, men and women, and enjoy himself. *Faire sans dire* was the motto of the house. Madame Jaubert was always an important member of the party; and of men there were Alton-Shée, Major Frazer, Prince Belgiojoso, Delacroix, and so on. The ways of the house were not over prudish. Musset enjoyed himself there. With his friends he was usually gay and debonair; but as Madame Jaubert says, "There never was a stormy sky, so streaked, so mare's-tailed, so lit by a March sun, whose changeability could be compared to his moods. . . . It was perhaps difficult to avoid the storm clouds, but in order to dispel them nothing was necessary but a spiritual caress.'' These spiritual caresses Madame Jaubert was able to give better than any one else, unless it was Sister Marcelline, who was sick nurse during an illness of his in later years. His letters to her are gay, sprightly, affectionate and intimate, they show the sun-illumined aspect of his character which reveals itself in his comedies. You would scarce believe that the same man had written the sobs, *les purs sanglots* of the *Nuits.*

April 1, 1836

Belle Madame,

I am shut up again, in Musset fashion, with my night cap on (a trifle less gay than your camelias) when I ought to be dining with Lamartine at Princesse Uranie's [Belgiojoso], but I excused myself for I didn't have the courage. I will confess to you that I am beginning to be completely disgusted to see that midnight outings— too much both for my head and chest—are not able to drag me out of a past that crushes me materially and morally. Amen. . . . *Compliments respectueux.*

A. de M.

This Princess Belgiojoso to whom he refers was destined to play an important rôle in his life. She was a creature of high romance. Heinrich Heine admired her greatly and describes her in *Die Reisebilder;* ''Hers is one of those faces that belong rather to the poetic region of dreams than to the rude reality of life. An outline that recalls Leonardo da Vinci, a noble oval, dimpled cheeks, and the pointed sentimental chin of the Lombard school. Her complexion has the sweetness of the Roman painters, that soft sheen of pearl, of elegant pallor, which Italians call *morbidezza*. It was a face, the like of which you can only find in some old Italian pictures that represent the great ladies, with whom the Italian painters of the six-teenth century were in love when they painted their masterpieces, or such as haunted the thoughts of French and German heroes when they girded on their swords and crossed the Alps," and added, "Italy has done well, she has produced Raphael, Rossini and the Princess Belgiojoso."

Heine's description was no exaggeration. Another ad-mirer, the Marquis de Floranges speaks of "her ascetic face, her blue black hair, her huge eyes, her close shut lips, her wonderful and haughty physiognomy." Balzac who saw her a few years later than this found her *très impératrice* but *horriblement bas bleu*. Nevertheless, in spite of her intellectual interests, she was universally acknowledged to possess rare beauty, elegance of carriage, nobility of gait, and a voice with a touch of magic in it. Berryer said of her: "An unusual mind, a passionate spirit liking to command, a look that impressed you by its power, remarkable courage and sang-froid, also the art of pleasing, and the need of adoration."

The Princess came of a noble Milanese family. She was brought up among people who were all conspirators for the liberation of Italy, friends of Silvio Pellico and Con-falonieri, all members of the *Carbonari*. At sixteen she was married to Prince Belgiojoso, the wildest of rakes, but *bello e giojoso*, handsome and gay, none more so. Tall, his fair hair curling on his forehead, regular features, a morning face, love-making eyes, a voice of magic and talents for music—he charmed what women he would, and he wished to charm many, and among them he charmed Christine Trivulzio, though she had been brought up with a strict and pious education. He had squandered his money; she was rich. He soon proved to be a bad husband; the two had nothing in common but their ardent patriotism and their daring; she rode bareback and handled gun and sword. Implicated in the revolutionary movement they fled to Paris in 1831, separately, and lived apart. Musset had been boon companion with the Prince for some time, but now he begins to notice the rare attractiveness of the Princess, who, however, had already chosen a man of elegance and charm, the eminent historian, Mignet, to whom she remained faithful all his life.

But for the present Musset merely saw that she was beautiful and intellectual, a Princess Uranie, and gazed without covetousness.

CHAPTER XIV

AIMÉE D'ALTON

IN THE years 1836 and 1837 Alfred de Musset is preeminently a man of letters. In his youth, prior to the episode with George Sand, he had been a dandy and a poet; in later life he was to be known as a novelist of short stories and a playwright. In the years I now speak of he is writing poems, plays, stories, artistic and literary criticism, in short he practises his métier, and takes it seriously, very seriously, it seems, from a letter he wrote to Buloz, editor of the *Revue des Deux Mondes* in August, 1835, a few months after the dénouement of the George Sand romance. He asked him please to recover from her a couple of sonnets that he fears, if published, might prove beneath him and sully his reputation: *"Que voulez-vous, mon cher ami,* I wrote the verses in a great hurry; I am a craftsman of verse; that is my profession, *c'est mon métier;* and I am now acting in my pecuniary interests. *Bien à vous."*

His literary career, though spasmodic and uncertain, may be divided into four periods: poetry, plays, tales, and the theater. The period of his great poetry, endured but for two short years, the *Nuits*, the *Lettre à Lamartine*, the *Stances à la Malibran*, the *Song of Fortunio*, that of *Saint-Blaise à la Zuecca*—the half-dozen poems that are most famous, included for instance, in the *Oxford Book of French Verse*—all belong to 1835 and 1836. The only exception is the *Souvenir* written in 1840 and this is a sort

of postscript to the *Nuits*. Of this period George Sand
was undoubtedly the tutelary genius; with the exception
of the *Stances à la Malibran,* all are due to her. But to
say that she was the inspirer of his great poetry is one
thing; to say she was the sole object of his invectives and
denunciations is another. She was the Pandora that un-
locked the chest of baleful memories; and all of them, un-
justly, are imputed to her.

In the period of his plays—these periods overlap—the
presiding genius was not a woman but the bright jewel
of gaiety, given by nature at his birth, set however, in the
somber frame of a gloom-loving temperament. Every
now and then in his letters, especially those to Madame
Jaubert, and in some anecdote concerning him, you
come upon the original of Octave in *Les Caprices de
Marianne,* of Valentine in *Il ne faut jurer de rien,* of
Fantasio in the play of that name, and so on. In every
hero he depicts something of himself. The gay plays
began with *Les Caprices de Marianne* (1833) before Musset met George Sand, and, at their best, continue for
about four years; in that period fall *André del Sarto,
Les Caprices de Marianne, Fantasio, On ne badine pas
avec l'amour, Lorenzaccio, Barberine, Le Chandelier, Il
ne faut jurer de rien* and *Un Caprice* (1837). And then,
it seems as if he lost a certain spontaneity, as if the
fountain of imagination no longer had power to gush out
in verse, as if

> *L'eau de sa source jazarde*
> *Qui trépillante se suit*

had lost its head, and now flowed forth less vivaciously in prose, although with the same melodious grace, and the same delicate fastidiousness of expression.

For the period of his tales, though they began with *Emmeline,* in which the heroine is the lady to whom the poems to Ninon are addressed, and though in others the tutelary genius seems to be the casual mistress of the hour, for all the tales are transcripts of his own experiences, nevertheless, one mistress stands out conspicuous, Mademoiselle Aimée d'Alton, and must be regarded as the tutelary spirit. After her time Musset produced no story of consequence, except *Histoire d'un Merle Blanc* (1842), which reverts to George Sand, and *Mimi Pinson* (1845), which is a memory of his youthful *vie de Bohême.*

The last period, that of his career as a playwright upon the stage, began in 1847 and was presided over by another divinity. So, to resume, we may for convenience' sake, while dividing his life into literary categories, look upon George Sand as the Muse of his poetry, the Pucklike spirit of gay insouciance that nature gave him as the genius of his plays, Mademoiselle Aimée d'Alton, as that of his tales, and Madame Allan-Despréaux of his theatrical career.

In 1835-1836, as I have said, he has not given himself up definitely to any of these categories, but practised generally his *métier* of *homme de lettres.* This was a happy period of his life, in which the friendship of Madame Jaubert played a large part, and diligence gave it dignity. On April 1, 1836, in the *Revue des Deux Mondes* he published an article on the *Salon* of the year, which still has a certain historical interest. Like his predecessor, Diderot, and his successors, Gautier and Zola, Musset was one of the eminent men of letters who interested himself in painting. Fashions in painting are as changeable as fashions in women's dress, and to glance at the ideas and tastes of the past generation might help one—though it usually does not—to be diffident of one's own present-day artistic convictions. Musset at the beginning of his essay lays it down as a rule that, if a painter pleases either the public or the connoisseurs, he must have some merit, and that, if he pleases both public and connoisseurs, he possesses real talent; he also lays down the postulate that no country at that time takes precedence of France, and that in art as in other matters the future is to be hers. He then proceeds to criticize individual painters. Delacroix always puts himself into his painting: "There has been an attempt [the critic says] to make Delacroix the head of a new school that is going to overturn the present taste," but to this he does not give credence. Baron Gros "is the greatest painter of our time." Isabey deserves "unlimited eulogy." Of Winterhalter he says nothing in particular. Corot's "Roman Campagna has received great admiration." Barye exhibits "a lion in bronze as terrifying as life"; Pradier, a Venus "admirable in execution," it is the ideal of what a statue of Love should be, a perfect symbol of "*volupté et caprice.*" But more than all he admired *The Fishermen, Les Pêcheurs,* by Léopold Robert, a painter who had been painting in Venice while Musset was there, and had died since then in great poverty. And so on, in moderate, sympathetic, intelligent criticism.

On July first, he published the little play *Il ne faut jurer de rien*; on August first, the *Nuit d'Août*, a joyous poem of old love forgotten and new love beginning; on September fifteenth, the first of a series of papers containing criticism of the Romantic movement, humorous, mocking, sensible; on October first, the lament of the death of the great singer Malibran. All this is not the performance of a *cadavre vivant*, as he had described himself in the *Lettre à Lamartine*, but of a man in the full exercise of his powers. It is fair to infer that this was the most temperate period of his life. That it was a happy period is clear from the jovial spirit in which his satirical papers on the Romantic movement were written, and by the early-morning air that blows through *La Nuit d'Août*:

> *J'aime, et je veux chanter la joie et la paresse,*
> *Ma folle expérience et mes soucis d'un jour,*
> *Et je veux raconter et répéter sans cesse*
> *Qu'après avoir juré de vivre sans maîtresse,*
> *J'ai fait serment de vivre et de mourir d'amour.*

> I love and I would sing of joy, and idleness,
> My madcap deeds, my sorrows of a day,
> And I would say and then reiterate,
> Without a mistress having sworn to live,
> I now make oath to live and die for love.

Evidently "the wound caused by black seraphim" had ceased to bleed, even to smart. George Sand is now, certainly, in the chapter before last, and Ninon-Emmeline is also a finished chapter.

Just who it was that caused the vow "to live and die of love" is not very sure. Paul tells of a *grisette* who lived across the court opposite their apartment. He speaks of looks exchanged between her and Alfred, then tells, like the *romancier* he is, how Cupid flits from looks to smiles, from smiles to signals, from signals to blown kisses, et *"finalement on tomba d'accord,"* for "in those days there were still *grisettes* who yielded freely and fully to the stirrings of their hearts." Her importance is that she served him, as all his loves did, in literature; she sat as model for Bernerette and Mimi Pinson in those two stories. But let us hurry on to a young woman of much greater permanence in his life, whom I have spoken of as the main inspiration of his story-telling period. Paul says little about her, for the reason that, after Alfred died, he in his turn wooed and won, and some months or years after having won, he married her; not that either he or she attached much importance to the rite, but their families were conventional, and they acquiesced.

In 1836 Aimée d'Alton was twenty-five years old. The sculptor, Auguste Barre, who afterward carved the poet's tomb at Père Lachaise, modeled a little figurine of her, with her blonde hair parted in the middle, with a knot behind, and hanging in curls on either side, her eyes set wide apart, her little nose turned appealingly upward, her mouth delicate. She is seated with her hands clasped in her lap, and looking up with a coquettish expression that says: "You are a man and I a woman, let us talk." She was a cousin of Madame Jaubert and frequented her

salon, and as she was as witty, or nearly so, as her
hostess, she soon had her circle of admirers. There she
and Alfred used to meet. At first he paid little attention to her; but one day while Madame Jaubert was
playing an accompaniment to some Venetian songs, he
was sitting next her, and she spoke of being bored; he
said that the only way never to be bored was to be in
love, to which she answered that she had nothing to do
with love-making. One afternoon a little later, while
Alfred was also calling there, she came to Madame Jaubert's bringing a pretty needle-box of black shell and
made her hostess a present of it. Alfred admired the
box and asked to have it. Madame Jaubert refused to
give up a gift, and Aimée protested that it was no longer
hers. Alfred kept up his beseeching all the evening,
until it seemed at last as if Aimée had become annoyed;
but when she left, she put on a little white hooded cape
that was very becoming, and he compared her to a little
white monk, and the next morning sent her some verses
beginning:

> *Charmant petit moinillon blanc,*
> *Je suis un pauvre mendiant,*
> *Charmant petit moinillon rose,*
> *Je vous demande peu de chose,*
> *Accordez-le-moi poliment,*
> *Charmant petit moinillon blanc.*

> Charming little monk in white,
> A beggar I in sorry plight;
> Charming monk in rosy mask,
> A trifling thing is all I ask,
> Give it to me and be polite,
> Charming little monk in white.

The lady replied by sending him a little box of sandalwood containing a pen, as a hint that he should not be lazy, and she followed that up with another hint. She knew that he gambled and lost money; so she knitted a purse and sent it with these words, but no signature:

To the Purse

Dear little purse how will you be received? Will you tell all the pleasure in your making, all the care that has been taken of your little self? You are not expected; there was a wish that you should not be seen, till you had on all your ornaments. Shall you get a kiss for your pains?

To the Recipient

Do not spend lightly, what I contain. When you leave the house, put one gold bit in me, that is enough for one day; and if something is left over at night, however little, you will meet some beggar who will thank you, and the Muses will pay you back.

He guessed who sent the purse, wrote her a sonnet and then a letter.

March 1, 1837.

My hand trembles as I write, and perhaps I ought not to, but your charming secret has not been betrayed, and it would be difficult for me to tell you how I know. I do not *know*; but I am sure, and whatever may come of it, it is impossible for me not to thank you. Nothing can ever deprive me of the courage, the pride, the hope, that this little treasure has given me. Please accept this letter as I have received your gift—with astonishment perhaps; but say to yourself that you have made a true heart beat. Is there anything else in the world? Is not all the rest a dream? . . . Yes, the hand that wrought this precious purse has a friendly feeling for me; in every little knotted thread there is a thought of yours, or at least a look of yours has fallen on each stitch. When shall I see you? One harsh word from you will do me more hurt than your gift has done me good—for I know you know that I love you, and neither you nor I can help that now. . . . I know what I feel, and never in my life have I lied to anybody, nor to myself. It is not a virtue. I am too *proud* to lie. . . . This letter at least will carry something of my heart to a noble heart in which I trust, and which shall do with me as it pleases.

ALFD. MT.

He had rightly read that *bouche mutine,* those eyes *candidement effrontés.* They are soon talking love. She protests that her health is an invincible obstacle, he does not agree, they argue. He writes her on March thirty-first: "You say that you know my character, you are mistaken. I am older than you in years by one, in experience by ten. Do not smile at the word experience. Mine is no great matter, but let me tell you what it has taught me:—To dream beautiful dreams, and to wish to realize them is the very first essential in a large heart. But after entering life, reality with its nauseating train sooner or later attacks our young virginal hope upon its upward flight and strikes it down. That is no mere moral apothegm, it is an everlasting truth. Aimée! the first experience consists in suffering, it consists in discovering that absolute dreams are almost never realized; or, if realized, that they wither and die when they come in contact with the things of this world. The heart bleeds, but it gathers up its courage, and at last says: evil is nothing, so long as happiness exists. . . . Let your heart beat. . . . You like the name of friend. My Child! Are friendship and love separate words? Your letter makes me thank God. It opens before me a world of hopes and desires, of torments and doubt, but also of heavenly pleasure—do not shut it again, my lovely Angel, do not doubt, do not look into the future, smile, answer, be kind and true, as you are beautiful. There is such strength in two together. Come as soon as possible. Could you not, if you would?''

More letters pass. He says that, although he has been loved by noble hearts—*moi aussi j'ai été aimé par de nobles cœurs*—never in such manner before, never has he seen so little coquetry. The month of May is spoken of: *"Quand je pense au mois de Mai—quand je me dis qu'une âme si belle, si candide, habite un corps aussi beau qu'elle, aussi blanc qu'elle—mon amour, qu'ai-je fait pour être si heureux? Aimée, la bien nommée!* [When I think of the month of May, when I say to myself, that so candid and beautiful a soul inhabits a body as lovely as itself, O my Love, what have I done to be so happy, Aimée, my beloved, the well named!]'' Then he proceeds more crudely. He asks how it is that her aunt can't give

AIMÉE D'ALTON

A. d. Musset
1841.

a room till the end of the month, or why Aimée should not go to her cousin's house. He calls her his *chère maîtresse.* She answered that one must not count one's chickens before they are hatched. On April fourteenth he gets word from her that she will come at daybreak a few days later. He protests that he loves her, repeating this three times, and reminding her that he lives with his mother, which is a great inconvenience. It would be necessary to go through the dining-room to reach his bedroom. Their apartment is not large, and his mother, brother, sister and three servants, live there. The best time to come, though it might seem early, for she came from a distance, would be seven or eight o'clock, because everybody, masters and servants, slept till half past eight or nine. Between seven and eight nobody would be stirring. His house was on the Rue de Grenelle, next to Bouchardon's fountain, *un assez vilain monument.* Their door is to the right. As the court was a sort of public passage, there would be no need to speak to the concierge. But she must be careful about the right door, as there were several. His was at the end of the court, at the right, with the word *Stairway* in large letters over it. He would be watching from behind his window curtain and go down to let her in, *ainsi point d'embarras.* Once up and locked in his room, she would be as safe as if she were in India, for there was an express prohibition against waking him, and he usually slept until two o'clock. *Je crois que l'amour n'est jamais venu sous de plus heureux auspices.* On April 22, 1837, this *charmante créature dont les mœurs n'étaient peut-être pas à l'abri de tout reproche* (as a rigid Frenchman says) made her adventurous way through the courtyard of No. 59 Rue de Grenelle. Part of the poetry of this romance is that she and Paul preserved this letter of Alfred's containing directions and deposited it, together with all others from Alfred to her, in the Bibliothèque Nationale for our profit and enjoyment for ever. But the *charmante créature,* supposing that she deserved happiness, had no bright prospects of it. Within a very few days thereafter Sainte-Beuve chanced to meet Alfred and wrote to Ulric Guttinguer (April 28, 1837): "I saw Musset the other day, very pleasant and looking well and in good color, considering that he is *si perdu et si gâté au fond et en dessus.*"

But the influence of Aimée d'Alton was good during the two years that the liaison lasted. Alfred wrote the admirable little comedy, *Un Caprice,* and a number of stories, *Emmeline, Les Deux Maîtresses, Frederic et Bernerette, Le Fils du Titian* and *Margot.* Aimée and himself are portrayed perhaps, with some greater accuracy of detail in the first rendezvous than to the uncurious eye might seem necessary, in the *Fils du Titian,* and the silk purse, which was the Galeotto that brought them together, furnishes the plot for *Un Caprice.* Their love does not seem to have touched any heights; on the contrary, one gets the impression that it is lodged in a low studded rather stuffy apartment. He calls her the *"bonne, belle et blanche fille* to whom I owe happiness, pleasure, repose and courage," but there is no sign on either side of any depth of feeling. The poet's emotional nature was losing the power of its wings. By June they had begun to bicker a little, but not as yet to quarrel. He goes out of town without seeing her, but he will write. In Paris they have a *nid d'amour,* Rue Saint-Nicolas; but it seems to have been too expensive and they look for another. When his mother is away, she is able to go to his house. By July they are quarreling. He showed her a letter from his last mistress [Emmeline] and she became jealous and said that he was deceiving her. In August he tells her that he has found a little apartment of two rooms, Rue Tronchet, behind the Madeleine, with a "splendid view of a pile of logs in the woodyard next door." It was quite new, situated on the *entresol* and had a private stairway. The tenant of the apartment across the court was conveniently away, in Algiers. For a time all goes well enough; he calls her *ma chère poupette,* a nickname not wholly to her liking. But he missed in her any lacerating emotional stimulus. His spiritual nerves craved spiritual alcohol, and he returned to his solitary and bitter broodings. In September (1837) he writes her that he has had a moment of *atroce tristesse* and says that he is going to try to write some verses. He wrote *La Nuit d'Octobre,* perhaps the most poignant and perfect of the *Nuits.* Paul suggests that the memory of his old wound was brought back afresh by his stories, *Emmeline* and *Les Deux Maîtresses,* but Paul is singularly disingenuous; in reality, Alfred was an emotional dipsomaniac, he needed the bitterness of loss, of anger, of reproach and invective, he needed the sharpness of pain to give his existence a fuller flavor, and in his subconsciousness he knew that only in such moods his Muse could sing her most thrilling notes.

The *Nuit d'Octobre* shows just how he worked himself up to an emotional pitch, cut loose the cords of self-restraint, unfurled all sails, ran out the spinnaker, and invoked all the storm winds of the passionate past. There is again a dialogue between the Poet and his Muse. How quietly it begins, how tender, how artistic!

THE POET

Le mal dont j'ai souffert s'est enfui comme un rêve.

The evil I have suffered has disappeared like a dream.

The Muse asks him what the evil was.

POET

C'est un mal vulgaire et bien connu des hommes.

It was a common ill, that men know well.

Then she urges him to tell her about it, but first, she asks, "Are you cured?" He answers "Yes"; and then he excites himself, says that the evil was caused by a woman, and recounts how, while he was waiting at his window for her to come, she delayed, he waited and waited. Jealousy, doubt, suspicion, certainty! At last she came. "Where do you come from, and what have you done? *En quel lieu, dans quel lit, à qui souriais-tu?*" and then he burst into a furious invective against George Sand:

Honte à toi qui la première
M'as appris la trahison,
Et d'horreur et de colère
M'as fait perdre la raison!

Honte à toi, femme à l'œil sombre,
Dont les funestes amours
Ont enselevi dans l'ombre
Mon printemps et mes beaux jours!

Shame to thee, who first
Taught me what treachery is,
And in wrath and horror,
Wrecked my reason!
Shame to thee, thou of the somber eye,
Whose fatal love
Has buried in the dark
My springtime, all my happy days!

But after his fierce invectives, having spewed forth the poison festering within, he ends in a calm, fatigued, purpose to forget her and says

Avec une dernière larme
Reçois un éternel adieu.

But how did Aimée d'Alton take this proof that she is really nothing to him, no more than the women in the stews? In October, shortly after the publication of the poem, he writes to her that he has not seen her for a hundred years and asks her to come to their trysting-place. In December he spoke insulting words; he had given her a ring, and then saw other rings also on her fingers and jumped to injurious conclusions. In January, he writes that he is working so hard that he must postpone seeing her. Thereafter, although their meetings continue and he calls her by endearing names, he has already returned to harlots and wine.

They see less and less of each other. They talk of the

dangers of estrangement; *"C'est ainsi qu'on finit,"* she said. But, on the other hand, if they were to be seen together in society, there would be danger of scandal. Then losses at gambling obliged him to give up the little apartment in the Rue Tronchet; they must do so at once, but if the landlord required notice, let it stay a week or a fortnight, in any case, give it up as soon as possible. It was obvious that he was drifting down-stream. She wished to help him. But the evil spirit that descended upon him from time to time was hovering near. He felt no grief, no anger, but life had become a useless, indifferent matter. The same feelings had come before, but now they are worse; he recognizes that he can not make her happy, nor fill her life, and he tells her that the simple fact is that they are poor and not happy, and that there is nothing to do about it, *Ma destinée est faite.* She proposed that they should marry. He is a little embarrassed to refuse, and not very clear in assigning his reasons, *"ma famille, ma position, l'avenir sont une necessité irrévocable qui disent: non."* Probably it was the best excuse that he could think of, but one remembers a less guarded statement of his, *"où sont avec le mariage, les rendezvous, le punch, la liberté?"*

Aimée appears in a much better light than he; she is willing to offer her small substance to him, but he will not face married life, and indeed as he says, his character was reason enough for not marrying. And so they went on, he always very generous with pretty epithets; *Ma chère poupette, Mimouche, ma chère âme, ma rose blanche, mon bel amour, ma blanche beauté, Nymphe poupette, mon bel*

et adoré amour; and keeps asking for rendezvous. Then
the letters grow short: "It is funny, isn't it," he writes,
"that I should be going into the country while you are
sick in bed?" (June 1838.) "You are sad, dear girl, and
you must be amazed that I don't ask you to come." (July.)
In August he drops in at Madame Jaubert's and finds
the ladies there convinced that he makes her unhappy.
"It is true," he comments, "that one must be happy oneself in order to make others happy." In October of that
year he was given a sinecure, the position of librarian of
the Ministry of the Interior at three thousand francs a
year, but that did not affect his attitude toward her.

So, in the beginning of 1839 the episode ends. Companionate marriage with a woman of genius had been
too exciting, too electrical, and companionate marriage
with a bovine creature was too dull, too phlegmatic. Both
had proved failures.

CHAPTER XV

RACHEL

MUSSET's liaison with Aimée d'Alton lasted into the year 1839, but other eyes than hers had caught his before that.

The Comédie Française had been playing, in accordance with tradition and its obligations, the great classical plays of the French stage, *Les Horaces, Cinna, Andromaque,* during the months of June and July, 1838. A young Jewish girl, seventeen years old, played the heroines. She was born in Switzerland, but her family emigrated to Lyons, where she and her sister picked up pennies and bad company, by singing in cafés and in the street. When she was eleven years old her family moved to Paris, where she went on the stage. She made such brilliant progress that Mademoiselle Mars, the great actress, noticed her, and the door of the Comédie Française was opened to her. Nevertheless the public was listless. Corneille, Racine, Voltaire, the whole classic stage, seemed on the point of disappearing. Then, by great luck, an eminent theatrical critic, Jules Janin, attended the theater, saw the young Jewess in the part of Hermione in *Andromaque,* wrote his enthusiastic approbation in the *Débats* for September tenth and twenty-fourth, and drew all that newspaper's public to see her. The receipts at the box office rose tenfold, and Rachel was become famous. Sainte-Beuve wrote to his friend, Juste Olivier: "The greatest news of the day is the appearance of a new actress at the Théâtre Français, Mademoiselle Rachel, a Jewess." Musset shared the general admiration and wrote an article *De la Tragédie* for the *Revue des Deux Mondes*. He describes the great actress: "Mademoiselle Rachelle is rather short than tall; those who picture to themselves a queen of the theater of great muscular power and of physical amplitude, enveloped in purple robes, will be disappointed. Mademoiselle Rachel's waist is not bigger round than one of Mademoiselle George's arms. At her first entrance, by her carriage, her gestures, her speech, she strikes the spectator with her perfect simplicity, and her air of genuine modesty. Her voice is penetrating, and in moments of passion extremely full of energy. Her delicate features that one can not look at near to unmoved, lose by being seen at a distance. Her health seems poor; a long part visibly tires her." He then praised her genius, and went on to expound his views of the respective relations of the romantic and classical schools to the theater.

Rachel next played the part of Roxane in *Bajazet*. Jules Janin, piqued to have a young man come forward as champion of the actress whom he himself had discovered, or disliking Musset, or moved by unknown reason, criticized her again in the *Débats* and this time found great fault. Other critics followed suit. Musset replied in the *Revue des Deux Mondes*, maintaining that Rachel was as admirable in Roxane as in her earlier rôles. He could not understand the opposite view. "My intelligence," he said, "may adopt a wrong opinion, but when my emotions are stirred, I am not mistaken. I can read a play, or hear it at the theater, and be wrong about its merits, but even if my taste were the falsest and most unreasonable in the world, when my heart speaks, my heart is right. This is no vain assumption of sensibility, it merely means that the heart is not liable to the mistakes of the intelligence, that it decides beyond contravention ... in other words it is the sovereign judge. That gives me the boldness to say once again that Mademoiselle Rachel will be another Malibran. That is why I have felt pain and sorrow to see her attacked; that is why I think, however little reputation one has, one should defend her as much as one can, and refrain above all else from destroying in the child's heart the sacred germ, the divine seed, that can not fail to bear fruit.''

This sounded a little tart to an older man who had long been recognized to be the first among critics of the theater. Jules Janin lost his temper and replied angrily: He sneered at ''third class poets'' at the *nouveau-nés de la critique*, who think that it is as easy to criticize as it is to write a novel, that to be a master critic one has only to put a dot on an i (an allusion to Musset's *Ballade à la Lune*) and sing it, to the tune *connaissez-vous dans Barcelone une Andalouse*—another reference to Musset's early poems, and so on. Monsieur Janin had indeed lost his temper. Alfred went to look for him in the foyer of the Théâtre Français, but fortunately did not find him, and wrote instead:

Saturday, December 8, 1838.

Sir,

I went to look for you last night at the Théâtre Français and at the *Opéra,* hoping to find you in the foyer, so that I might tell you publicly what I thought of your last Monday's article. As I did not find you, I am compelled to write.

It is understood, I know, that as soon as one writes one becomes a critic; and I am not unaware of the ridicule that attaches to wounded vanity. But if you, as a journalist, have the right to judge me, I have the right to tell you my way of thinking. I had written in the *Revue des Deux Mondes,* with politeness and sincerity, my opinion upon Mademoiselle Rachel. I did not designate you. You have answered without regard to conventions. Your article is boorish. From a literary point of view you are a child on whom one should put a fool's cap; you are a clown who should be forbidden to enter the Théâtre Français.

There, Sir, is what I would have said to you yesterday had I met you, and what I shall repeat the first time I see you. Take your revenge for this letter, if you wish, by fresh insults. I expect it and I don't care in the least.

ALFRED DE MUSSET.

Aimée was alarmed, it seemed to her as if a duel might be on foot. A note from Alfred reassured her: "There is nothing in it, but my telling a clown his true name," and the next day he sends her a second note to say that *"l'affaire est arrangée,* Janin has swallowed the insult." But this championship of her cause roused Rachel's interest and gratitude; and Alfred's constant attendance at her representations had stirred again his interest in the theater, which had been nearly quenched by the ill success of *La Nuit Venitienne* at the Odéon in 1830. For two months, night and day, he was haunted by an *idée fixe,* concerning the theater, and what a tragedy should be; and became most eager to write a play, to be acted by Rachel. He was aware that, under French customs and conventions, there would be innumerable obstacles in the way, but he was full of enthusiasm and hope. On December twenty-seventh he writes, "*ma rage théâtrale va toujours son train* [my theatrical fury proceeds at full speed.]" His plans, of course, revolved about Rachel: "that woman, all instinct and ignorance, a true Bohemian princess, a lump of ashes in which there is a sacred spark." His enthusiasm for her and her young companion in genius, Pauline Garcia, a great singer, Malibran's sister, who had also just appeared, grew and grew. In a letter to Madame Jaubert, December seventeenth, he says: "Really I believe that a wind is stirring in the world of art. The classic tradition was an adorable convention; the romantic extravagance was a flood that had its good aspects, but now we have arrived at unalloyed truth. I would give a hundred crowns down, as Vernet says, to be but twenty [he was twenty-eight] and able to fly away upon this wild gust, in company with Pauline and Rachel, and lose myself in the clouds with them! I am too old for such a flight through time and space; and my wings have been pretty well singed. What does it matter? If I do not follow them, at least I can see them go, and drink a stirrup cup to their good health. Will you not come and touch your glass to mine, dear Godmother?"

The plan of some tragedy was turning in his head, and he would go from time to time to see Rachel, who lived with her family in a little back street, but somewhat cautiously for fear of gossip. On May 29, 1839, on coming out of the theater, where he had seen her play in *Tancrède,* he met her by chance close by in the gallery of the Palais-Royal. She invited Musset to come home for supper. He went, passed a most interesting evening, and that same night wrote a long account of it to Madame Jaubert, for he knew that she, as well as he, recognized that Rachel was one of the greatest of actresses.

May 30, 1839. 1 A.M.

Chère Marraine,

First let me thank you for Paolita's letter [Pauline Garcia]. She is a very amiable but less so than yourself, for you never lose an opportunity to send any possible pleasure to your friends. You are the only person, man or woman, that I know, who does that. A kindness is never wasted. In return for Desdemona's letter [the rôle sung by Pauline Garcia] I invite you to a supper at Mademoiselle Rachel's, which will amuse you, perhaps, if we still think alike. This little episode is for you *alone,* first because that noble child detests indiscretion, and also because, as I go to see her sometimes, there is such a lot of gossip, and scandal and nonsense, that I have decided not even to say that I have seen her at the theater.

It was the night that *Tancrède* [Voltaire] was given, and during the entr'acte I had gone to compliment her on her costume which was charming. In the fifth act she read the letter with a deeper, more touching, tone than ever. She told me that she had wept while reading, and had been so moved that she was afraid that she should be obliged to stop. At ten o'clock, as I was leaving the theater, chance made me meet her in the gallery of the Palais-Royal. Félix Bonnaire [Editor of the *Revue des Deux Mondes,* since Buloz had been made *commissaire royal* of the Théâtre Français] had given her his arm, and a troop of young things were following, Mademoiselle Rabut, Mademoiselle Dubois of the Conservatoire, and others. I bowed, and she said: "I am going to invite you home to supper."

So we went to her house. Bonnaire, vexed at our meeting, went off to drown his disappointment in *plusieurs petits verres;* Rachel smiled at his slinking away. The rest of us went in, and sat down, each demoiselle with her swain next her, and I beside my dear *Fanfan* [Rachel]. After some insignificant remarks, Rachel noticed that she had forgotten her rings and bracelets at the theater, and sent the *bonne* to fetch them. That left no servant to get the supper! Rachel got up, went to change her dress and then into the kitchen. A quarter of an hour later, she came back in her dressing-gown and nightcap, with the ribbon at her ear, pretty as an angel, holding a platter with three steaks which she had cooked herself. She set the platter down in the middle of the table, saying, "Help yourselves;" then went back to the kitchen, and returned with a soup tureen full of steaming soup, and a dish of spinach. "There's our supper!" There were

no plates nor spoons, for the *bonne* had taken away the
keys. Rachel opened the sideboard, found a bowl full
of salad, took a wooden fork, unearthed a plate, and began to eat by herself.

"But," said Mama, who was hungry, "there are tin
plates in the kitchen."

Rachel went to fetch them, brought them in and gave
one to each of the guests. At this point, the following
dialogue began, in which you will readily perceive I have
made no changes.

The Mother: My dear, the steaks are too much cooked.

Rachel: It's true; they're tough as wood. When I used
to take care of the household, I was a better cook than
that. It's a talent lost. Well! I have lost on one hand;
I have gained on the other. You are not eating, Sarah?

The Sister: No. I can't eat off tin plates.

Rachel: Oh! It's only since I bought a dozen silver
plates with my earnings that you can't touch tin. If
I get richer, you will soon require one valet behind your
chair and another in front. (Brandishing her fork) I
will never turn these old tin plates out of the house.
They have served us too long. Haven't they, Mama?

The Mother (with her mouth full): What a child she is!

Rachel (to Musset): Just imagine, when I began to play
at the Théâtre Molière, I only had two pairs of stockings, and every morning—(Here Sister Sarah began to
jabber in German to prevent Rachel from continuing)—
No German here! Haven't you any manners?—I only
had two pairs of stockings, and in order to have a clean
pair to play in I had to wash one pair every morning.

It hung on a clothes line in my room, while I wore the other pair.

Me: And did you do the household work?

Rachel: I got up at six o'clock every morning, and by eight all the beds were made. I then went to the market to buy the dinner.

Me: Did you contrive to save some pennies for yourself?

Rachel: No, I was a very honest cook. Wasn't I, Mama?

The Mother (eating the while): Yes, that's true.

Rachel: Excepting just for one period, then when I spent four sous I wrote down five, when I spent ten sous, I wrote down twelve. At the end of a month, I found myself three francs ahead of the game.

Me (severely): And what did you do with those three francs, Mademoiselle?

The Mother (as Rachel did not answer): Monsieur, she bought a copy of Molière for herself.

Me: Did she really?

Rachel: Yes I did. I had a Corneille and a Racine already. I had to have a Molière. So I bought it with my three francs, and then I confessed the crime—why is Mademoiselle Rabut going away? Good night, Mademoiselle.

Three quarters of the other nuisances, getting bored, followed Mademoiselle Rabut's example. The servant came back with the forgotten rings and bracelets. They were spread out on the table. The two bracelets are magnificent; they must be worth 4000 or 5000 francs. A gold circlet goes with them, most costly. All the jewelry caromed about the table, with the salad dish, the spinach, and the tin spoons. During this time, taken aback by the idea of associating Rachel with household drudgery, cooking, beds to make, all the fatigues of poverty, I stole a look at her hands, a little fearful lest I should find them ugly or disfigured. They are charming, plump, and tapering like a spindle; a very princess' hands.

Sarah, who was not eating, continued to scold in German. It is as well to know that that morning she had skipped away from under the maternal wing, with somebody or other, no one knows where, and had only received forgiveness and her place at table through her sister's repeated prayers.

Rachel (answering to German grumbling): You tire me. I want to tell the story of my youth. Yes, I do. I remember that one day I wished to make a punch in one of these tin spoons. I held the spoon over the candle, and it melted in my hand. By the way, Sophie [the servant], give me some Kirsch. We'll make some punch.—We've done; I've finished my supper.

The Mother: Sophie's made a mistake. This is a bottle of absinthe.

Me: Give me a little of it.

Rachel: I shall be delighted, if you will take something at our house.

The Mother: They say that absinthe is very good for the health.

Me: Not at all. It's injurious and detestable.

Sarah: Then why do you ask for some?

Me: In order to be able to say that I have taken something in your house.

Rachel: I want to drink some.

She drank a *petit verre*. The servant fetched a silver bowl; she put in sugar and Kirsch, struck a match and set fire to it.

Rachel: I like that blue flame.

Me: It is much prettier when there is no light in the room.

Rachel: Sophie, take away the candles.

The Mother: Don't, don't! What an idea! Good gracious!

Rachel: Oh, you tire me!—Oh, excuse me, Mama dear, you are sweet, you are charming [she kissed her], but I want Sophie to take the candles away.

A guest took the two candles and put them under the table. An effect of twilight. The Mama, now green, now blue, in the light of the flaring punch, stared at me. The candles reappeared.

Sarah: Mademoiselle Rabut was very ugly to-night.

Me: You are hard to please. I thought her very pretty.

Mother: Mademoiselle Rabut is awfully stupid.

Rachel: Why do you say that?

Mother: I say it because it's so; she's an idiot.

Rachel: Well, if she is stupid, she's not both stupid and bad. She's all right. Let her alone. I don't want to hear my friends spoken of in that way.

The punch was brewed. Rachel filled the glasses and helped everybody. Then she poured the rest of the punch into a soup plate and drank it with a spoon. Then she took my cane, drew out the dagger in it, and used the point as a tooth pick.

Me: How wonderfully you read that letter to-night. You were greatly moved.

Rachel: Yes, I seemed to feel as if something in me were going to break . . . But I don't care. I don't like the part of Tancrède. It's not real.

Me: You prefer Corneille's plays, and Racine's?

Rachel: I admire Corneille: and yet he is sometimes trivial, sometimes turgid. That is not consistent with nature.

Me: Oh! Oh!

Rachel: Think a minute. Where in *Les Horaces,* for instance, Sabine says

On peut changer d'amant, mais non changer d'époux,

One can change a lover, but not change a husband,

well, I don't like that, it's vulgar.

Me: At least you will admit, that it is true?

Rachel: Yes, but is it worthy of Corneille? I adore Racine!

Me: Apropos of Racine, do you remember to have received, some time ago, an anonymous letter giving you advice about the last scene in *Mithridate?*

Rachel: Perfectly. I followed the advice it gave me. Since then I have always been clapped in that scene. Do you know the person who wrote it?

Me: Very well. It's the woman who has the greatest intelligence and the littlest foot in all Paris.—What rôle are you studying now?

Rachel: This summer we are going to act *Marie Stuart*

for transients, but I don't like those whining rôles; then in the winter *Polyeucte,* and perhaps——

Me: What?

Rachel (striking the table with her fist): Well, *I want* to play Phèdre. They tell me that I'm too young, that I'm too thin and a hundred other nonsensical things. To that I answer, It is Racine's highest rôle, and *I intend* to play it.

Sarah: My dear child, you're wrong.

Rachel: Oh, leave me alone! Let them try and see if I'm too young, if the part doesn't suit me! Confound it! There were many more objections to my playing Roxane. And what do I care anyhow? If they consider me too thin, I assert that it is silly. A woman [Phèdre] with a shameless love, but who had rather die than yield to it, a woman who has shriveled from passion, from weeping, such a woman can't have a bosom like Madame Paradol. That would be absurd. I have read the part over ten times during the last week. I don't know how I shall act it, but I tell you that I feel it. The newspaper critics are disgusting. They won't change my mind about it. They rack their brains to hurt me, instead of helping me and encouraging me. But *I will* play it, if need be, before four spectators. (Turning to me): When they write articles that are frank and conscientious, nothing is better or more helpful; but there are so many people who use their pens to tell lies, to destroy! They are worse than robbers or assassins. They kill the soul with their pinpricks. Oh, I'd be willing to poison them!

The Mother: My dear, you are talking all the time; you are tiring yourself. You were up at six o'clock this morning. I don't know what possesses your legs. You have chattered all day long, and this evening you have acted; you will make yourself sick.

Rachel (vivaciously): Not a bit, let me be! I tell you I won't. It keeps me alive (turning in my direction). Do you want me to get the book? We will read the play together.

Me: Should I like to? You couldn't suggest anything more delightful.

Sarah: But, my dear, it is half past eleven!

Rachel: Well, what's to prevent you from going to bed?

So Sarah went to bed. Rachel got up and went out of the room; in a moment she was back with a volume of Racine in her hand. Her manner and bearing had something solemn and religious, like a ministrant bearing sacred vessels to the altar. She sat down beside me, and snuffed the candle. The mother smiled and dozed.

Rachel (opening the book with reverence and bending over it): How I love that man! When I put my nose in that book, I could stay so for two days without eating or drinking.

So the book was placed on the table between us, and she and I began to read *Phèdre*. Everybody else left. Rachel made a slight bow to each as they went, and continued reading. At first she read in a monotonous tone, as if it were a litany. Little by little she became animated. We talked over every passage, each saying what we thought. At last she came to Phèdre's declaration. Then she extended her right arm on the table,—her head resting on her left hand, supported on her elbow,—and let herself go entirely. At first she read in a soft voice. She turned pale, then red. I never saw anything so noble, so interesting; at the theater she never produced such an effect upon me.

Fatigue! A slight hoarseness! Punch! The late hour! An almost feverish animation on her little cheeks, half hid in her nightcap! A mysterious charm shed all over her! Brilliant eyes looking for my opinion, and a childish smile that managed to slip into the midst of all this! Add to these the disorderly table, the flickering of the candle, the mother dozing beside us—the whole composed a picture worthy of Rembrandt, a chapter in a novel worthy of *Wilhelm Meister,* and a souvenir of theatrical life that I shall never forget.

It got to be half past twelve. The father came back from the opera, where he had been to see the first night of Mademoiselle Nathan in the *Juive.* As soon as he sat down, he addressed his daughter a few boorish words to bid her stop reading. Rachel shut the book saying: "It's revolting! I shall buy a night light and read in bed." As she spoke there were tears in her eyes. It was indeed revolting to see such a creature treated in that fashion! I got up and went away full of admiration and respect and much moved.

On my return home, I sit down at once to write you, with the fidelity of stenography, all the details of this strange evening, thinking that you will keep them, and that one day this letter will come to light.

Pray accept *mes hommages*,

A. de M.

Not long after that evening there followed the plan of a tragedy. He got hold of the story of Frédégonde and Chilpéric, of Merovingian times, and believed he had found the proper intrigue and a rôle that would suit Rachel. He sketched a plot, and wrote a monologue for Frédégonde. Rachel read it, and asked him to finish the play. He meditated about it, read Merovingian history, sketched the incidents of his drama, and neglected the better paid tales which the editor of the *Revue des Deux Mondes* pressed for. Nevertheless, Paul, aided by an adverse balance in his budget, persuaded him to make a contract to deliver three stories in the course of three months. But no sooner had he done this than he railed at Paul: "You have turned me into a factory hand, a galley slave, a serf attached to the glebe. Give me back my debts and my creditors!" He became so depressed over these shackles that Paul, fearful of what he might do, took the caps off the pistols in the house. The next morning a letter came from Rachel asking him to spend a few days at the country house she had taken at Montmorency. It is probable that he took with him sundry scenes of his play which he called the *Servante du Roi* and that Rachel was pleased with his ideas. At any rate he went off and came back in good spirits. Paul, the *romancier,* who always thinks in terms of amours, attributes more signif-

icance to this visit than there is any justification for.
Rachel, to be sure, had never had, so far back as she could
remember, any conventional scruples on such matters,
and nothing turns on Paul's hypothesis, other than that
it serves as offering superfluous testimony that Aimée
d'Alton has been thrown into the discard. At any rate,
the *Servante du Roi* was dropped. Rachel had set her
heart on playing the rôle of Phèdre, as she had told Musset at the supper party. She now said, "When I shall
have played Phèdre and have no more battles to fight,
when I shall have won all along the line, then you can
write for me and I shall be wholly at your disposal." So
she took her separate way, and the poet seems to have
dropped *Frédégonde* and to have taken up *Alcestis* as the
subject of a tragedy. The actress wished to have him at
hand when she might want a tragedy, and he was eager to
have a play of his acted by her. So they kept on terms with
each other, but they were too high strung, each of them,
not to quarrel. As usual Alfred writes to Madame Jaubert about the occasion of it:

Nov. 24, 1842

Ma chère Marraine,

As for news there are only two items. I have quarreled
with Rachel, and here's the reason. A few days ago, as
she was coming out of the Théâtre Français, while her
father was trying to hail a hack, she was on the arm of
some gentleman of the press. Just then Buloz came up
and said: "What! You take the arm of such people as
that?" "Pooh," she answered, "when I have had enough

of people, I know how to get rid of them." Thereupon she named me, and boasted, if you please, that the reason I never went to her house was that she had dropped me a hint.

Your very humble servant and godson, to whom these remarks were carefully brought by his best friends, did not think it well to put up with them, nor to have it said that he had been put out of her house. He took the liberty of writing to the Princess, very politely, that she had lied about it, that no justification existed for any such story, and that he was greatly surprised. The Princess did not show herself unworthy of her sex or of her position. She answered with a long cock and bull story in which she denied formally the things she had said before three people, and at the same time she did not fail to be much offended, not because she had been caught in this way but because there were these words in my letter. "Permit me to tell you, Mademoiselle, a thing of which *you are perhaps ignorant;* it is unusual for a gentleman to say or do anything rude enough to forbid him the house etc., etc."

It seems that the phrase *of which you are perhaps ignorant* was not readily digested. And, as for her age she does not lack a certain poise, she answered that the phrase had not, for a gentleman, been well chosen, etc. In other words, we insulted each other, very courteously, as you see. After that I reflected a long time on what I ought to do, and after mature reflection, I came to the conclusion that I would do nothing at all. What do you think about it?

A. de M.

He refers to the quarrel again, in another letter to Madame Jaubert; by this time he is rather ashamed: "I left Rachel *plantée là* for no reason but that I was in ill-humor; Rachel was piqued, and said that it was she who had left me *planté là*, at that I became jolly mad— there were letters, a rumpus, bawlings, and then at last it ended in smoke." The tragedy to be written by him, however, though occasionally talked of, came to nothing.

Three years later these famous personages came together again. In April, 1846, Rachel gave a dinner at her house and invited Musset. During the meal the guest on her left drew attention to a very handsome ring that she wore on her finger. It was passed round the table and everybody praised it. "Gentlemen," she said, "since this work of art has the honor to please you, I put it up at auction. What will you bid?"—"Five hundred francs!" "A thousand!"—"Fifteen hundred!" The bids got up to three thousand. She turned to Musset: "And what will you give, my Poet, will you not bid?" "I bid my heart," he answered. "The ring is yours," she said, and dropped it on his plate. As they left the table, thinking that the joke had lasted long enough, he tried to give back the ring. "By jove," she cried, "this is no jest. You bid your heart and I would not give it back to you for a hundred thousand crowns. The bargain is struck; you can not get out of it." He continued his protestations; she bent her knee like a suppliant: "Dear Poet, you would not have the courage to refuse this little present, if I offered it to you the day after I played the famous rôle that you are to write for me and which, perhaps, I shall have to wait for all my life. So, I beseech you, keep this ring as a gage of your promise. If ever, by my fault or otherwise, you shall definitely renounce writing the wished-for rôle, bring me back the ring and I will take it." Musset was really affected by her earnestness and went home full of kindly feelings toward her and of purpose to write such a play. But Rachel went to England and Alfred was lazy. But once again, four years later, 1851, she invited him to dinner, asked him to take her down, recalled the old days of the supper party, and said that she would show that she was *aussi bonne fille* as in those days. He asked how? and she answered: "By going to see you to beseech you once more to write me a play." And the next day she came and talked "theater" for an hour, but she could not extort a definite promise from him. Again she went to England, and on coming back, again returned to her suit. He acceded and prepared a plan of a five-act drama, to be called *Faustine*, the scene of which was to be laid in Venice in the fifteenth century. Then again he heard nothing from her; so he laid his manuscript aside, and the poet and the great actress parted for ever.

CHAPTER XVI

THE PRINCESS BELGIOJOSO

Alfred de Musset's acquaintance with the Princess Belgiojoso was due to his godmother, Madame Jaubert. The first letter that we have from him to Madame Jaubert is addressed to her, care of the Princess, *à la Jonchère, près Reuil*. Next year he is familiar enough to refer to the Princess as the Princesse Uranie, after he had refused her invitation to dinner to meet Lamartine. This was shortly after he had published his *Lettre à Lamartine*, the poem which, added to the *Nuit de Mai* and the *Nuit de Décembre*, had made him famous with young men and with those persons in society who cared for poetry. A year later the Princess asked him for some verses to be sold at a fair; she wished for a comedy, for he had already published *Caprices de Marianne, Fantasio, On ne badine pas avec l'amour*, and *Le Chandelier*; but he preferred a story. They could not agree on the subject that he proposed, and she said that it would be necessary to give that subject up, unless Madame Jaubert could find a way of compromise. But unfortunately Madame Jaubert did not find a compromise and neither comedy nor story was ever written.

This was just at the beginning of Musset's liaison with Aimée d'Alton, and such notice as he bestowed upon the Princess was merely due to his intimacy with his godmother. For instance:

Thursday, June 28, 1837

Madame

As your departure vexed me a little, I am not sorry that my silence disquieted you a little; but when will you know me? That day you will lay aside forever your diffidences, and at the same time you will excuse my faults. Please remember what you said once on our way back from Augerville: "There may be laziness, there may be negligence, but never coldness or forgetfulness." Diffidence is a miserable fault that witty people should never fall into. I am going to prove to you at once that it is not always one of mine, for when I heard of your departure, my first thought was to say to myself, "How I should like to make a third at the back of the carriage between the mouth of her Highness [the Princess] and the ear of the Privy Councillor [Madame Jaubert]!" And my second thought was that "the Privy Councillor could very easily, in spite of the distance, make me such a third by her letters, and write me some little scandals." I could hear the carriage roll along in the moonlight, and see the [Princess's] little sister Valentine asleep on the front seat; in the back the other two travelers stretched out side by side, chatting in a low tone, laughing or dreaming, and I said to myself, "Some of it will be coming to me." You see that while you were doubting me, I was relying on you.

Then he rallies her about her suddenly leaving Paris in company with the Princess (he calls it an elopement) and says that he was on the point of writing her a letter

about it, in which, among other things he was going to
say: "Be so good as to tell the Princess that if at her
age she goes in for elopements, people will certainly talk.
But I suppose, and I like to think so, that you will get
married *incognita* at the blacksmith's in order to legalize
your escapade. And what can the Princess say if, while
she is carrying you away in your dressing-gown and
slippers, they impress post horses, gallop after, and take
you off, while she is bathing in the sea in her bathing
wrapper? She will be getting just what she deserves.
Behold the consequences of imprudence!" (It seems that
the two ladies had gone to England to see Queen Victoria's coronation.) He continues: "However, you shall
both be pardoned on one condition, that you will appear
at the coronation in trains longer than the Queen's. See
that you don't fail. Present my compliments to your
lovely traveling companion. I should like, also, to know
three things: Were you seasick? Is Miss Talbot [an
actress] pretty? and, When do you mean to come back?"

It rather seems as if the letter were as much intended
for the Princess, as for his godmother. Perhaps the contrast between this Italian lady and Aimée d'Alton drew
him on. Aimée was a young woman, a minx, circum-
scribed in experience, and over ready for adventure, but
the Princess Belgiojoso was indisputably a great lady,
a jewel set in a most romantic setting, a very unusual
personality. Her admirer, Floranges, says: "The Princess Belgiojoso was then writing books, great heavy

books. Not content with conspiracies, with being a
beauty, with playing the guitar or with a dagger, or
painting fans, or telling all Paris that Austria was per-
secuting her, she was reading Hebrew and composing
books, and what books! A gigantic mass, a pyramid of
pages!'' This pyramid became in due course an *Essai
sur la formation du dogme catholique;* Sainte-Beuve said
it was ''solid, of Catholic sympathies, but at bottom semi-
pelagian and origenian, written in a simple, strong style,
enfin une très précieuse curiosité.'' The semi-Pelagianism
may not have attracted the poet, but the Princess' exotic
character, like attar of roses, certainly did. Nevertheless, Aimée d'Alton still maintained a certain influence
upon him. One *amour* with him may have been an obstacle to a second contemporaneous *amour,* although his
story *Les Deux Maîtresses* (1837) seems to imply the
contrary, but it did not interfere with *amitié.* Indeed it
would be very unfair to the poet if one, in passing from
Aimée d'Alton to Rachel, and from Rachel to Princess
Belgiojoso, did not pause to lay stress on his charming
friendship with Madame Jaubert.

To His Godmother
Tuesday, October 17, 1837

Chère Marraine,
There is a rumor that Madame Jaubert is returning
to Paris in the month of November. I hope that she will
tell me, perhaps, when she comes why I have not written
to her during her absence. If I were to try to find the
reason for myself, I should certainly make a mistake; and

perhaps, Madame the Privy Councillor, in spite of her wit, may make a mistake, too.

She will tell me that I am lazy, distraught, in love, a waster of time, that is to say a loafer, a Parisian; that is true; but those are not good reasons, for Madame knows better than anybody how completely I should forget men and things before any forgetfulness of her could creep into my heart.

No, Madame, for my part at least, my silence does not prove that the smallest blade of grass has sprung up on the path of our friendship; but, is it the same on your part? That is a question I dare not ask myself for fear of being in the wrong,—for I am certainly in the wrong; it was for me to recall myself to you. A pretty woman, from the mere fact that she is a woman, does not write first, even to a friend, any more than she invites men to dance at a ball. Tell me if I have lost, and what I have lost. I fear that it may be a little trustfulness; Have I still any aces in my hand? You will agree that, if life is a game of cards, I cheat sometimes pretty well, but that I play very badly.

For a prospective diplomat [through the influence of the Duc d'Orléans at this time he might have joined the Embassy at Madrid] I have no qualifications, my knowledge of the world scarcely extends to a visiting card. Madame de Girardin told me one day that I was, *Un élégant qui n'est pas mondain.* She would have done better to say: *Un élégant* who has rips in his evening jacket, and *un mondain* who does not go into the *monde.*

Apropos of ennui, I have made a discovery. *L'ennui*

m'ennuie, and I don't want to hear the thing mentioned; which makes me feel better.

Adieu, Madame. Have you grown?

Â. de M.

To his Godmother

October 27, 1837

Madame,

You have found the real name of the sentiment that unites us, in calling it a sentiment without a name. It recalls that saying by one of my friends who said to a woman, "We are on the road that divides *amour* and *amitié.*" What do you think of the comparison?

"I am greatly concerned," says Madame the Privy Councillor, "that you should not become too much of a rake. I mean it seriously."

But, I ask in my turn, do you seriously mean that I am becoming a rake, when I tell you that I am holding myself back with both hands? Am I a rake, because I find a row of pearls white and have a desire to touch them with the tip of my finger?

You say, "I like that."

Very well. If I like what you like, it is, first a proof of good taste, and second that even in another lady's company, I miss you.

Unluckily Madame the Privy Councillor knows very well that, sweet as they are, the pearls in question are far too sour for your humble servant.

You have not asked me how I have passed the summer. No, and why not?—Because

A. de M.

It is too late to discover what lies behind these allusions; it may be that Madame Jaubert has just discovered his liaison, it may be that she suspected that Musset was already losing his interest in her young cousin. For, although, if as yet the Princess Belgiojoso has not taken the first place in the poet's thoughts, the *Nuit d'Octobre,* just published, showed that he had not forgotten George Sand. Or, it may be that she refers to the Princess Belgiojoso or to his more degraded habits.

At any rate Madame Jaubert used to lecture him on his manners in society. He took the lectures with a good grace, for he knew that he deserved it, and that she had written out of kindness. That his manners were careless at times seems certain. An Austrian diplomat took away a very unfavorable impression of them. Musset came, the diplomat says, to the salon of their Ambassador's wife, smelling of his pipe *à faire horreur.* The conversation fell upon Léopold Robert, the celebrated painter, who had recently died in Venice. Musset remarked that he, too, had nearly died there.

Hostess: It must be horrible to expect to die when alone in a foreign land.

Musset: Yes, indeed. But I had a faithful and adorable companion.

Hostess (sympathetic): Is Madame de Musset dead?

Musset: No, I have never been married. It was Madame Dudevant, with whom I was traveling in Italy. I owe her my life. She took care of me with an affection, a tenderness of which she only is capable.

Embarrassed silence. And the scandalized diplomat

says that at Madame de Girardin's, among other *bar-bouilleurs de papier,* Musset lounged on the sofa, put his feet on the table, wore his hat in the drawing-room and smoked cigars. Musset was aware that he was subject to criticism; he agrees that his mode of entering a salon is displeasing, to himself, most of all, and says that it is due to pride and shyness, and, also, that on certain days he is in an extremely nervous condition. Even when people are polite to him he is embarrassed; compliments he can not bear, he will not say that they wound him, nor that he thinks them hypocritical, they merely make him wish to slip away. "And please believe," he writes, "that I detest myself at those times." It had not been so when he was a boy, and he wished that it were not so, now; he admits to a disinclination for the society of men, even when intelligent and friendly, and though he does not like to analyze his feelings, he supposes that it is because he is indifferent to men, or worse, possibly he hates them. As to little tokens of social civility, bowings, hand-shakings, and so forth, he will do his best. "But as to sympathetic relations between man and man, even when slight and merely suggested, that is a different matter. Permit my old experience not to decide such a question boldly. Your letter has made me ponder over it a long time; you were lecturing me on politeness, but you have made me think of friendship. I have considered myself; and I have wondered whether, under my exterior, which is stiff, morose, impertinent and little sympathetic, whatever the lovely little Milanese lady [the Princess] may say about it, whether (I say) underneath that exterior there was not originally something exalted and passionate in Rousseau's manner. It is possible; I tried once to throw myself into a friendship, a strange sentiment, unheard of in me, an emotion stronger perhaps than desire in love. According to all that I know, it must be a terrific sentiment, a very pleasant but very dangerous one that makes the happiness or misery of a whole life, and I understand how Rousseau went half mad, being so shaken by that passion. No, by all means, no; I do not care for it. Love is quite enough, that is all one wants of you, *Mesdames,* and besides I haven't the time.

"This is too serious for so slight a remonstrance; but in talking to you my heart opens, as with other people it shuts up. So forgive this dissertation, and if you think of what I have said, you will understand me better. I am not tender, but I go to extremes. That is my fault, and it makes me very angry.

"A. de M."

One suspects that this talk about friendship and the reference to the *la belle petite Milanaise* may fairly be interpreted, involved though it is in a general analysis of his own character, to be a rejection of that sentiment with regard to her.

By the spring of 1839 the liaison with Aimée d'Alton had come to an end. Musset's thoughts were on Rachel and a possible play, but his heart was untenanted, and had begun to be weary of its emptiness. In a letter to Madame Jaubert he refers to the Princess simply as *Elle*: "So then, *She* is coming back and you too; one will be able to live a little." His reference suggests that *She* has begun to be of consequence to him.

In the beginning of the year 1840, Musset was very ill and insomnia made him nearly crazy; he refused to obey orders. He cried out that he must eat, sat up and demanded his clothes and said that as long as they would not give him anything to eat he would go to the baker's and get some bread. The household could do nothing with him. Fortunately, Madame Jaubert came and quieted him; "Get into bed," she commanded, and laid her tiny hand on his forehead. The Princess Belgiojoso also came several times, and sat at his bedside and gave him medicines, which (Paul says) he did not dare to refuse from the hands of a *si grande dame*. One day while she sat beside him he felt very ill, but she said quietly, "Don't be alarmed, nobody dies in my presence." He made her promise to come again, for he said: "I shall not die on that day." At the end of March he was convalescent, and writes his gratitude to his godmother, *"Vous m'avez vu tant et si bien gâté, tous et toutes,* that I should like to go back to bed in order to see you again." He then left *cet ennuyeux Paris que j'adore* and made a visit to Bury where he wrote the melancholy verses,

J'ai perdu ma force et ma vie

which show that he had not wholly recovered his strength; but he was really doing well. A letter from the Princess to Madame Jaubert says: "I have seen Madame et

Mademoiselle de Musset, who gave me very good news of that one of the two [sons?] whose health disquieted me. The country is just what he needs they say, and he expects to make a long stay there. I know some one who will not be sorry.'' As the letter is full of a quarrel between her and Mignet, it is a fair surmise that she means that Mignet was jealous of Musset. From what she says it seems virtually certain that a passage in a letter from Musset to the Duchesse de Castries written at this time (September, 1840) refers to the Princess. The letter starts out with a description of his religious faith, for the Duchess was a very religious person, and much concerned with his piety, then he proceeds: ''That which I lack now is a much more terrestrial thing, as I have told you. I explained to you how an extravagant passion, very useless and a little ridiculous, made me, nearly a year ago, change all my habits. I quitted everything about me, men friends, women friends, all the current of life in which I lived and one of the prettiest women in Paris [evidently Aimée d'Alton]. I did not succeed, of course, in my crazy imagining, and to-day I am cured, but dried up, like a fish in the middle of a wheat field; well, I have never been able to live alone like this, I can't and I never shall be able to, nor to agree that it is living. I had as lief be an Englishman. That is my whole trouble. I don't think it very hard to cure me, nor will it be very easy. I have never been *banal*. What are called women of the world, on the one hand, seem to me to be playing a play, and don't know their parts. On the other hand my lost loves have left scars that will not be effaced by ointment. What I need is a woman who has some quality, no matter what: beauty, goodness, wickedness if need be, or is very witty, or very stupid, but one who has some quality. Do you know any such, Madame? Twitch my sleeve, please, when you come upon one.

"Believe, Madame, in my very sincere and respectful friendship.

"ALFRED DE MUSSET."

But not till the end of the year does he really let the secret out, and then in a letter to his godmother, dated October 9 (1840): "As for *Her,* now that I have made up my mind not to see her again, I can tell you frankly what I think of her. I love her, I love her, I love her, and I love her very much."

The Princess liked to be loved, and to be made love to: she said, "I can't guess what interest there is in life, when eyes no longer look at us with love!" She flirted with him. Madame Jaubert remarks: "Always interested in one another, these two people were either quarreling or making up." The Princess went to Italy in the beginning of 1841, and stayed away until midsummer, 1842. There is a reference to her in a letter of his to Madame Jaubert. He is in an unhappy mood and derides society and its pleasures—"*Le monde! Les petits cancanneries, les gros rieurs sur une chaise qui craque* . . . but, *Ohime!* There was a person with a thoughtful brow and disturbing eyes who persuaded me to believe for a time that I could live in that trough! . . . I wrote to Uranie [the Princess] and as well as I could. But Destiny rules. Writing was unsuccessful before, and would be unsuccessful again.''

The Princess came back to Paris in the summer of 1842. Then a more serious quarrel took place. Madame Jaubert says that one night Musset was drawing caricatures; and the Princess challenged him to caricature her, she said that attempts had often been made but never with success. He retorted that regularity of features offered no difficulty, took up his pencil and drew a likeness exaggerating a trait here and there, in order to make it comic. Everybody was amused but the Princess, who remarked in a tone of indifference, ''There is something in it.'' Madame Jaubert thought that he had taken too bold a step. Musset replied that he had never felt the Princess's charm so strongly as while he was drawing. But so trifling a matter could not seriously have vexed a lady busy with the Italian *Risorgimento* and matters of dogma that bordered on semi-Pelagianism. Another incident seems to approach nearer to probability. The Princess at this time had recovered her Italian fortune and had hired a very fine house, Rue d'Anjou, and there she used to receive on Wednesdays and Saturdays. Everything was individual. A negro in a turban, looking as if he had come out of a Paolo Veronese, introduced the guests into the antechamber adorned like a Gothic oratory with skulls and cross-bones. The salon was hung with dark velvet, nearly black, spangled with silver stars and the furniture covered with the same stuff. The bedchamber beyond was all in white silk, the bed of ebony incrusted with ivory, standing on a platform, raised three

RACHEL

From the ivory by Auguste Barré in the Louvre

PRINCESS BELGIOJOSO
Portrait by Chassériau

steps from the floor, like a cenotaph, and the great can-
delabra were of silver. The Princess was wont to wear
a black dress, that set off the alabaster of her neck and
emphasized the pallor of her beautiful regular features.
Her guests were usually men of distinction in literature
and art, Mignet, the historian; Victor Cousin, the philosopher; Ary Scheffer, the painter; Henri Martin, another
historical scholar; Thiers, the statesman; Rossini, Mey-
erbeer, Bellini, the composers; Franz Liszt, the charming
and fashionable musician; Chenavard, the sculptor; Heinrich Heine, Musset, Alton-Shée, Major Frazer and so
on. The evening receptions were more select than those
of the afternoon; the Princess, crowned with a wreath
of fuchsias, lay on a sofa smoking a narghile, with *la
Guiccioli,* the Romagnole rendered famous by Byron, but
now quietly married to a French gentleman, and other
ladies, beside her, while the savants talked, or Heine
jested. Sometimes there was a *soirée dansante.* At one
of these Musset saw a beautiful young woman, Mademoiselle de C., who had come up to Paris from the provinces. He asked to be presented. She had read his
poetry. They danced a *galop à deux temps* together. Both
were excited, *troublés.* It is said that she murmured,
"Ai-je donc trouvé un maître?" So, Lady Caroline Lamb
wrote in her diary on meeting Byron, "That beautiful
face is my fate." They danced again together. When
Musset went to speak to the Princess, he felt in her manner *l'impertinence voulue.* He decided on the spot that
he would leave her and go into the country. His godmother, who tried to calm his impatient childish moods,

disapproved of his going. The Princess on her part, went to see Madame Jaubert, praised Mademoiselle C.'s grace, her carriage, her blue eyes, her little feet, extravagantly, and said: "I hope that Monsieur de Musset will appreciate her beauty as much as I do; that will create a happy diversion for the sentiment that he *thinks* he feels for me, and which absolutely ruins our friendly relations." Madame Jaubert laughed and said that she was skeptical of curing one wound with another, and that she thought that Alfred was more likely to overload his heart than to lighten it. Before leaving Paris, Musset came, in his turn, to say good-by to *la marraine*. He seemed to be very irritated with the Princess, and kept saying: "I will show her that she has no right to treat me so lightly."

Besides Mademoiselle C., there was on the horizon a Countess Kalergis. But the cause of the rift between the poet and the adventurous Princess lay in their respective characters. He, a child as he himself said, *tergiversant, tournaillant, débraillé,* turning and shifting, like a field poppy that has lost its petals tossed in the wind; she, an intellectual woman, with *sang froid,* fond of adoration and accustomed to receive it. At any rate they quarreled; and he was very sore. His letters to his godmother now are full of allusions to the Princess:

1842

Dear Godmother,

Are we, too, at odds? Have you gone over entirely to the enemy? Is susceptibility so contagious, and are you piqued by a jest? You, who are the personification of good sense and indulgence? Example must have great authority with you.

I do not mean to say that I am right, nor that I am wrong, because you are too Lombard [the Princess came from Lombardy] at the present time; I merely wish to state a fact, and that is that I have suffered sorely, and for that reason I deserve to be forgiven. Those that suffer should be pardoned. To cudgel soundly, and also to maintain rancor, you know, is a little too feminine. It is also proper to say that as I broke the cups, it is fair that I should pay for them. So I do, and I say nothing.

The Princess Turandot [an allusion to a character in a fairy tale of Carlo Gozzi] (I am not Kalaf) does not know how much she has hurt me, otherwise she would have been less ferocious. She would not listen to the plainest facts, to wit. First: that the cares, material and very serious, which hang about my neck, have made my wrong attitude toward her a great deal worse. I may say that I defy anybody to keep an even temper under the circumstances in which I am. Second, that I can not confide to her matters that concern others besides myself. It seems to me that she ought to be able to understand that there are moments in this earthly life when a man's disposition changes in spite of himself; and that when he has, besides, the privilege of having been born peevish, he may become more so.

The beautiful Turandot takes me at my word whenever I am sulky; and on the other hand she gives me no credit for my good impulses. I spoke to her with the utmost

frankness, foolishly, awkwardly; and she replied with
the calm gravity of a mandarin. I repeat, dear Godmother, that I do not claim to be in the right, but that I
regard you as completely under her influence at present.

A. de M.

Lovers' quarrels. But one must read, in these letters
to his godmother, more than the words, for it is thought
that next to his passion for George Sand, Musset's love
of the Princess Belgiojoso was the great emotion of his
life. In July, 1842, on her return from Italy, the faithful
Mignet had found her a house with a pleasant garden
on the Avenue de Paris, at Versailles, and there she invited Musset, who had been writing her letter upon letter,
to pay her a visit. He went and stayed a week. She
avoided every occasion of a tête-à-tête, and treated him
like a stranger. He did not know what to make of this
behavior. He wrote his surmises to his godmother. Perhaps she was afraid of herself, but he thought not; perhaps she enjoyed making him suffer, knowing that she
ran no risk of really calming him; or, as was most likely,
she was merely haughty and indifferent. One day he
made some jest at the table not to her liking; and in the
midst of a game of chess she took him to task for it. He
became petulant, and to make matters worse, she made
him mix water with his wine, and when he coughed insisted upon his putting a plaster on his chest, which
he found very uncomfortable. He joked about it to his
godmother, but it was easy to discover that he was really
out of humor and had not been polite; so Madame Jaubert

advised him to make a penitent call upon the Princess. He felt reluctant, like a child dragged by his nurse to apologize; like a child he called upon all his resolution before he could get out of the carriage and walk up to the house, and again before ringing the bell. The butler's calm aspect scarcely reassured him, nor the friendly greeting of Monsieur Mignet. At last, as he writes to Madame Jaubert, "When the star arose, half asleep and veiled in thin clouds, but very sweet and charming, shedding the fairest rays, then I felt revived, and so, sunburned on the way out, I began a game of chess by moonlight (this is a romantic metaphor)." He says that he drank four tumblers of *reddish water* and went back to Paris with the sense of having done his duty, and more than that, for, though but a few days before he had been saying to himself, "What ferocity! What cruelty!" his words now were, "How charming! What a delightful person!" And he adds: "P. S. Please tell me what you think of the following sentence, it refers to Origen: 'He experienced the temporary preference for material comfort over intellectual pleasure, which is so precious when it is unaccustomed.' I do not cite it exactly, but it is about like that. Is it not a goodly sentence well expressed? It is in a very serious work. Without the presumption of thinking that I am like Origen, my sick stomach took note of it!

"A. de M."

That little fling at the Princess's book on the *Formation du dogme catholique* does not sound as if the poet's feelings had been really hurt. And yet they were. What took place is not known, but the poet became very angry; it seems that he must have brooded over a too scornful rejection of his suit. She had said to him: "The only good effect of *too easy* success, is to keep a man from an obstinate pursuit of an impossible success." At any rate in September, 1842, the *Revue de Deux Mondes* published a poem under Musset's name entitled,

On a Dead Lady

Elle était belle, si . . .
Elle était bonne, si . . .
Elle pensait, si . . .
Elle priait, si deux beaux yeux,
Tantôt s'attachant à la terre,
Tantôt se levant vers les cieux,
Peuvent s'appeler la prière.

She prayed; if handsome eyes
Sometimes commercing with the skies,
Sometimes with earth and earthly care,
Can be called a prayer.

So the stanzas ran, stating a virtue, only to deny it, and ending by saying that she had never done more than appear to live, that the book of life had fallen from her hands unread. The verses were bitter and undoubtedly intended to give pain. But though they were read freely, nobody knew to whom they referred; some thought George Sand, some Rachel, but there was nothing definite in them except that they pointed to a lady who had hurt his feelings. Madame Jaubert thought that he had behaved improperly. "A gentleman, especially after staying at a lady's house, should never write about her in a magazine"; but in her usual fashion of trying to smooth matters out, told him that the Princess had not read the poem. Alfred thought that he smelled a rat; he wrote, "So, Urania has not read the *Revue!* I hope that you do not believe that I believe that you believe that I believe that! I am not used to this kind of jest, and my pretty little godmother knows her godson's heart too well for her to imagine that he tumbles to that trick. As to having a magazine before one's eyes *dove di voi si favella* (which speaks of one) and not opening it, No, my dear Lady, I don't believe it." So he continues in his tone of boyish cynicism to assert that, say what she will, he will never believe that. Then he says that he is thinking of writing a novel to be called *See-Saw,* the plot being: I love you— you do not love me; I go back—if you advance, etc. etc., adorned with some veracious facts. And that if *She* did not read it, there were others that would. He tries to affect a care-free manner, but, child that he is, he bursts out with his wounded feelings: "I tell you, she has made me mad. You don't know, Godmother, you can't know to what degree she has killed me, scourged me, wrecked me, how she drew me on and encouraged me, how cold-blooded she was, how her malignant, perverted, deep-revolving coquetry worked on a poor devil who loved her with all his heart, who followed her like a dog, who went off quietly a half-hour before dinner to shed hot tears, and hardly dared to tell her so in a whisper when he offered her his arm on the way to the dining-room."

He sought comfort and distraction in his usual diversions, and went to bed for a week with a fever, *fruits de sa sagesse,* as he says. Paul preached sermons to him. Fever, restricted food, medicine, nursing and sweats under innumerable blankets brought him to reason, and then he felt regret and shame for having published his verses. He wrote his godmother that he did not love the Princess any more, did not care two sous, and had no wish to make it up, but that he was dissatisfied with himself and would like to make reparation, and asked her how, and says that it is perfectly certain that nobody thought the poem referred to the Princess: neither Paul, nor he, had even heard it suggested. He asks her advice. "Remember," he says, "I don't want any reconciliation in any way." He had had enough, and was done with her, only he had gone too far, and wished to undo what he had done. His arguments with his godmother carried him to Byron and Mary Chaworth and Lady Byron. Never, he said, had he been angry with a woman who said that she loved another man; and if a woman had said that she did not love him at all (a situation in which he had never been) he would have said nothing. Then he burst into complaint: "I have letters from Urania in which she says, 'I thought that my friendship might be of some benefit to you'! and 'With me you would have suffered, but not without some compensation.' I held her hand, I kissed it for a whole minute, and she let me do it. I told her a hundred times that I did not aspire to be her lover, that my vanity was not concerned, that I only asked for one word of friendship in order to be happy all day long. And besides letting me kiss her hand, there are a thousand things that one can't say, because one can't explain them to a third person. But you may be sure that she drew me to her out of idleness in order to amuse herself merely to make me play the part of *patito* [a lover borne in hand]—you know what that is. I would not. And for that reason she has ill-treated me. As for me, I really believed in this false show of friendship, which was merely comedy, a pastime, and stopped short when she saw me come back and yield. It is that which wounded me! She had no right, first of all, to treat me so; and, second, she misjudged me in a manner mortifying to me, by trying to do it. I shall always retain a bad impression of her conduct.

"A. de M."

But, fickle and changeable as ever, his good feelings got the upper hand and he wrote to the Princess with candor; she answered with perfect indifference. He was deeply hurt. He put a brave face on it in his letters that autumn to his godmother, but the light tone of badinage can not conceal the bitterness within. There was talk of their meeting the next year, but Musset avoided it. Years afterward (1849), before leaving France, she went to see his comedy *Louison* at the Théâtre Français, and wrote him that it was a masterpiece, *"Votre Louison est adorable de grâce et de verité, de finesse et de sensibilité.* You think and feel like Shakespeare and you speak like Marivaux; it is a strange union, but the effect is very successful. Perhaps you do not remember that I exist; no matter. You have taken good means to perpetuate your memory even in the most forgetful. I thank you for some hours, more than agreeable, that I owe to you.

"CHRISTINE TRIVULCE DE BELGIOJOSO."

She threw herself into the *Risorgimento* in Italy, and Alfred went sliding down his withering primrose path.

CHAPTER XVII

MADAME ALLAN-DESPRÉAUX

THE *Souvenir*—a poem due to a chance return to the spot in the forest of Fontainebleau where he had been with George Sand—written in 1841, was the last of Musset's poems that have wings. He needed the spur of pleasure rendered poignant by pain; this George Sand had given him, and once more he lifted aloft "the pageant of his bleeding heart." Had he been younger, had his powers not been enfeebled by debauchery, the Princess Belgiojoso might have roused him again, *"Poète, prends ton luth et me donne un baiser."* As it was, his genius rested in its scabbard. He could do nothing without the stimulus of outside help. Bonnaire, the editor of the *Revue des Deux Mondes,* kept dunning him in vain. There is a letter written in 1842 to Madame Jaubert, always his good angel, which says:

Monday morning

Madame,

Do you want to do a good deed? If you feel better, take a pen one of these evenings, and as you may chance to be feeling, but very definitely, write me reproaches upon reproaches for my idleness. It's an odd proposal. Please be brave and accept. I will answer your letters in a poem (*without any name,* of course) but I need the stroke of a battledore to send me the shuttlecock, and only you can give it. I can only write when I get a fillip, I can't invent.

231

Start off with a laugh at this nonsensical scheme and then send me one of your heart beats, and I'll send it back.

She accepted the proposal, and he wrote his verses:

On Idleness

Oui, j'écris rarement et me plais de le faire:
Non pas que la paresse en moi soit ordinaire;
Mais, sitôt que je prends la plume à ce dessein,
Je crois prendre en galère une rame à la main.

Yes, I write seldom; on my pleasure it waits,
Not that to be idle is one of my traits;
But as soon as I take a pen in my hand,
It's like plying an oar at the word of command.

But nothing further of consequence for a year, when he published in 1843, on the anniversary of the death of his old schoolmate, Duc d'Orléans, and heir apparent, an elegy called *Le Treize Juillet.* There followed a few sonnets, and some stanzas, *Réponse à M. Charles Nodier,* that dwelt upon the happy days, *le bon temps,* when he, Victor Hugo, Alfred de Vigny and Sainte-Beuve were young.

In 1844 he had an attack of pleurisy. He was but thirty-three, and returning strength, aided by the benefit of a forced rest, brought back his good humor.

To Alfred Tattet

May, 1844

My dear Friend,

I have just had an inflammation of the chest, and I

take advantage of the occasion to give you my news. When I say inflammation of the chest, I should say pleurisy; but the name does not matter much. The important thing is that they put on fifty leeches and bled me three times; after that, on the third day, they opened my bowels, just as if I had swallowed the crown diamonds, then they put me on a restricted diet. With all that, old Boy, they cured me quickly and admirably. I will whisper in your ear that without that, joking aside, my trunk was on the *diligence* and my place booked for a better world. I have lost my deposit by not going.

I am now exemplary, really, quiet, content, pretty religious—but of all things don't preach to me, I beg you in the name of friendship and of all the purges I have taken, unless you feel sure that you are a better preacher than the fever and more ethical than the diarrhœa.

Now that I have told you all about myself, tell me a little about you. What are you doing? What are you reading? Do you see anybody? Write me in your turn all about yourself—just as if you had lost a thousand crowns.

Good-by, old chap. I am at work. I have started on some stuff that I must finish. I shall go one of these days and knock on your door and ask for a glass of milk. Of such is your friend's nourishment.

A. de M.

The reference to work concerns the little story, *Pierre*

et Camille, published in the *Constitutionnel.* He also wrote
a poem when Paul came back after a year's absence, *A
mon frère revenant d'Italie.* But the years rolled by, and
little golden grain was garnered. He was very idle. He
went little, or not at all, into society, played chess and
read a great deal. Or, in the need of distraction, went
night after night to the opera. Paul suppresses all the
story, familiar to his friends and acquaintances, of
drunken habits. But the silence of the poet gave Paul
great concern; he went to Madame Jaubert and asked
her to use her influence, she said that she would see what
she could do. She tried, but when Paul went to ask her
of her success, she said: "Don't speak to me of it. I hurt
our dear boy badly, and myself, too. He vanquished me
at every point. He is a hundred times right. His silence, his sorrow, his scorn are but too well justified. If
he were to publish them, they that blame him would crawl
into the ground. Soon or late, his immense superiority
will be recognized by everybody. Leave it to time: let us
not play with fire, for we are but children compared to
him."

How much of this is godmother and how much Paul,
among whose virtues veracity limped in the rear, there
is no telling. Some critics have inferred a secret malady,
a sort of *intellectual epilepsy,* as George Sand called it;
for it is sure that all his life he had some mental or nervous disturbances, at times hallucinations, wild fancies,
suspicions, morbid imaginings that set him apart from
sane, healthy, commonplace men. But the less charitable
ascribed his ailments, physical and mental, to debauchery.

He himself, after his interview with his godmother, wrote
her this sonnet:

> *Q'un sot me calomnie, il ne m'importe guère,*
> *Que sous le faux semblant d'un intérêt vulgaire*
> *Ceux même dont hier j'aurai serré la main,*
> *Me proclament, ce soir, ivrogne et libertin.*
>
> *Ils sont moins mes amis que le verre de vin*
> *Qui pendant un quart d'heure étourdit ma misère;*
> *Mais vous, qui connaissez mon âme tout entière,*
> *A qui je n'ai jamais rien tu, même un chagrin,*
> *Est-ce à vous de me faire une telle injustice,*
> *Et m'avez-vous si vite à ce point oublié?*
> *Ah! ce qui n'est qu'un mal, n'en faites pas un vice.*
>
> *Dans ce verre où je cherche à noyer mon supplice,*
> *Laissez plutôt tomber quelques pleurs de pitié,*
> *Qu'à d'anciens souvenirs devrait votre amitié.*

He cares not how fools call him drunkard and libertine,
even those that pretend to be his friends. He has a better
friend—the cup that drowns his grief for half an hour.
But he entreats his real friends not to be unjust, not to
make a vice of a misfortune; let them rather shed some
tears of pity in his cup.

But he was still young, not yet *nel mezzo del cammin,* and
though his lyrical power had diminished, it was not too
late to cultivate his two other gifts in literature, for
sentimental tales and for the theater. In 1845 he wrote
the proverb *Il faut qu'une porte soit ouverte ou fermée;*
it was published in the *Revue des Deux Mondes.* And the
director of the Odéon proposed to put *Un Caprice* on the

stage. Musset writes to Tattet that it was necessary to postpone his visit, "for it is probable that I shall be obliged to attend rehearsals at the Odéon and watch over my fiasco, for I am sure it will be a fiasco. Everybody says that it will be charming, delightful, etc., etc. Alone, against all, strong from the past, and certain of the future, I heroically await the rotten eggs." For some reason the director abandoned the play, but Alfred continued his interest in the theater, and went often; and then an unexpected event, fraught with strange consequences, happened.

Madame Allan-Despréaux was born, in the same year as Alfred de Musset, in the town of Mons in Belgium, where her father, whose name was Ross, managed a theater. The little girl was taught to play children's parts. When she was ten years old the great Talma came to Antwerp to play *Athalie;* and she was brought to him to take the part of Joas. He asked her what her name was. "Louise Rosalie Ross," she answered. "Louise Rosalie will do," Talma cried, "but I can't in decency put the name Ross on the bill-boards!" "It's my name, sir," she said. "Yes, but you have got to have another. What is your mother's name?" "Despréaux." "Good! Louise Despréaux, that at least is a theatrical name. From now on that shall be your name, and if your parents consent, and you play Joas well, I will take you with me to Paris." So she did, and played with Talma again at the Théâtre Français. She then took lessons at the Conservatoire, fulfilled her childish promise, and at sixteen was established at the Théâtre Français. Here she

had a tiff with an older actress. This older actress came
to a meeting and found all the chairs occupied. Going
up to Louise Despréaux she said, "Come on, little girl,
get up, I'm tired." Louise replied coolly : "Mademoiselle
if you had asked me politely for my seat, I should have
given it *out of deference to your age,* but since you speak
as you do, I was here before you and I keep it."

Louise was pretty, with handsome eyes, a good figure,
a little hand and a little foot. She left the Théâtre
Français and went to the Gymnase for several years, married one Allan, an actor there, and then the two went
to St. Petersburg to play. She was very much of a lady,
very good-natured and agreeable, and was well received
by the Russian aristocracy. After the play, the Empress
often invited her into the imperial box, an honor only
accorded to herself and Mademoiselle Taglioni. A better
evidence of her amiable disposition is that while she was
in Russia, Rachel commissioned her to buy Russian stuffs
for her costume as Roxane. She acted in Scribe and others,
and then in Musset's *Un Caprice* which was very well
received. In 1847 François Buloz, the former editor of
the *Revue des Deux Mondes* had become director of the
Théâtre Français, and he engaged Madame Allan-
Despréaux to act there. She came, leaving her husband
behind, with *Un Caprice* in her muff, as Théophile Gautier
said, and insisted that on her first night she should play
it. The first night was November 27, 1847. Madame Allan-
Despréaux showed imagination, powers of unexpected
gaiety, and an extraordinary naturalness of tone and gesture. The play was an immense success. In the follow-

ing June, *Il ne faut jurer de rien* was put on the stage, and in August *Le Chandelier.* The town was talking about them, the dramatist became known and admired. Royalties replenished a lean purse, and most opportunely, for after the Revolution of 1848, that deposed Louis Philippe and established the Republic, Musset lost his place as librarian at the Ministry of the Interior which he had held for ten years.

On May 3, 1849, *On ne saurait penser à tout* was played in a private house by Madame Allan-Despréaux, Got, and others of the Comédie Française. Musset was in great spirits over the way in which it was given. Not very long before this he had begun to frequent her society. She lived in a pretty apartment, No. 15 Rue Mogador; and there she used to receive once a week. Sometimes there was conversation, sometimes she sat at the piano and sang, for she had a very pleasing voice, or she recited verses. Madame Allan-Despréaux was not far from forty, with some embonpoint, but her frank honest eyes, her laughing lips, her pretty young face were very attractive, and her manners were not only cordial but distinguished; she was intelligent and cultivated; and it is believed had been faithful to her marriage vows. Musset became an assiduous visitor. A dear friend of hers, Madame Samson-Toussaint said: "Take care, Louise, you are receiving Monsieur de Musset very often." Louise answered: "My dear friend, don't be afraid. I am, assuredly, much flattered by Monsieur de Musset's attention, but as for anything further that is quite another matter. I am acquainted with his character, and I feel sure that this is a mere passing humor.'' However, the poet wrote a sonnet in eulogy of platonic love,

Vous, dont chaque pas touche à la grâce suprême;

and Madame Samson-Toussaint, leaving her friend in May to go to Brazil, must have felt some uncertainty. Two months later this letter followed her:

Paris, July 17, 1849.

Dear, good Adèle

While your life has been changing, mine has changed, too; perhaps you foresaw that the last months would cause some change, although there was nothing serious then. . . . When things are not serious, they may drag on indefinitely, but when they are, they rush with frightful rapidity to a conclusion. That is what happened to me, my poor Friend. I need make no preface, you know whom I am speaking of. On parting from you I spent several days in profound trouble. O how I missed you, kind, friendly Heart! You left at an evil time for me. However you must know the story. On May 13, a notable day—you were still in Paris—I dined at Scribe's house; before I went, I received a visit from a man—discontent, grumbling, afflicted, as lovers are. His manner seemed to me rather rude, so I gave no sign of anything, and left him alone to quiet himself. I did not see him for a week, and I said to myself, "So much the better. I have paid too much attention to him, and my conscience pricks me." You were gone, and I fixed my thoughts on you—that is to say—thinking a great deal about him and making up impossible romances, or such as I thought impossible.

On my return from Havre [where she had gone to see her friend off] I found a penitent letter which told me of his illness during the week of my absence. He was sick, and begged me to write him a line, even in anger. In consequence of this correspondence, which lasted two or three days, one fine evening he escorted me from the theater to my door, and in a very simple, sincere and eager manner said he loved me, thought of nothing but me, and confessed that his illness was the consequence of the follies into which he had plunged to escape the pain I caused him. As he had been well behaved for five months, this attack had been more violent than before, and he had nearly died. As I have other evidence of this, and as besides, with all his faults, he has the superlative trait of never lying, I believed him. He showed both love and respect. I was touched. However, I struggled and held back. Things had come to the point where it was necessary to say yes or no. I took a whole day to summon up enough courage to say no, for I regretted to say no, I won't conceal that from you, but I had so many reasons for refusing!—At last, not feeling myself strong enough to say no in my own house, I wrote him to come that night to my box during the second act of *Adrienne Lecouvreur*. He mistook the meaning of my note and thought it was consent. And when we were alone, he burst into such transports of joy, so natural and full of feeling, that it went like an arrow into my heart.

Nevertheless, I held my purpose to refuse, but, to speak the truth, awkwardly and without the decision that I had promised myself. If he had not been really in love, he would have noticed it, but, far from that, he mistook and fancied that I was a cold coquette who wished to play with him. I was no coquette at that moment, I assure you.

He took my refusal sweetly and sadly, he said that I was wrong as to the nature of his feeling for me, that it was neither a caprice, nor a passing fancy, but a serious and lasting affection, a tender friendship based on similarity of mind, of tastes, of talent, also because I was attractive to him, and that he loved me deeply and should suffer much. After he had said all that with sweetness and kindness, and with a note of resignation, all of a sudden the mad fellow exploded, and his very unreasonableness showed clearly that he was in love. He left pretty angry. As for me, the interview upset me, and since then I can't say that I have been wholly myself. I shut my eyes and ears in order not to see my madness. Well, let me finish. Before the end of the play I wrote him a note, and at midnight took it myself and left it at his door. I passed a most agitated and feverish night, and when day came, I had to admit to myself that I could not bear it. I considered my situation, and persuaded myself with the aid of sophistry that I was free. I felt sick, sore and excited all at once. A note came from him asking me to forgive his outbreak of the night before; then he came himself and I surrendered without resistance, swept along by an irresistible inclination, but with deep sadness. Make what you can of that. That is the first part of my story, I now take up the second.

After spending the first days in getting to know one another, a terrible storm broke out between us, in which much love was mixed with things I could not endure. He went home, and had an attack of delirium. He is subject to them when he gets excited; it is a consequence of his old disastrous habits. When an attack comes on he has hallucinations and talks with phantoms. There, in his room, *he beheld me* angry, sad and refusing to forgive him. His tears, supplications, his despair, revealed everything to his mother, and when he came to himself again, he told her all. She was delighted by the news, for he had, long before, given his family an idea of me with which you would be satisfied. Well, I forgave him, and then, a few days later one of his fits of jealousy came to spoil all. His head is weak, and he went wild again; this time he disappeared for four days, and nobody knew what had become of him. I was horribly anxious; I wrote three notes (during the first day), went to his house at seven o'clock, and said that I should come again at ten. Well, as my carriage drew up, who should I find waiting for me at the door? His mother, who is seventy-two years old, dying of anxiety. She clasped my hands, spoke to me with tender and touching kindness, begged my pardon with the tactfulness of a well-bred woman used to society, and told me how happy she was that I loved the son whom she adored. Our conversation lasted two hours, in my carriage. We held one another's hands, tears in our eyes, and she confirmed all that he had told me. She told me besides much that he had not said, and proved to me that he had not deceived me, that he really loved me. His mother said: "Save him, you can, he loves you enough for that. He was cured of dissipation, and he plunged back on your account! (That was just what he told me.) Save him, I entrust him to you, help me." Then she said, "As soon as he comes home I will send you word, even if it is in the middle of the night."

There was an epidemic of cholera, and she trembled lest he be brought back on a stretcher; you can guess my feelings, for I was saying to myself that it was my fault. At last the mother went off to her daughter [Madame Lardin, married, and settled in Angers] without being able to learn what had become of him. When he came back, several days later, miserable and ashamed of himself, for he was to have escorted his mother, who had to go alone, he begged me to write to her, as he dared not himself. I did so, and she wrote me back a charming letter. And he, in addition, later, wrote her about how he was, and he showed me his mother's answer. I could picture the joy she felt at knowing him as happy as he said he was; and, as for me his gracious and affectionate behavior, straight from his heart, convinced me that he really loved me.

The love of Alfred de Musset did not strew her path with roses. She hired from the sculptor, Pradier, a villa at Ville d'Avray, which lies just beyond Sèvres in the direction of Versailles, and took possession as soon as her vacation began. She said nothing of this to third persons, and looked forward to a honeymoon of six weeks. The villa was in the style of an Italian pavilion, small but pretty, with a delightful big garden adorned by great trees and full of flowers, and with a miniature lake, on which there was a boat. She expected to be very happy. Both were fond of music and she betook herself with delight to the piano; and she found that their tastes in music, literature, in any matter that concerned art, were identical. As to their characters, though alike in some ways, they were very different in others. She wrote: "In this creature there are two men—one that I should adore, if he was always so, but the other, I admit frankly, I don't like." She understood him better than any of the other women that had come into his life. She put her finger on the spring of evil. He ought to work, she said. His disposition was variable, independent, fantastic; he would never even pretend to interest himself in work unless the inspiration came upon him, and he never went out of his way to invoke it. Tears would come into his eyes when reading poetry that he liked, or listening to music; and when his imagination turned to something noble he became like the heroes in his books. He wrote some verses, read them to her, he listened to her singing, or sketched her portrait. But the Gods were envious. Musset would disappear for three or four days. No word of him at the Musset apartment. The housekeeper, Mademoiselle Colin, a devoted servant but jealous, would answer dryly that she had not seen him. It was impossible to scour the slums of Paris. Madame Allan-Despréaux would go back to the villa and wait.

When the prodigal returned, there were tears, embraces, songs sung, verses recited. Then, boredom, jealousy, whim, the call of the brothel carried him off. So night succeeded day, and day night. When he was his good self, it was delightful, love, adoration, joy; when he was his evil self she could not bear it. There were *crises de nerfs,* hallucinations, delirium; but the touch of her hand would calm him. When he was penitent, his regrets were as immoderate as his jealousy or his rudeness. His disordered past had set its seal upon him in distrust, suspicion, grossness. Life with him was like sinking into a foul slough, and rising again to see the sunlit sky. ''I have never seen,'' she repeats, ''such a striking contrast as between the two beings housed in a single body. One, good, sweet, tender, enthusiastic, poignant with wit and common sense, naif (extraordinary thing!), naif as a child, a good fellow, simple, modest, without pretension, sensible, excitable, weeping for a nothing that touched his heart, an exquisite artist in every kind of art, sensitive to everything that is beautiful in music, painting, literature or the theater, and expressing his feelings in the most noble language. Then turn the page, look at the reverse. You confront a man possessed of a devil, weak, violent, arrogant, despotic, mad, hard, petty, distrustful, insulting, blindly headstrong, egotistical as possible, blaspheming everything, and exciting himself in evil as much as he ever does in good. When once he is astride of his diabolic horse, he must ride till he breaks his neck. *Excess,* that is his disposition, in good things and in bad. In the latter he ends in illness, which has the advantage of restoring him to reason and making him feel penitent. I don't understand how he has endured such a nature so long, or why he has not died a hundred thousand times.''

So the pair went on. Before the year was out they had quarreled and separated twenty times. Once he stayed away over a month. She vowed to break the liaison. But she found that he had been very ill; so ill that they had had to give him chloroform. He went back. She said that there could only be friendship between them—''*mais* [she wrote to Madame Samson-Toussaint], *ma chère, vous savez comme on se trompe quand on se rabat sur l'amitié.*'' At last a new element came up as a cause of quarrel. Alfred was very exacting as to his plays; they meant reputation, they meant money. It seems that the director of the Théâtre Français put on Legouvé's *Bataille des Dames,* at a time when Alfred wished him to put on *Le Chandelier* and imputed the blame to Madame Allan-Despréaux; and when *Le Chandelier* was played, June 29, 1850, he was displeased to have her play the heroine Jacqueline, for he thought her too old and too fat for the part. However she achieved a brilliant success, supported by Samson, the father of her friend, Madame Samson-Toussaint, Delaunay and Got, glittering names in the archives of the illustrious theater. By the beginning of 1851 the lovers had separated. She says: ''We all, men and women, are but dupes, and we are wrong to throw the blame on one another. The human heart follows its course *en se moquant de notre raison.*'' But the separation was a drifting apart rather than a quarrel. Three years afterward she wrote him a kind, generous, magnanimous letter on the representation of *Bettine* at the Gymnase, when Rose Chéri played the heroine. It was not the poet who enacted the *beau rôle* in the tragicomedy of their loves. When her husband returned from Russia, she confessed and he forgave her. She died a year before Musset. He followed her bier to the grave in Père Lachaise, and showed his emotion. Tattet wrote to Guttinguer: "Alfred is much more affected by the death of Madame Allan than I should have believed. It is true that he owed her much! She was his best friend."

CHAPTER XVIII

LIFE AT HOME, 1846–1851

I MUST go back a little, in order to recount certain episodes that did not concern his liaisons directly. In the year 1839 the Musset family had moved from the Rue de Grenelle to the Quai Voltaire. In 1846, the daughter, very much younger than Alfred, married a Monsieur Lardin and went to live in Angers. That left Madame de Musset without feminine companionship. She engaged a superior woman, Adèle Colin, *sage et laborieuse,* to be half servant, half companion. When Madame de Musset was alone, Adèle came to table with her, and even when Paul was at home she would stay in the room. Alfred at first paid no attention to her, but soon after her coming he fell ill and she helped take care of him, and from that time on, for the rest of his life, became an important personage in it. The poet, as we have learned, had a very ill-poised nervous system, and his ways of living put it out of joint. Even in early youth his dreams of corpses and skeletons when a student at the medical school point to some deep-seated disequilibrium. His illness at Venice for moments deranged his reason. The illness which he had in 1840, during which, as I have said, Madame Jaubert and the Princess Belgiojoso came to see him, was very serious. The doctor's diagnosis at first was cerebral fever; Paul says that the doctor was mistaken, and that Madame de Musset was able to correct him. Whichever was right, it required three people, aided by a sister

248

of Bon-Secours, Sister Marcelline, (one of the nuns who in those days played the part of trained nurses) to take care of him. He had insomnia for ten days. As he got better, while Sister Marcelline and Paul were sitting beside him, he was a little delirious, and saw visions. Alfred has described one of them. The table, at the time, actually covered with bottles and drugs, looked to him in its old state, littered with books and papers; then four little winged cherubs flew down, carried off the books, and brought vials in the very order in which they had come from the apothecary. Another cherub brought the old remedy which Pagello had given him in Venice, and had been approved by the French physician. Alfred waved his hand, after the manner of an Italian greeting, and said: "It is Pagello who has saved me again." Following that, two cherubs with melancholy mien and gesture fetched, in the midst of vials, a bier on which stood a bottle of champagne. Then other cherubim came, carrying a carafe of water, with a crystal stopper, crowned with roses, while still more cherubim scattered flowers in its path. At the end, the cherubim carried away the vials, and replaced books and papers just as they had been before the poet was ill. Alfred remarked: "That is not quite right; there was dust in several places, notably on the inkstand." As he spoke a little man, three inches tall, came carrying on his back a miniature itinerant cocoa-fountain with a spigot, and walked over the table, turning the spigot and scattering here and there a fine layer of dust. "That is perfect," Alfred said, "now I can go to sleep; I think that I am cured." The physician, when he heard of the vision, said: "Try to profit by it, but the apothesis of the carafe of water is not sufficient; you must remember that nature created day for waking and night for sleep." "That aphorism," Alfred answered, "is less profound than those of Hippocrates, but I promise to meditate upon it."

In this illness Sister Marcelline had been a good angel to him. She was devoted and tender, and her sweet spirit had a most tranquillizing effect upon him; she gave him gentle counsels for his body and his soul. He wrote some stanzas upon her to record his gratitude. He promised her to be mindful of what she said, and she gave him a penholder on which she had stitched in silk: "Remember your promise." By his wish, almost his last, the pen was buried beside his body in the coffin. When he needed a nurse after that he always asked for her, but only once was she able to come.

In the illness of 1847 that came on soon after Adèle Colin entered into the Musset household, he suffered from nervous attacks that ended in convulsions. Mademoiselle Colin was obliged to hold him down on the bed. She put on mustard plasters that did him good. But the physician insisted on bloodletting. It carries one back to Tobias Smollett and the French doctor at Montpellier. Adèle stood firm for mustard plasters. Madame de Musset said to her sternly, *"Vous n' avez rien à dire; pas d'observation."* The bloodletting was administered. The delirium returned. Alfred thought he was in the presence of a criminal magistrate, gave his name and his age; the pillow was the magistrate. The next night the doctor gave him a bath; and he went completely out of his head. He kept asking for food; but the doctor forbade any. The delirium lasted for four days; the patient kept crying out that he was hungry. Adèle was in charge that night. A bowl of consommé and a *gâteau Saint-Honoré* were left for her to eat. She let Alfred eat them. He then went to sleep for the first time, and slept well, while she dozed on a sofa beside his bed. He did not wake till eleven o'clock the next morning, gazed about, recognized his room, looked at her. "Mademoiselle," he asked, "what are you doing here? You have been sleeping in my room. Who are you?" Then he added, "I recognize you now, you are the *petite ouvrière* whom my mother employs." He was so much better that he ate lunch with the family.

After this Madame de Musset went to Angers to visit her daughter and made Adèle promise to take care of Alfred during her absence. Adèle, who had had some experience with a sick person before, happily for her master, happened to read a book by Doctor Raspail who said that bloodletting was very bad in every illness, especially if the fever was a consequence of excesses; in fact the doctor said that bloodletting without any food, under certain conditions, might make a man crazy. Adèle imparted her information to Paul, and he to Alfred; so the regimen was changed. Whenever indispositions, due to excesses, came on, Adèle gave him a little vegetable soup, *une legère purgation,* and then some good beef bouillon with an egg in it, and then a simple quieting liquid. During these attacks Alfred usually had visions.

In order to prevent visions from developing into fits of insanity, Uncle Desherbiers used to come in, chat and play cards and keep him distraught. The good Adèle adds, *"c'étaient les beaux jours."* She stayed with her master continuously for three or four days during these attacks. After a few good nights Alfred would go to work again.

That September he went with Paul to Croisic, in Brittany (the birthplace of Hervé Rielle) for bathing, and then he passed a month at Angers with his sister. After his return to Paris that autumn, in consequence of the success of *Un Caprice,* he set at once to work to have his other plays, written merely to be read, also produced upon the stage. Then came the Revolution of February 24, 1848, which forced the abdication of Louis Philippe and established the Republic. As Musset's friend, the Duc d'Orléans, the heir apparent, had died, he was not touched in his affections; the old King had been, if not rude, very little condescending, when his son had attempted to obtain a friendly commendation from him for some verses by Musset, written when the King had escaped assassination. But the Revolution affected Musset in another way. The republicans in power wished to find places for their supporters: like other politicians they adopted a rule to that effect: *Prenez comme règle que les fonctions publiques ne peuvent être confiées qu'à des républicains éprouvés.* Ledru-Rollin, the new Minister of the Interior, wished to reward a friendly editor, and in May, 1848, removed Musset from the post of librarian of the Ministry of the Interior, which he had held for ten years. It must be

said that the poet had done extremely little to deserve
his salary of three thousand francs per annum; so little
that this jest upon it ran the rounds: some friends met
him at the library door and asked him what he was
doing there. "I have come," the poet replied, "to see if
there really is a library here." And the head of the department had asked that he be dismissed. On the other
hand, the post was undoubtedly regarded as a sinecure.
All the papers in opposition cried out that his removal
was an outrage. Alexandre Dumas, *père,* in his paper,
La France Nouvelle, June 16, 1848, wrote most indig-
nantly: "What! Here is a writer who has endowed our
language with admirable poetry; here is a poet, the
brother of Lamartine, of Hugo and Byron; here is a
story-teller the rival of l'abbé Prévost, of Balzac, of
George Sand; here is a playwright who with a single
play enabled the Comédie Française to take in more
money than you grant it in six months; here is a man of
intellect who has not once sacrificed the dignity of art
to the ambitions of fortune and position; here is a genius
who asks nothing of God or man but liberty to live and
think as he will, who has never belonged to a political
club or a literary coterie. And here is a transitory
minister, who, in transit, expels the poet in order to make
room—for whom?"

Musset was much pleased and wrote back at once:

My dear Dumas,
    I have read *la France Nouvelle,* and I shall go to shake

your hand. But I must express to you, without waiting, the lively emotion of gratitude that I feel. You have made me proud, my Friend, and you have given me the right to be proud, when a man like you deigns to crush a little blunder with such noble, courageous, admirable words,

à vous de cœur

ALFRED DE MUSSET.

The loss of his salary would have been serious, had it not been that theatrical royalties were coming in. The *Caprice* had run extraordinarily well. Sainte-Beuve said that its success did honor to the public. Théophile Gautier wrote that it was a great literary event; "Since Marivaux nothing has been produced at the Comédie Française so subtly delicate, so exquisite, so refreshingly playful as this charming little masterpiece tucked away in the pages of a magazine, which, before we could accept it, had to be discovered by the Russians of that snowy Athens, Saint-Petersburg." In April Madame Allan-Despréaux was also acting *Il faut qu'une porte soit ouverte ou fermée.* And in June preparations were made for putting on *Il ne faut jurer de rien,* and on the twenty-second the first representation was given. Here Sainte-Beuve was alone in his disapproval. "Alfred de Musset," he said, *"est le caprice d'une époque blasée et libertine."* The public entertained a very different opinion, but at the outset the play was temporarily suspended by political misadventures. The new government was in difficulties. In order to secure the support of the proletariat of Paris, it had organized national workshops to provide work for them; the scheme had failed, and a decree was made that the workmen in these shops should either enlist in the army or go off into the provinces to work on roads. On June twenty-third, the proletariat of Paris sent its delegates to the government to protest against such action. The speaker for the government replied: "If the workmen will not go voluntarily, we will send them by force." The next day at six o'clock in the morning a great crowd of workmen assembled in the Place de la Bastille, and soon barricades were thrown up in all the working quarters of the city. The government had an army of fifty thousand men and for four days there was continuous street fighting, when it was officially announced: "Order has triumphed over anarchy, *Vive la République!*" Alfred and Paul were members of the National Guard, at that time a body representing the middle and upper classes, and were called out. Adèle Colin watched them go from the window. Alfred has described the consequences of this revolt upon himself and his affairs in a letter to Alfred Tattet:

July 1, 1848

My dear Friend,

Thanks for your letter. My brother and I suffered nothing worse than considerable fatigue. I have just now, before beginning to write, taken off my uniform, which I had not done since the beginning of the insurrection. I will say nothing of the horrors that have taken place; it was too hideous.

In the midst of these pleasant idylls, you will understand that Uncle Van Buck [in *Il ne faut jurer de rien*] remained in the soup. He had, however, had a success, I may say without exaggeration, a complete success. It was the night before the insurrection. The theater was full, and well furnished with pretty women, and intelligent people. The pit was very friendly to me and the actors were capital; everything first rate. I had my evening's entertainment. I caught it, so to speak, on the wing. After the curtain, all the actors were called out, and even the author, who, as you can guess, did not appear.—The next day—Good-by! Actors, director, author, prompter, all of us, gun on shoulder, had cannon for orchestra, burning buildings for lighting, and a pit of mad *Apaches*. The *Garde mobile* behaved so courageously that the mere sight of them, happily, set our hearts beating proudly. They were almost all mere children. I never dreamed anything like it. A thousand compliments to Mme. Tattet. I write in a hurry. A handshake from my heart,

A. de M.

It is said that he and Jules Sandeau, also in the National Guard, met at bivouac in front of the *Institut* one night, and chatted about George Sand, *cherchant à s'expliquer la nature ènigmatique et fatale de cette femme*, and next day took part in carrying the insurgent barricades at the Petit Pont. There were no further consequences to the poet from these political troubles, and he addressed himself again to his plays. *Le Chandelier* was given in August at the Théâtre Historique, but had little success.

In December Prince Louis Napoleon was elected President of the Republic. Alfred attended the soirées at the Élysée palace, where the Prince received him kindly, and he met many charming ladies. One day he remarked to the Prince: "I saw your Highness at *Marion Delorme* [a play by Victor Hugo] at the Français last night." The Prince answered, *"Oui, Monsieur,* for my sins." Alfred, always extraordinarily ignorant of political concerns, had renewed his old friendship with Victor Hugo, and felt it his duty to say a good word for him: "Your Highness must not think that Victor Hugo is a man who would be politically hostile to you or your course of action. No poet is evil-minded. He is not to be taken too seriously, I shall gladly be his surety in this case." The Prince turned on his heel without a word. Musset, who was so self-centered that he did not know Victor Hugo's hatred of Louis Napoleon, never could understand this behavior in a Prince usually so polite and gracious. Several years later, after the *coup d'état* of 1851 which made Louis Napoleon Emperor, he recalled the incident to a friend, who said to wait a minute, went and got one of Victor Hugo's pamphlets, and they took it to Musset's apartment to read. Victor Hugo was at his best in his passionate eloquence of denunciation. During the three years Musset had continued to notice little besides women and wine and the swelling or ebbing of his own emotions. He read the pamphlet and cried: "Is it possible to write and print such insults! I did not know of this pamphlet!

I understand now why the Prince turned his back and did not answer me.''

The year 1849 contained its miscellany of episodes. Alfred, in spite of his service during the insurrection of 1848, was not much more attentive to his duties as a member of the National Guard than he had been to those of librarian. Adèle Colin has recounted her troubles when the poet sent her with a doctor's certificate to excuse his failure to perform sentry duty. In March of this year he again failed to report, and as he had no doctor's certificate he was placed under arrest and lodged in ''l'hôtel des Haricots,'' a prison for delinquent members of the National Guard, in cell No. 14, reserved for artists and men of letters. It was not the first time he had been there. He amused himself writing a poem

Le mie Prigioni

On dit: ''Triste comme la porte
D'une prison,''
Et je crois, le diable m'emporte,
Qu'on a raison.
D'abord, pour ce qui me regarde,
Mon sentiment
Est qu'il vaut mieux monter sa garde,
Décidément.

Je suis, depuis une semaine
Dans un cachot,
Et je m'aperçois avec peine
Qu'il fait très chaud, etc.

[They say ''A prison door is sad! The Devil take me but I think they're right. First, from my own personal point of view, my feeling is that it is decidedly better to perform sentry duty. I have been locked up for a week, and I have a disagreeable perception that it is very hot here," etc.] And yet, in obedience to the proverb concerning an ill wind, it has been suggested that these days of obligatory temperance were highly beneficial to the delinquent. While there he wrote a letter to a popular actress, Mademoiselle Augustine Brohan, who had been a good friend to him, and done her best to stop his drinking. They had been real friends. For years he used to call her his *amie*; and with her friendship was a boundary not overstepped. He was delighted to have a fresh ear in which to pour the horrible sufferings that had embittered and changed his nature; and she was ready with sympathy. As usual, the poet told her that if there were a remedy to save him from the incurable weakness that undermined his health, it was she that could find it. To this she returned wise words; but all her wise words went for nought, the need of forgetfulness plunged him back into follies. He had hardly begun to woo Madame Allan-Despréaux yet, and he seems to have been looking about for some actress who would save him from debauchery.

March, 1849, Des Haricots,
Friday

O my dear Brohan,

I am in fetters. I groan from the dungeon's depths. But that will not prevent me from going to see you tomorrow, Saturday. I am writing this epistle from the bottom of the cellular system. I am in the famous Cell

No. 14, which was depicted in *Le Diable à Paris*. I
haven't killed anybody; it's for sentry duty. This cell
has a lot of new things in it, and some, joking apart, are
charming; but there is no space left, even for an improper
word. The door is padlocked; the rest of the prison is
whitewashed. However, I notice that the poetry here
is inferior to the paintings.
(He copies some)

> *Acrostic to her I love:*
>
> *C'est toi*
> *La vrai flamme!*
> *O mon âme,*
> *Tais toi . . .*
> *Ici, mon bel idole,*
> *Le cœur qui t'est voué*
> *Désire ton obole*
> *Et puis mourir . . . aimé*
>
> A. L. . . . 72 hours

This acrostic represents the name Clothilde; it is easy
to guess. The poet forgot the *h*.

You see that there are people bold enough to challenge
your beautiful couplet on *la Vièrge en patache*. I have
been thinking of it. You might add

> A young man full of life
> Pierced his heart with a knife.

But I shall go to see you to-morrow. Shall you be at
home; perhaps not. No matter. On thinking it over, I
think I am fool enough to fall in love with you, and that

Top: Alfred bowing to Madame Joubert; drawing by Alfred de Musset

Middle left: A pen and ink sketch of Alfred de Musset by Roger de Beauvoir

Middle right: Drawing of George Sand by Alfred de Musset

Bottom: Pen and ink sketch of Rachel and Alfred de Musset, by Musset

A Sketch of Alfred de Vigny
By Musset

it will be a sensible thing to do. I mean that I shall always love you, not more one day than another but never less.

A vous

PIERROT

And there is another letter written to her after he was at large again.

My dear Brohan,

I have not written you that you are charming because I wanted to tell you so; and yet I suppose that you know it. But I want you to be sure of this, that your kind present gave me the greatest pleasure and that I shall always cherish the memory of a friendship that is worth many a love.

Tout à vous,

ALFRED DE MUSSET.

And when she went for a tour in the provinces he wrote her some charming verses:

Adieu, Brohan, rapportez-nous vos yeux,
Si charmants quand ils sont joyeux,
Si doux, quand vous êtes pensive!
. . . .
Regardez-vous dans un miroir français
. . . .
Ce rond visage au nez pointu,
Amusant comme un impromptu,
Cette taille leste et gentille,
Ces perles fines, où babille
L'esprit charmant de la famille,

Cette fossette à l'air moqueur,
Ces bonnes mains pleines de cœur.

.   .   .

Ah! Brohan, ma chère, en voyage
Est-il bien prudent, à votre age,
Que vous emportiez tout cela?

Adieu, Brohan, bring back those eyes
So charming when joy in them lies,
So sweet, when pensive thoughts arise

.   .   .

Go look at what the mirror shows,

.   .   .

The rounded cheeks, the dainty nose,
Pleasant as wit that unexpected flows:
That form of grace and ease combined,
Those teeth of pearl, as if designed
From sparkles of the Brohan mind.
That dimple full of mocking art,
Those hands whose kindness match your heart.

.   .   .

Ah! Brohan dear, when you star,
Is't prudent, at the age you are,
To take those riches off so far?

There had been a tiff at one time, because Mademoiselle
Brohan wished to play Madame de Léry in *Un Caprice,*
after Madame Allan-Despréaux, but Alfred refused because he said that she was excellent as a soubrette but
could not play the part of a high-bred lady, and that the
public would agree with him. The poem, however, proves
that a complete reconciliation had taken place.

In 1849 the family household at Quai Voltaire were
on the verge of separation. Madame de Musset went to
Angers to be with her daughter, leaving Alfred in the
charge of Adèle Colin, and from that time on Mademoi-

selle Colin felt that this gave her proprietory rights over him. One day she saw him going out during convalescence without asking leave of her; she immediately told him that the lady by whom she had been employed before going to the Musset family asked her to come back as soon as she should be free. He replied, "Go, and stay as long as you like." So she went, but the next day a letter came from him: "I would not have believed that you could go and leave me this way, when you knew I was ill and all alone, for the servants are of no use. I had expected, after the care you took of me, to find some permanent affection in you, independent of what might happen. If I displeased you, you have revenged yourself, but rather cruelly, for I confess that this solitude and suffering have cast me into an insupportable melancholy."

Adèle came back, and took as much care of him as if he had been her invalid son. She wrote often to his mother while she was away to tell her about him; repeated that he went to the theater every night but came home afterward. At last one night after Madame de Musset's return, it must have been the day that Madame Allan-Despréaux described in her letter to Madame Samson-Toussaint, he came in after the theater about eleven o'clock and said: "Don't wait for me to-night, Madame Allan wishes me to take supper with her. Be sure to tell my mother not to feel badly, for Madame Allan is a very nice person. She is not a bad woman. Make it clear, and I shall be obliged to you. The lady is waiting for me in her carriage." Adèle promised, but said nothing that night for fear that Madame de Musset would not sleep well. The next morning when the old lady spied his bedroom candlestick still in the hall, she said to Adèle: "Then he has not come in?" At this she received Alfred's message, and was very unhappy. "Oh," she cried, "I came back to Paris in good spirits, I hoped that we had finished with these disorderly ways, and there he is gone again." Adèle argued that it was much better that it should be Madame Allan-Despréaux, who was no longer young, than some outcast woman. And the mother's alarm quieted down.

That summer Madame Allan-Despréaux hired the Pradier Villa at Ville d'Avray, and Musset asked Adèle if she would go with him. Adèle hesitated; Madame de Musset said to stay as near him as possible. So it was arranged that if he had need of her she would go to him, and anyhow she would see him from time to time, and keep his mother informed. Madame de Musset was urgent *"je vous prie, ma chère Mademoiselle Colin,* to learn about his condition, even if he is at Madame Allan's villa, you can go there under the pretext of carrying him a letter, and if he falls very ill you can offer her your services, for nobody knows how to take care of him in his nervous fits as you do. And write me every day." In consequence Adèle went very often to the Ville d'Avray, and it ended by her staying. Madame Allan had two servants, but Alfred would not have Adèle eat with them, so she had her own table. As we know, the honeymoon was troubled. One day Musset would tell Adèle to pack his trunk; and they went to Paris. A letter followed

them, Adèle repacked the trunk, and they went back to
Ville d'Avray. Once he fell ill with an attack such as he
had had before. Adèle had her medicine chest and slept
in his room on a mattress. This attack lasted a week.

The next attack came at a time when Musset had returned to town. Adèle took care of him all alone and at
first slept in his room on a mattress laid on the floor.
That was not restful; so she found a folding-bed and
brought that in, laid the mattress on it, and made a comfortable bed, hoping for a regular night's sleep, as up
till then she had not taken her clothes off. But no, that
night Madame Allan arrived, maid and trunk, and immediately attired herself *"en toilette plus que negligée"*
and said that she would sleep in the bed next Alfred.
Adèle was obliged to get dinner for her and then go off and
sleep on a sofa. *"Servir Monsieur, servir Madame,"*
seemed to her rather too much, and she complained to
Madame de Musset, who wrote back: "My kind Mademoiselle Colin, I am so sorry that you are put out by something not worth it. If you will but consider that your attendance on Madame Allan is merely transitory, it's a
mere caprice of hers, and you will play your part easily.
You know that my son is attached to you, and that this at-
tachment will outlive many others, for men are fickle. At
all ages they need care and affection. Believe me, he will
always return to appreciate yours. I advise you to be very
patient and very, very gentle. Be sure that with his tender
disposition and with his eye, which lets nothing escape
it, he will be grateful for your sacrifices. Above all, don't
complain, and always speak in a friendly tone. I hope

you understand, dear Adèle, that the advice I give you is all in your interest and my son's. I want you to stay with him.''

When Madame de Musset returned to Paris, she and Madame Allan-Despréaux went to look for a little apartment for Alfred, for she was going to give up the large apartment at the Quai Voltaire and go herself to join her daughter at Angers. One was found at Rue Rumfort (now disappeared), on the *entresol,* two bedrooms, a salon and a dining-room. Madame de Musset provided the silver and linen; Alfred would not accept any furniture. Paul went to live in the Rue des Pyramides. Adèle Colin took charge of Alfred's apartment. The furniture was scanty; Alfred bought a sideboard for one hundred and twenty francs, and some blue china, but the way he always did was merely to choose the purchases, then Adèle was to go to see them and buy them if she deemed them suitable.

Adèle Colin was jealous of Madame Allan-Despréaux and not wholly just. Alfred's illness came from his gross debauches; Madame Allan says that he disappeared twenty times during their liaison, but Adèle Colin attributed these disappearances to quarrels with his mistress. And she showed her jealousy and dislike in many ways. The doctor had ordered (Adèle reports) that Alfred should have the greatest possible quiet during his attacks. One day he was very miserable, and it was understood (she says) that nobody should be admitted. Nevertheless Madame Allan wrote that she was coming at a certain hour, that Monsieur should open the door himself, and that she did not propose to ask any other person's consent. Adèle suspected that she would come with maid and trunk, as before. She says that "the mere reading of her letter made him the more ill." He left the letter open on his table and Adèle read it. He dozed for ten or fifteen minutes at a time, waking up to ask what o'clock it was, so that he should be ready to open the door when Madame Allan came. Each time he dozed, Adèle turned the hands of the clock back a quarter of an hour. She also shut all the doors very carefully. When the clock reached the appointed hour, the poet said, "You may go out now, and do any shopping you have to do. I will stay here alone, I feel an inclination to sleep." Adèle went out, but the hour of the tryst was well past, and Madame Allan had come, knocked in vain and gone. On the ensuing days Adèle refused to open the door. When Alfred was well enough, and Madame Allan came, and wished to know why he had not let her in at the hour named, he replied that she hadn't come, although he had waited for two hours. Quarrel and reconciliation. Finally Madame Allan carried him off to her own apartment, Rue Mogador, where she said she would take care of him, and Adèle went away to her sister's in a huff. But the next day came a piteous little letter:

"I haven't closed my eyes. My attacks of delirium are beginning. You alone understand them. Come. Don't forsake me. You hurt my feelings last night, but I admit that I hurt yours the first. Come, I can't get on without you.

"Alfred de Musset."

And with it came a note from Madame Allan:

"Come, Mademoiselle Colin, please. Take your patient away, and I will only go to see him when you say I can do so without danger to his health or tranquillity."

When he got home, he reproached Adèle for letting him go; he said that he might have died, that he cried all night long aloud for her, shouting "Mademoiselle Colin! I want Mademoiselle Colin!" till he frightened them.

It is clear that by this time the poet and the actress had reached a place where they did not always make each other happy.

CHAPTER XIX

LOUISE COLET

THE poet, after leaving his mother's apartment, was a great deal perturbed by the necessity of supporting himself, especially as he had lost his sinecure as librarian. He established himself in Rue Rumfort with Adèle Colin as housekeeper, and started out with rigid economy. Accounts were new to him. He gave Adèle five francs at one time and then five at another, and did not understand why, when she rendered an account of her expenses in her little book, at the end of the week, he should have more to pay. "I can't afford to spend fifteen francs a day," he said. She answered that she would run the house, not counting wine, for seven francs, only he must not say that to-day he wants such and such a dish; he must take what was set before him, and she would do her best. He said that he was glad not to have to decide what he would eat, and would try the seven-franc allowance a day. Then he reflected: "How shall I be able to bring a friend home to dinner?" "All you need do," she answered, "is to give me an extra franc that day for each guest." So he did; and at the end of the month she was able to save twelve francs out of her allowance. "Keep them," he said, "buy a hat, or shoes, or whatever you want."

But even so shrewd and little-exacting a housekeeper as Mademoiselle Colin did not find it always easy to live with Musset. He was very irritable, and now and again she would say that she could not bear it, and was going to

269

leave; she gave him a key, any key, but she said it was
that of the front door, put on her bonnet and went out.
Madame de Musset and she had arranged what should be
done. She went in again by the back door, and waited.
After a few hours the poet would call the concierge and
say that Mademoiselle Colin had gone to her sister's, and
bade him fetch her, that he did not feel well, and feared
that he was about to be sick. After waiting the necessary
time required for going to and back from her sister's
Mademoiselle Colin put on her bonnet and walked in the
front door. He asked: "Why did you go? I don't know
any reason." "Nor I," she replied.

With Mademoiselle Colin's economies stopping the out-
go, and royalties from the theater coming in more liber-
ally, the budget was successfully balanced, and the whole
charge of his finances put into her hands. She collected
his revenues, and paid his debts. She heard him say re-
peatedly, "What! I am going to live out of debt. How can
one live out of debt?" Still they lived very simply; occasionally Adèle would cook a tender chicken *à la recette de
Lons-le-Saulnier,* or a dish of *riz au safran,* or of maca-
roni little cooked in the Italian fashion, a taste he had
acquired in Venice, and sometimes *le père* Colin, Adèle's
father, would send up a basket of trout or char from the
Jura. Adèle was kept very busy; she went to bed late, got
up early, dressed, valeted her master, went to the market,
prepared lunch, arranged everything, ordered about the
femme de ménage, and did not even have time to go to
Mass. But she liked to control, as one can see in her picture
a determined French face, straight lips, irascible nostrils

and hawk-like eyes. Later on Monsieur de Musset allowed himself sundry extra expenditures: he hired a cook, Clemence, who however had to give way to Adèle when it came to making fish sauces, he bought some pieces of mahogany furniture, a copy of a Giorgione by Vanloo, a marble clock, a table and so on.

That summer of 1850, on June twenty-ninth, *Le Chandelier* was put on at the Théâtre Français, and was greeted with great applause. But the dénouement aroused criticism; you remember how Jacqueline, the errant wife, after having played her husband false with the foppish Clavaroche, an officer, a coarse-grained man without sentiment, discovers that Fortunio, the sentimental apprentice, really loves her with all his heart, and therefore transfers her favors to him. This was in accordance with the Mussettiste code; but did not appear seemly to the conventional-minded, nor to Prince Napoleon's Government, which affected high domestic propriety. Léon Faucher, the Minister of the Interior, suppressed it. There was nothing personal to Musset in this; for a few years later the brothers Goncourt were prosecuted for licentious passages in their writings, Flaubert also for *Madame Bovary,* and Baudelaire was put in prison for the *Fleurs du Mal.* Musset received speedy compensation for on October 21, 1850, the Odéon brought out *André del Sarto,* which was a great success.

The next year Mademoiselle Madeleine Brohan, sister to Augustine, played the *Caprices de Marianne.* Madame Rose Chéri, another charming actress, also played *Bettine* at the Gymnase, but it was a failure, and indeed

the plot in which a virtuous prima donna is deserted by
a scalawag suitor and consoled by a "lover true" is not
exciting, and the dialogue lacks Musset's peculiar charm.
His last play, *Carmosine,* based on a story in Boccaccio,
was published in the *feuilleton* of a newspaper, *Le Constitutionnel,* but not acted till years after his death. The
publication in this newspaper came about in an odd way,
for Musset had always written for the *Revue des Deux
Mondes.* He was then in the habit of going to the Cirque
d'Été, and there he met Doctor Véron, the editor of the
Constitutionnel, an oldish man of the world who, in
Alfred's gay youth, used to preside at a table in the Café
de Paris, with Eugène Sue and other successful writers
gathered about him, and whom gossip linked in an un-
usually ignoble fashion with Rachel. Doctor Véron and
Alfred talked literature, and Doctor Véron said, "If you
will write me a comedy, I will pay you one thousand
francs an act; if there are five acts, I will pay you five
thousand francs and publish it in my *feuilleton.*" Alfred
said that he had a subject in his mind, and that when it
was finished, he would submit the manuscript. So he
composed it, and as he had cut a finger of his right hand,
he dictated it to Adèle Colin. Once begun, it went fast,
and three acts were written without interruption; then
a day was fixed for Doctor Véron to hear it read. Musset walked to the meeting-place with the manuscript,
leaving Adèle in a flutter of anxiety. He came back
radiant; cited certain passages that they had liked during
the composition, and said, "When I paused there, Doctor
Véron looked at me and said, '*C'est beau.*' " Adèle noticed

a tear of joy on his face. Alfred went on; "Although the play has only three acts Monsieur Véron wished to pay me five thousand francs. I wouldn't accept; it was too much. At last he obliged me to take four thousand francs, and here they are. During our discussion, Monsieur Véron said, 'It is you who will get the worst of it; with your permission I mean to keep the manuscript.' Then I thought, 'It's in Adèle's handwriting! I haven't written one word in the whole play; what will Véron think, I must disclose the fact to him.' " "Don't do anything," Adèle replied, "my handwriting looks like yours; when the play has been copied, it will be sent to the press, and the manuscript will be locked up carefully."

No trouble arose on Doctor Véron's part, and the play was published; but unluckily a mistaken punctuation had been made in some verses inserted in the prose, a period had been put where a comma should have been, sadly damaging the sense. Musset was ill, and the error appeared to him of highly exaggerated importance; he was violently disturbed about it. Adèle did not know how to calm him. Then she advised him to write to Doctor Véron, and that she would take the letter to him at once. The poet did so, but was troubled to know whether he had expressed himself clearly, so he read the letter aloud to Adèle, and made her say what she understood by it, to state exactly in what she thought the fault consisted and how it should be corrected. It was a long letter, and when the explanations had been finished, it was too late that night to disturb Doctor Véron. So the poet went to bed, slept well, reread his letter and decided not to send it. You can see by this how well Mademoiselle Colin had learned to handle her patient. But, unfortunately, his friend, the Comtesse Kalergis, wrote him a letter, complimenting him on the play, but saying that she could not understand the verses in question. Alfred wrote Paul that he was greatly worried about the mistake, that he had not supposed that a period in place of a comma could keep a sane man from sleeping for three nights, and please to tell the Comtesse what the error was. Evidently illness made him nervously sensitive to an abnormal degree. Uncle Desherbiers made fun of his worry, and said that nobody would notice the mistake; but the only conclusion that Alfred drew from this supposition was that, if readers were so obtuse, it certainly was not worth his while to write.

Moreover, by this time his theatrical fame had called general attention to his genius as a poet, and he was recognized to be of sufficient distinction to propose himself as a candidate for the Académie Française. Prosper Merimée encouraged him. Under the practise of the Académie the candidate must go the rounds of the members and ask them to vote for him. Victor Hugo wrote back enthusiastically: "I am yours from head to foot. I shall vote unblushingly for you in face of all possible Falloux and Montalemberts. V. Hugo." But on the first application he received only five votes. So he tried again. He was encouraged by the approbation of Monsieur le Comte Mathieu Mole, an Academician not as well known to us as perhaps he should be. When Alfred went to make his visit of request, the Count's two great dogs received the poet as if he were a friend. The Count said: "Sir, you must be a good man, for my dogs acknowledge you." Alfred's friends worked for him; chief among these, Charpentier his publisher and Madame Ancelot the wife of a member. The very night before the vote, Monsieur Ancelot met Charpentier in the garden of the Palais Royal and said to him: "Poor dear Alfred, he's a delightful fellow, most charming socially, but, between you and me, he never could, and never will, write a line of poetry." He was admitted and took his seat; when the new member, with his fair hair and the look of a man not over thirty, stepped forward in accordance with the long established procedure, to pronounce a eulogy of Monsieur Dupaty, to whose seat he had succeeded, the young ladies in the audience (so Paul de Musset says), accustomed to gray beards and bald heads, could not refrain from murmurs of satisfaction. The task of devising a eulogy upon Monsieur Dupaty, whose literary endowments had been rather lean, was not easy, and the poet, like a brave man struggling with adversity, went to the limit of possible praise, but it can not be said that his speech was a success. Flaubert thought it very poor. A serious consequence, however, flowed from his admission to the Academy.

Louise Colet was born in Lyons in 1810. Her father was a drawing master and poor. She was very pretty, her eyes bright blue, her cheeks pink and white, her lips very red, her figure "like that of Venus," and her spirits were gay. She flirted with what young men she could, and read poetry and romances. At twenty-six, a little desperate, she married Monsieur Colet, a music-teacher, and went to Paris, where they lived on the left bank in rather poor quarters and in very bourgeois society. Louise was bored and longed for a larger and livelier life; she wrote many poems, and in 1839 the French Academy awarded her a prize for the best poem on the *Musée à Versailles*. She went to the judges to thank them, and learned that the eminent philosopher, Victor Cousin, had been her strongest supporter. It was of him that Roger de Beauvoir, one of Musset's early friends of the Boulevard de Gand had written, when the Pope put his books of philosophy on the Index:

> *Victor Cousin, je bénis ton martyre*
> *Et cet index qui maudit tes écrits,*
> *Car le pape à coup sûr aurait mieux puni*
> *En nous ordonnant de les lire.*

He praises the Pope's clemency in putting Cousin's books on the Index rather than ordering them to be read. Cousin was forty-seven, but very distinguished and looked it, and withal he was a brilliant talker. In less than a month she had become his mistress. The affair lasted for years.

As time went on she became *plantureuse, massive, tapageuse;* and more and more she manifested her desire to live to the full. However, she had her standards, and accepted no money from him. But his influence got her poems published, her plays acted, and when he became a Cabinet Minister he procured her a pension of twelve hundred francs a year. The best laid plans of mice and men, alas! A baby, inopportunely, was on its way. Alphonse Karr, a journalist, published a vulgar article about her. She took a knife and stabbed him in the back.

In 1846 she became Flaubert's mistress, and there is a great deal about her in his correspondence. He lived at Croisset, near Rouen, she in Paris; he wrote to her almost every day. She is believed to have served more than Flaubert would admit, in the picture of Madame Bovary. Her husband died in 1851, but Flaubert, in spite of her tears, would not marry her. It is said that at last he slapped her face and ran away. That was in 1854.

As a means to keep herself before the public, she had tried to make Sainte-Beuve devote one of his *Causeries du Lundi* to her and nagged him abominably. He replied: "I only ask one thing of you, Madame, that is to be allowed to admire you in silence, without being obliged to explain to the public the exact point where I cease to admire you."

Madame Colet was proposing to compete again for some prize of poetry for which the Académie Française was judge, and she wished such support as she might be able to get. The day of Musset's reception (May 27, 1852), she met him coming out of the *Institut*. She said that they had seen each other in early youth at Monsieur Charles Nodier's, but had never been introduced. He was very polite with that *grand air de gentilhommerie* that he affected. She asked when she might come to see him. He said that he was at home every morning. She went to see him. She wrote about it to Flaubert. He answered: "Your long account of Musset's visit made a strange impression on me. Take him all round, he is an unhappy fellow. One can not live without religion. That kind of person has none, no compass, no goal, he floods and ebbs from day to day, *tiraillé* by all the passions and vanities of the town. The origin of their decadence, I think, lies in the common mania which he has of mistaking sentiment for poetry. For instance, take his verse,

Le melodrame est bon où Margot à pleuré,
[Margot's tears are proof that the play is good],

which is a very good line in itself, but of a too easy theory, or 'For poetry, to suffer is enough,' and so on. Those are the axioms of that school. In ethics they lead to anything, in art to nothing. Musset will have been a charming young man and then an old man, but nothing solid, nothing enduring, nothing four-square or serious in his talent (*comme existence, j'entends*). Alas! Vice is no more fecundating than virtue; you need to be neither, not vicious, nor virtuous, you should be above all that. The part that seems to me most foolish,—even drunkenness does not excuse it—is his wild anger at the cross. That is lyrical stupidity in action; it is so forced, so little felt. . . . Musset's ideas always keep the highroad; his vanity is thoroughly bourgeois. I don't agree that what he has felt most are works of art; what he has felt the most are his own passions. Musset is more poet than artist, and now much more man than poet, and a meager man."

However, Flaubert did not succeed in persuading Madame Colet to forego her admiration for Alfred de Musset; she persisted and established an intimacy, the duration and extent of which it is hard to determine. Our only authorities are what Madame Colet herself says in her autobiographical romance called *Lui,* published after the poet's death, and a page or two by Adèle Colin. There is undoubtedly some truth and a great deal of fiction in *Lui,* but the three main characters, Alfred de Musset, Flaubert and herself are unambiguous, and the story concerning Alfred de Musset and George Sand, which she purports to tell as she heard it from Alfred's lips, is full and unambiguous. I offer the outline of her tale for what it is worth, with a few corrections, taken from Adèle Colin. Madame Colet begins with an account of her first visit to the poet at his flat, No. 6 Rue du Mont Thabor. She went there, in company with a friend of Musset, in order to ask him to read some of her verses at the next meeting of the Academy. She and her companion passed through a little antechamber, wainscoted with oaken panels. There was a picture on the wall of the Venetian school, a Venus, lying nude on a purple counterpane. Madame Colet judged it exceedingly lifelike. The guests then proceeded into the little salon, used as Musset's study. The farther wall was lined with well-loaded bookshelves from floor to ceiling. Two drawings, one of Rachel, one of Malibran, were hung to match. There were armchairs, a piano, a rosewood desk, and a clock surmounted by a classical figure in bronze. Madame Colet was struck by the sad change since she had seen the poet at the Arsenal, fifteen years or more before. He was thinner, but still more distinguished-looking, perhaps, than before, for the increased pallor gave his face a more ideal expression. His cheek-bones showed, his hollow eyes shone with a strange fire, his lips were nearly white. The bitterness of his soul sat upon his mouth. But there were no wrinkles on his forehead, and his hair, well *frisé,* framed it as in youth. He was dressed with elegance. He looked at her so fixedly that the diffident Madame Colet lowered her eyes. She said that she had seen him one Sunday evening long ago at Monsieur Nodier's. "What! It was you," Alfred exclaimed, "who would not waltz with me. You were wrong, Madame, we might have loved each other."

"How you go on!" said the gentleman who accompanied Madame Colet. "You are always the same, Alfred. Can you never see a woman without talking to her of love?"

"What would you talk to them about?" Alfred asked, laughing. "Madame does not look like a blue stocking, and I should suppose that she would not care for strong doses of socialism or metaphysics."

"And what makes you think she would care about love?" the other said.

"That shows you are in love and jealous!" Alfred answered, laughing harder than before.

So (I am giving you her story) she and Musset became friends. They talked of his drinking. He said, "I only get drunk when I suffer too greatly, when an imperious desire to forget life makes me envious of death. . . . I

know what I do." Then they approached the borderland
of flirtation. "Madame," he said angrily, "you are a
coquette like all the others, and I am an incurable fool
to be unable to come into a woman's presence without
feeling my old bruised heart flutter again."

One day they went to the Jardin des Plantes, wandered
about and saw the animals, he said that her eyes were
like those of the antelope, that the dark blue in hers
produced the same effect as the animal's black eyes. They
stopped before the lion's cage, the lion Marzo, whose
acquaintance Musset had already made, as he had been
there before with Adèle Colin. He bade her do as
Mademoiselle Colin had done, to put her hand on the
lion's head and pat him. Madame Colet did not dare,
but touched the beast (so Mademoiselle Colin reports)
with the handle of her umbrella. The lion roared so that
the building shook. Alfred recounted this to Mademoiselle Colin and they laughed over it. That is Mademoiselle
Colin's story. But the poet wrote a sonnet addressed
to Madame Colet: *After a walk in the Jardin des Plantes,*
in which he says that her sweet breath rivals the fragrance of May, that she may be doubtful of his sorrow,
but that she must not doubt his love, and closes with the
lines,

> But who will ever know my torturing pain?
> They say that the wild flowers guessed it once.
> Black-eyed Antelope, *dis qu'elle est mon amante.*
> O Lion, you know it, O noble prisoner,
> You who saw me turn pale when her charming hand
> Slowly descended on your bending head.

You see that Alfred agrees with Madame Colet's story
that her hand touched the lion's head, but in recounting
the anecdote to Mademoiselle Colin, who was always a
little sniffy with regards to the poet's ladies, he may have
deemed it more prudent to substitute the umbrella handle.
As to the intimacy of the friendship between the poet
and Madame Colet, there is her story that he was in love
with her, and she recounts several exceedingly highly
colored scenes of Musset's wooing, but she asserts that
she was true to Flaubert, for she recognized the great
space she filled in Flaubert's life.   She was (she says)
*la volupté radieuse, la frénésie, la recompense adorée,
et cætera de son cœur.*   On the other hand, Musset's
biographers, following the well established tradition of
French biography that rejects the hypothesis of platonic
love, wherever possible, asserts that there was a liaison.
One must remember that Cousin and Flaubert were still
in the background.   All that Adèle Colin says is: "The
lady, still very pretty, *chercha à plaire. Relations assez
suivies* were established but did not last long."   Her
story of the break is probably true.   The poet was soon
weary of Madame Colet.   Nevertheless her visits continued.   He took her picture that she had given him,
to the concierge (a woman), and bade her not let that
person go up to his apartment.   But so feeble a barrier
could not stop Louise Colet.   She came, saw her picture
in the concierge's room.   She pushed past the concierge,
got into the apartment, and demanded: "What have you
done with my picture?"   Musset was ill, but she forced
him into a corner, corporeally and mentally, and

Mademoiselle Colin felt herself obliged to come to the rescue.

Mademoiselle Colin ends her references to this episode by saying that the novel *Lui* "is a tissue of unworthy things, in which the author boasts of what passed between her and the poet; that there are things in it of a cynicism such that no woman should say, much less write them." In this judgment most decent people would concur.

CHAPTER XX

I REPEAT, the dominating influence in Musset's life was the passion of love, and a biography of him is obliged to deal primarily with this passion, for from it came his purest poetry, the *Nuits,* the *Lettre à Lamartine,* the *Souvenir,* poems that made Heinrich Heine say of him, "A great poet of all time, the greatest poet of modern times," a judgment uttered no doubt in a moment of enthusiastic sympathy. The poetry of love, triumphant, ruinous, desolate or dead, constitutes Alfred de Musset's claim to glory; but though his loves overshadow they should not obscure a very pleasant side of him, the side turned toward his friends, the aspect that made his mere acquaintance, Monsieur Ancelot for instance, find him *un aimable garçon, un homme du monde charmant.*

Nothing could be pleasanter than his relations with Madame Jaubert, and her affection for him offers admirable testimony to the bright aspect of his character. Here is a letter written to her during the troubled time when the Princess Belgiojoso dominated his heart:

Saturday night, 1840

Madame,

I have just come in. It is two o'clock. I came in, not sad, but a little weary, and with that kind of presentiment of ennui [with him a state of mind more than boredom and less than sorrow] that causes weariness, and, like *Scapin,*

I almost expected some ill tidings. Instead of that, I
found your kind and delightful letter. When I read such
noble sentences, so frankly thought, so gracefully said,
addressed to me, it restored my soul to its own place.
A thousand thanks for this beam of sunlight that you
send me. It shone in your heart and in your eyes while
you were writing. I am not worthy enough to ponder
over it to-night, but I can't go to sleep without thanking
you, even though I must beg your pardon for doing it
so badly.

With my respectful and devoted compliments

A. DE MUSSET.

Here is a letter to Maxime du Camp, a lad of eighteen
or nineteen, who like all the literary youth of France
went mad over his poetry and had sent him some verses:

1841

Sir,

I am very late in answering you. An indisposition,
that has kept me in bed, has prevented me for thanking
you before for the verses you have sent me, and which
give me the greatest pleasure. Your verses, Monsieur,
are youthful, so no doubt are you. They remind me of
happy days, still not very far behind me. I should be
delighted if my lucky star could make me better acquainted with you.

I am, Sir, your very obedient servant

ALFRED DE MUSSET.

Here is a letter to Tattet, that wild gallant fond of Cypriote wine and other men's wives, whom Pagello found sympathetic but Mademoiselle Adèle Colin did not like:

Mirecourt, May, 1845

Dear Alfred,

Nothing elevates the heart and beautifies the mind like a grand tour through the Kingdom. You wouldn't believe the number of houses, peasants, flocks of geese, glasses of beer, stable-boys, dishes of meat warmed over, village curés, educated people, high officials, hop vines, vicious horses, broken-backed donkeys, that have passed before my eyes. . . . I came back in the coach with a young beauty of forty-five to forty-six years, who was on her way from Warsaw, by *diligence,* to Batignolles. It's a historical fact. She was eating a Polish cake, the color of *fromage de Marolles,* and she was weeping because a tall monsieur, seven or eight feet high, and of very little width, had been squabbling with her. His name was *mon bien-aimé;* at least I didn't hear him called by any other. . . . Judge, old boy, of my situation. Luckily the face of this Ariadne made me think of Bacchus. So at Voie I bought a bottle of excellent wine for ten sous, really capital, and so, she weeping, I drinking, we went on our way sorrowfully. O friend, what piquant tragedies, what sufferings, what palpitations there are in the three compartments of a diligence!

By reading these letters to his friends one sees, that,

contrary to one's first impressions, he was not always begging a woman to rescue him from debauchery, or bewailing her hardness, or her faithlessness, or drinking in order to forget her. With his friends he was a good fellow. Here is an earlier letter to Tattet:

Saturday, October 17, 1840

My dear Alfred,

I am well enough, neither gay nor sad, but kept in the house; and yet, as the newspapers say, my mind and my heart are elsewhere. I think that I must hurry up and write my memoirs, to prove that once upon a time I laughed and cried. I really can't sympathize with you for losing your money; it's something to lose money, and it is quite as pleasant to think of that, as to read the *Moniteur* when you go to bed. To remain quiet at home is the most atrocious of punishments; I don't understand why it is not employed in hell. Why didn't Dante think of a man in his dressing-gown in the 4th or 5th circle of Hell, sitting in his armchair beside his hearth with his feet in his slippers? It would have been the highest degree of the horrible; perhaps he didn't dare to draw so terrible a picture. O misery! No cares, no worries, no hope, no nothing!—Only wood, oil and flannel! O horrible, horrible, horrible, as Hamlet's ghost says. It's worse than Ugolino, more tantalizing than Tantalus, duller than Ixion! You see, old fellow, in what a happy mood I am, and I repeat that I am well enough; I have a new hat, new shoes, in short all that is necessary to happiness.

You say that the *Revue* [*des Deux Mondes*] is mortally dull, and I am too disinterested not to believe you. Nevertheless, I can't help regarding the *Revue* as a kind of old relation, a great-aunt, and respecting it as such. She's a respectable woman, who has had her fling, and is now being consoled by Sainte-Beuve. You know that he holds a monopoly of consolation for forlorn ladies about forty-five years old.

Good-by, dear boy; if, when you ride in the woods or drink a glass of wine, you should run across a hope or an illusion, put out your hand and catch it, like a fly, and send it to me, please, and direct it "to a gentleman who has not taken a drop."

> *A vous de cœur*
>
> A. de M.

Perhaps, next to Musset's relations with his Marraine and Tattet those with his Uncle Desherbiers, show best his good aspect, his pleasant disposition and his power to attach and to be attached. Uncle and nephew had been friends since boyhood. When the poet wrote his first verses he discussed them with the sympathetic older man, and it had been so always. They were very much alike, so that Alfred's father used to say to him: "You are indeed the son of your uncle." It was with him that Alfred stayed at Mirecourt, where he was *sous-préfet,* a position to which he had been appointed through Alfred's influence with the Duc d'Orléans.

As the story goes, about 1840, one evening when the family were gathered together at the Château de Bonneaventure, Alfred said to his uncle, who was poor: "We are going to celebrate your birthday in three days, Uncle, do you want me to make you a present of a *sous-préfecture?*"

"By the Lord! I should;" Uncle Desherbiers answered. The poet sat at his desk, took a pen, wrote a note to the Prince d'Orléans. The next day but one came the nomination as *sous-préfet* at Mirecourt in the Vosges.

"The deuce! That's pretty far away," was Uncle Desherbiers' first comment.

"Oh," said Alfred, "just a little selfishness on my part. I have been ordered to take the waters at Plombières which is only two steps away from your town, and I shall go to see you every year."

Before the week was out, Uncle Desherbiers was performing his duties as *sous-préfet*.

After Madame de Musset had given up her apartment in Paris, and Alfred was in his own little apartment, Rue Rumfort, under the care of Mademoiselle Adèle Colin, Uncle Desherbiers was frequently there whenever Alfred was ill. In the very first illness, when Mademoiselle Colin had declared in favor of Doctor Raspail's doctrine of no bloodletting, Uncle Desherbiers had concurred, as well as Paul. Perhaps this ready concurrence had something to do with Mademoiselle Colin's favorable opinion of Uncle Desherbiers. She says that he was the tenderest and most devoted of friends, and that there was no sacrifice that he would not make for his nephew. Indeed he was both a father and a companion. Alfred loved him dearly, and they could not get on without each other, although they did not always agree. They disputed over matters of literature, politics or philosophy, and they would quarrel over chess or piquet and separate in very ill humor. After such an occasion Alfred would send a letter of excuses round in the morning, and when they met again that night no reference was made to the dispute of the night before; or, often, Uncle Desherbiers, feeling that it was he who had been to blame, would arrive at Alfred's before the letter of apology had gone off, and apologize himself. Of this sweet friendship Mademoiselle Colin gives several instances.

The poet had neighbors in an apartment opposite upon the same landing. The man of the family died. Alfred, who was morbidly sensitive about death, was not told, though he knew that the man was attended by a physician. Nevertheless, Adèle was nervous lest her master be upset and asked Uncle Desherbiers to come to spend the next day. That evening Alfred went to bed soon after dinner, which he ate at a late hour. At two o'clock Adèle, awakened by a loud ring, rushed to her master's room; she hardly recognized him, he was a prey to such terror. "Sit there," he cried, pointing to the foot of the bed, "sit there in place of that undertaker, he says that he is waiting for me and he has a band of crêpe on his sleeve. As soon as you stop talking, he reappears!" Adèle lighted candles, flung open the windows, and the welcome dawn dispelled the vision. He asked news concerning his neighbor. She said that he had gone into the country and was doing well. "Oh!" Alfred replied, "when I saw the vision, I supposed that he was dead." Good Uncle Desherbiers came as he had promised at ten o'clock, saying that he had come to spend the day. Alfred said: "Oh, dear Uncle, you never had a better inspiration than to come this morning."

The last game of piquet the two ever played was not long before the poet's death. They used not to play for money, but for honor, and the vanquished was never pleased. That night Uncle Desherbiers had the bad luck to misdeal; he misdealt three times. At the third misdeal, Alfred said nothing but got up, left the card table and went into his bedroom. As he did not come back, Adèle followed to see what was the matter. He was out of humor, very cross, and while undressing himself he said: "Three times to deal thirteen cards in one evening is intolerable!" Adèle reported this to the uncle. "Yes," he said, "that is true. I made a mistake three times, I am very sorry. But if Alfred gets angry for that, I can't help it now." And he went away without saying good night.

Once Musset had cut his finger badly; Adèle bandaged it and he went out. He did not come back that day, nor the next, nor the next, but a messenger came asking for a handkerchief. Adèle was alarmed and at once wrote to Monsieur Desherbiers, who wrote back:

January 10, 1851

Dear Mademoiselle,

I think that there is nothing better for us to do than to stay quiet and do nothing. Since the persons who sent the messenger did not ask you to go to Alfred, it means that his indisposition, if he is indisposed, is not dangerous, for if it were not so, they would not be willing to incur so serious a responsibility.

Let us calm ourselves and wait. If Alfred does not come home within a few days, we must find out where he is. I wish you had asked the messenger the name of the street and the number of the house where the friend lives to whom he is gone.

Recevez, ma chère Adèle, l'assurance de mes senti- ments, etc.

DESHERBIERS.

There is something about Monsieur Desherbiers that re- minds one of Tristram Shandy's Uncle Toby. On that occasion things turned out as the uncle anticipated. The poet returned in good spirits and said that a charming woman had carried him off as he was leaving the theater. Madame Allan-Despréaux was quite right, by this time he had grown aweary of her, and needed a new person to catch his wandering fancy.

But the real test of good-fellowship in a man lies in his friendship with animals. Alfred had a dog and a cat. He understood that a neighbor's cat was about to kitten, and asked for one of the brood. A hideous little kitten of dirty gray color and short fur was sent. "I have no luck," he said as he looked at his four-footed companions, "I like only the beautiful, and I am sandwiched in be- tween an ugly cur and a gutter cat. But what can I do? I did not choose them. Such as they are, Chance presented me with them, and in these poor beasts I admire and respect the phenomenon of life and the handicraft of mysterious Nature.'' This, however, was not fair to the dog, Marzo, but perhaps he made the remark before Marzo's remarkable qualities were conspicuous. The ugly kitten never was beautiful, but she developed *grâce et gentillesse,* and Marzo became renowned in the *quartier*. He went alone every evening holding three sous, wrapped in a paper, in his mouth, exchanged them for a copy of a newspaper and brought it home, and then opened the door himself. He adored his master; and long after his master's death, and he had become old and feeble, when Mademoiselle Colin spoke of Monsieur de Musset, the faithful dog pricked up his ears to testify that he understood. This name, Marzo, was borrowed from the lion in the Jardin des Plantes, which Alfred de Musset had gone to see with Louise Colet. He was acquired in this way.

Musset and Mademoiselle Colin used to dine at the Bœuf à la Mode, go to the theater, and stop on their way home at the Café Drançay on the Quai Voltaire. Here Musset would take a glass of beer. And usually a little bitch that belonged to the proprietor would come forward and Musset would fondle her. One night, Mademoiselle Colin discovered that the woman behind the counter had been crying. She asked what the matter was, and the woman told her in a low tone that her husband was going to drown the little bitch. As Musset started to go he asked: ''Where is the little dog? She hasn't come to say good night to me.'' Mademoiselle Colin explained the situation. Musset felt very badly. ''What can we do?'' he asked. ''We can't take the little bitch.'' Adèle suggested: "Ask Monsieur Drançay for one of her puppies." So Alfred walked over to the proprietor who was playing cards in an adjoining room. "Monsieur," he said with his customary politeness, "I am one of your regular customers." "I know it," the proprietor answered, "it is an honor. This is Monsieur Alfred de Musset, is it not?" "The same," the poet said, "and I am going to ask you to be so kind as to do me a slight favor." "Only too happy; what can I do?" "Will you be good enough to keep one of the puppies of your bitch for me?" "What, that nasty beast!" "Well, she is not very pretty, but *que voulez-vous?* It's a caprice." "Caprice!" the proprietor replied, "nobody has a better right to a *caprice* than you! But you can boast that you have saved her life; I was going to drown her." "Not really?" "But I forego in your favor." "You will give me a puppy then?" "Sure."

Not long afterward Mademoiselle Colin was invited to come and choose one of the litter. She chose the littlest, which was quite black. Alfred approved her choice. But the poor little puppy whined so, away from its mother, that Mademoiselle Colin had to take it back for a week. Then it came to stay. Alfred was delighted; he and Mademoiselle Colin spent all their time fussing over it. The question of a name came up. Alfred asked Mademoiselle Colin what she thought; she said, "I think it should be a name of two syllables." Monsieur de Musset did not agree; "He shall be called Vercingetorix." Adèle cried out, said that he must be joking. "Well, would you rather name it Marzo after our lion?" She assented.

Marzo turned out to be intelligent. He learned the proper behavior in a house very quickly, for propriety was rewarded by lumps of sugar; no sooner had he learned the causal connection between going to his private quarters and the sugar received, than he would go there frequently, and quite unnecessarily, and come back for his lump. But he was no beauty. As he grew bigger, one friend said that his ears must be cut, another that his tail must be docked. Monsieur de Musset absolutely refused: "Nothing shall be cut off," he said, "his Creator gave him useful appendages, and they shall remain." Marzo's second lesson was to lie quiet on his mat when they went out; but when they came in, there was a grand explosion of joy, leapings, waggings, attempted kisses, a sort of Bastille anniversary celebration. Monsieur de Musset, did not like to have his face kissed, but he allowed the puppy to lick his left ear; and that remained a permanent privilege. For the sake of health, it was prescribed that Marzo should have no meat; but, after this régime had lasted for some time, the dog went limping about on three feet, and finally one of his hind paws appeared to be lifeless, and the household did not know what to do about it. Mademoiselle Colin took him to a veterinarian; the paw was virtually withered. The doctor pulled it, put it in splints, and bade her keep the dog perfectly still for several days by tying it with rags to a mattress. This cost, as Mademoiselle Colin records, five francs. She did exactly what the veterinarian said; then she went out to do an errand, when she came back the dog was gone, only mattress, rags and splints left. The dog was hiding in his master's room. Mademoiselle Colin reported this behavior to Monsieur de Musset. He answered: "If the dog has torn all those things off, it shows that they must have been bad for him. Let him alone." The little dog listened attentively; but Mademoiselle was not satisfied. She happened to speak of it to an acquaintance, who said that her father was a veterinarian at Fontainebleau, that he was coming to dine with her the next Sunday, and bade Mademoiselle Colin bring the dog for him to see. So she did. The veterinarian asked what the dog ate. She told him. "Doesn't it get any meat?" he asked. "No, never," she said. "That's all wrong. You must give him a mutton chop, as a medical remedy, every day until he is restored to his normal condition. When he runs on four paws again, give him a pâté of boiled beef, some bread soaked in cold water with a sprinkling of salt." This veterinarian, as Mademoiselle Colin also records, gave his advice gratis. In less than two weeks Marzo was well again.

The dog's position in the household was now well assured. Sometimes Monsieur Émile Augier, author of *Le Gendre de M. Poirier,* a great friend of Monsieur de Musset, would say: "Marzo, you have fleas." The dog became very indignant, and seemed to call on his master to testify. Then Musset would say: "You are mistaken, Augier, Marzo has no fleas," and Marzo, having obtained justice, would go away satisfied. When Mademoiselle was assisting Monsieur de Musset to dress in the morning, he would come and stretch out his neck for her to tie Musset's night neckcloth on it; and sometimes, in preparation for bed, he would sit in an armchair beside the chess table with this neckcloth on and never lie down for fear of disarranging it. Mademoiselle Colin suggested to Musset to ask the dog for his neckcloth; the dog got up and went to Mademoiselle Colin for her to untie it. If one is to believe Mademoiselle Colin, Marzo understood almost everything. When she was going to market, and went with her book to Monsieur de Musset to ask for money, Marzo always went with her. She told the dog that they were to get money to buy some beef of which he always had some. Monsieur de Musset would sometimes say, in order to tease the dog, "I shan't give you a cent." Marzo would look up at her, then yelp at his master, and so on, yelping louder and louder till he really got angry. Then when Musset had given the money, he would catch the hem of Mademoiselle Colin's skirt and drag her to the door, en route for the market.

Marzo, also, had the drumstick of a chicken occasionally. He got into very fixed ways. Once Alfred took Marzo along when he went to dine with his mother; Paul was there, too, with his white poodle, Tobie, whom Marzo detested. Madame de Musset was feeding Tobie with scraps of biscuit, and offered some scraps to Marzo, who turned up his nose at them. Madame de Musset said: "Marzo doesn't like biscuit." "Oh, yes he does," Alfred answered, "he eats biscuit every day, but he always has a whole one." So Madame de Musset then offered the dog a whole one, which he took and retired to a corner to eat. In the evening (Mademoiselle Colin's anecdotes are strung together, inartistically, the scene is here shifted to Musset's own apartment) when it was time for Monsieur de Musset to come home, Marzo always recognized the sound of his carriage, and barked to notify Mademoiselle Colin; he never was mistaken. He could not endure a hand organ, but the moment he heard the piano played he ran up to listen. After Musset's death, Mademoiselle Colin stayed on for three months in the apartment that they had occupied the last few years of his life, No. 6 Rue du Mont Thabor, and every night the dog listened for his master to come home.

A second dog appeared among them for a time. This was a black dog Loulou, who used to nose round in the street, in front of their apartment-house, and one day, not getting much satisfaction, followed Mademoiselle Colin up-stairs. Monsieur de Musset bade her feed the dog, and in order to make sure that it should not be obliged to sleep in the street, paid some person to give it night's lodging. Loulou now followed Mademoiselle Colin through the streets, and unluckily met his old mistress, who scolded it, beat it and carried it away. The next day Loulou reappeared at the Musset apartment and hid there all day. This touched Alfred's sympathies; and he was uncomfortable until Mademoiselle Colin had found the owner and persuaded her to sell them the dog. That cost five francs. Mademoiselle Colin had to go to the woman's house to pay the money; Loulou went too, but stayed outside the door for fear of being kept. Loulou, in spite of its name was a male dog, old and intelligent. Mademoiselle Colin washed him, made him respectable, and he soon was established as a member of the household. It was

From the medallion by David d'Angers in the Louvre

La Malibran

Marzo's privilege to carry the morning mail to Monsieur de Musset, but Loulou one day was quicker, took the letters and presented them to its master on its hind legs. Marzo's nose was out of joint; but Monsieur de Musset made him understand that Loulou was only a servant and to be considered such. Unfortunately, Loulou had the mange, and gave it to Marzo. The veterinarian said that he could cure Marzo, but that Loulou was too old, so poor Loulou was put *en pension* with an old woman, and paid for, till its death. Marzo was taken to stay with the veterinarian, shaved and treated.

During Marzo's stay with the veterinarian the household moved from Rue Rumfort to Rue du Mont Thabor. After they were settled in the new apartment, Mademoiselle Colin went to fetch Marzo and brought him in a carriage. Monsieur de Musset was out. Marzo sniffed round the rooms, recognized the furniture and then disappeared, nobody knew where. When Monsieur de Musset came home for dinner, he inquired for the dog. It had gone back to Rue Rumfort and persuaded the concierge to let it go up to the old apartment. It was quite empty. The dog went into Alfred's room, whined and howled, and then ran across the street to Mademoiselle Colin's sister's, where he was found. When Musset saw him shaven and shorn, he said, "He is *very* ugly," but the dog was so delighted at the reunion that his master had to admit that he loved him just the same. Adèle said, "Talk to him about little Baptiste, the veterinarian's apprentice who had had charge of him." So Monsieur de Musset asked Marzo about Baptiste; at this hated named Marzo looked round and growled and gave them plainly to understand that he had been very miserable while away.

This pleasure in the ugly dog makes one understand how lonely the poet was in the last years of his life, with no woman's hand other than that of the faithful but unlovely Adèle Colin. He made her promise to stay with him till he died. "I have no more friends," he said, "my mother is far away. If you leave me, I shall die in a hospital." This thought often troubled him. Adèle promised; his other friend, the dog, was equally faithful. During his last days after he had been unconscious he came to and asked: "Where is Marzo?" The dog had been taken out of the room while his master was asleep, but then came in with great protestations of joy and love. Alfred patted and fondled him: "You should stay beside your master, little dog." Marzo turned toward the *bonne* who had taken him away, and yelped until his master understood that his going had been against his will.

CHAPTER XXI

THE END

During Musset's latter years the effects of his irregular habits told more and more upon his constitution. His will became less and less master of his actions, and as one reads anecdotes and recollections concerning him, he seems like a man walking in a world unrealized, looking about him with the helplessness of an undernourished child.

Some of his friends had always thought that marriage perhaps might save him, might enable his genius once again to flare up and cast a bright light. One of such friends was the Duchesse de Castries. This lady was afflicted by a partial paralysis, but though obliged to remain in her armchair she liked to distract her spirits by pleasant company and animated conversation. She was very pious, and rather more conservative and conventional in the choice of her friends than Madame Jaubert. In her salon the conversation was more guarded and kept within narrower bounds than at Monsieur Berryer's. The old Duc de Fitz-James, a descendant of the Stuart Pretenders, was a privileged guest, and his *historiettes gauloises* were permitted, but persons of less illustrious descent had to mind their p's and q's. The Duchess was fond of Alfred, and made much of him; in her invitations she would say, "Come, you may smoke," and Alfred fully returned the Duchess's affection, and enjoyed the restrained manners of her friends. And, he was not too

301

tightly curbed, for, as Paul says, "Alfred knew how
to say everything without giving offense to the most delicate ears."

The Duchess sometimes talked to him, or wrote to him
about religion; she went to see him when he was ill, she
gave him a copy of *Thomas à Kempis,* and she concerned
herself particularly with making a match for him. The
first time, however, Alfred was young and had no mind
to put his head in the yoke; he says, *"C'est un serpent
doré qu'un anneau conjugal,"* and he waived the chance
aside. The second time the young lady in question pleased
him very much, but—it is Paul, now married to Aimée
d'Alton who says this—"nevertheless he had the courage
to surmount his inclinations." A third suggestion was
received more hospitably.

He and his friend Chenavard, the painter, were playing
chess. By this time there must have been a conspiracy
to turn the poet into a married man, for the procedure
points to cooperation and careful forethought. "By the
way," Chenavard said, "if you are wanting to marry,
come to me. I can indicate the very girl to suit you."
"I might," Alfred replied, "and, anyhow, you may as
well tell me." So, Chenavard with the chess-board between them, setting up the men for the second game, went
on: "I have known Monsieur de Mélesville for some
time. This morning I went to his house, and was shown
into the parlor. A charming young girl invited me to
sit down until her father came. I had never seen her
before and I was struck by her beauty, her good sense
and amiable expression. She is a brunette, with big

black eyes. Her father is the best fellow in the world. The family are people of taste and intelligence. It flashed into my mind that this was the match for you, and I made a resolution to tell you. That's my proposition. You better think about it.''

Alfred was interested, and the two talked the matter over; a brunette with black eyes appealed to him. He had had an acquaintance with Monsieur Mélesville ever since the time when his family lived at Auteuil, and he had liked him, and he recollected that he had seen the little girl play a small part in a comedy, and that she had played it well. He knew that she was intelligent and well-bred. As they talked, Alfred became much excited by the project, and Chenavard repeated that Mélesville was a capital fellow, very simple, a man of patriarchal ways, who owed his fortune solely to his own ability, and attached more value to talent than to money. ''Why,'' he said, ''any man would marry the daughter for the sake of having such a father-in-law.'' Everything, Chenavard reiterated, was just as it should be, most suitable on both sides. The only question left was as to the proper procedure. Alfred cast about immediately for some excuse for calling on Monsieur Mélesville, as it seemed better not to say that he was in love with the girl until he had seen her, and he did not wish to begin, in notarial fashion, with a consideration of *dot*. Chenavard was prepared with a suggestion: ''You shall go,'' he said, ''and propose to Monsieur Mélesville that you and he collaborate in a play. It will be easy for you to think of a plot for a comedy. Armed with a plot, you present yourself, you work with the father, you talk to the daughter. As soon as you have had the time you need to perceive her charms and her intelligence, you send me as your ambassador! I carry your proposal! I am received with favor, and you make a marriage fit for the Opéra Comique!''

Alfred was delighted with his friend's ingenuity, and taking down *The Arabian Nights,* set himself to convert the story of *Noureddin Ali* into a comic opera. More than that, Chenavard warmed to his rôle of match-maker, and profiting by the fact that Mademoiselle Mélesville's name was Laura, drew a picture of Petrarch's first meeting with Laura, and gave Petrarch the features of Musset and to Laura those of Mademoiselle Mélesville. What could be happier, or better calculated to catch the fancy of a romantic girl? Having finished the sketch, Chenavard told Alfred to write some lines underneath. So, Alfred imitated Petrarch's eulogy of the place and time when he first saw Laura, and rendered into French the famous lines:

Benedetto sia'l giorno, e'l mese et l'anno,
e la stagione, e'l tempo, e l'ora, e'l punto,
e'l bel paese, e'l loco, ov'io fui giunto
da duo begli occhi che legato m'anno.

Everything was ready. Alfred remained at home with the plot of *Noureddin Ali,* while his ambassador, bearing the rich gift of sketch, verses and autograph, went to knock at Monsieur Mélesville's door. Alas! The ambassador had hardly begun before Monsieur Mélesville

interrupted him to say that his daughter was already be-
trothed and soon to marry. Alfred felt badly; so did
Paul. But the reader thinks of the young girl so lightly
cast in what Chenavard considered a comic-opera rôle of
bride, and charged with the duty of reclaiming a de-
bauchee twice her age. Paul, in his optimism says: "Alfred would have been the most faithful, the best-behaved,
the happiest of husbands. He respected his plighted
word." And then, in the next sentence he goes on to say:
"Years and experience had no power to cool Alfred's
heart. Quite the contrary, its sensibility continued to
increase, more and more, up to the very last minute. Agitation, anxiety, perpetual emotions brought with them a
continual need of confiding, of recounting everything with
circumstantial details, either to Uncle Desherbiers or to
me. Alfred would make us stay by his fireside. We could
not tear ourselves away, and he could not make up his
mind to let us go. In these feverish moments, we had to
share his feelings, and profess ourselves miserable, sentimental, or indignant, by turns. These extreme excite-
ments, these violent agitations of a spirit, singularly sensitive and mobile, were sometimes fatiguing to those with
him." Well, at least one may comfort oneself by re-
membering that Mademoiselle Mélesville had what, from
our point of view, was an escape.

As I have said, the poet's irregular mode of existence
told upon him more and more. He became easily troubled, flustered, unable to cope with the vexations of life.
When his plays were not played at the Théâtre Français
as often as he thought they should be, he complained

querulously to the director. When, as I have related, a period was put where a comma should have been in *Carmosine,* he lay awake for three nights in unpunctuated pain. An episode of more consequence shows how pitiful his nerves had become.

The poet had been reappointed a librarian by the government of Napoleon III, and the Minister of Public Instruction thought it appropriate that the recipient of a sinecure should make some show of gratitude, and suggested a poem, which should draw a happy parallel, in some fashion, between Napoleon III and Augustus Cæsar. Musset set to work to write the words; Gounod to compose the music for them. Musset was to read the poem, *Le Songe d'Auguste,* in the Imperial presence. Poems written under such circumstances seldom have a permanent interest, and the *Songe d'Auguste* is no exception to that rule. However, Musset made ready to go to the palace of the Tuileries to read the poem before her Majesty, the Empress Eugénie. A functionary of the court in charge of the ceremony, Monsieur Conti, was unwise enough to make some hint of remuneration; as Musset was particularly sensitive on any matter that touched upon his *gentilhommerie* his feelings were hurt; he told Monsieur Conti, who begged his pardon. But the affair had begun badly. On the appointed evening Musset was asked to go first to the Théâtre Français, and see Monsieur Arsène Houssaye, the director, and an old acquaintance. It seemed to Musset that he was being subjected to an examination to see whether his dress, and so forth, were appropriate for the occasion. One can not but sus-

pect that this ceremony was to make sure that the poet
was completely sober. At any rate, Musset's sensitiveness was again irritated, but this time he said nothing.
From the theater they went to the palace. Monsieur
Conti was standing at the foot of the stairway to receive
him. Musset, already in a bad humor, became more irritated as he deemed this an excess of ceremony. He remarked that he was *astonished*. By this time he had
become quite nervous. However, he took his place before
the audience and began to read the poem. In the middle
of an important scene, a personage entered the drawing-
room without being announced. There were greetings
and whisperings. Musset stopped reading and rolled up
his manuscript. This action called forth some unfriendly
remarks. Houssaye whispered: "It's another royalty,
Monsieur de Rothschild," and Musset continued his reading. He was very much vexed, but made up his mind
to go on without stopping to the end. But a parrot
suddenly broke in shrieking and laughing. Poor Musset
was quite upset, but he managed to continue and finished.
Even so, his annoyances were not over. As he was on
his way out, the actress to whom a part had been assigned in the proposed public performance of this dramatic poem, stopped him and begged to be excused from
acting in it. The angry poet replied: "You shall not
play in this piece, Madame, nor in any other written
by me." And the poor, harassed, nerve-broken poet
went home to his faithful Adèle Colin and burst into
tears.

Another incident troubled him. An impudent vulgar

fellow, named Jacquot, who wrote under the name of
Mirecourt, was seeking to make money by publishing
short biographies of distinguished literary contempora-
ries. He published one of George Sand, another of Gérard
de Nerval, and so on. He wrote to Musset asking for certain dates and facts, Musset returned a peremptory and
unwary refusal. The consequence was that Jacquot took
what revenge he could, and among other things said that
a book entitled *Comte Gamiani,* which consisted of a *tas
d'ordures* against George Sand, had been ascribed to Alfred de Musset, but added that when the book was brought
to Gérard de Nerval, he exclaimed against such an ascrip-
tion as a most foul outrage. There can be little doubt
that Musset did not write any such book; but, as if to
prove the truth of the adage that, if you throw enough
dirt, some will stick, there lurks here and there, among
persons acquainted with the murkier regions of French
literature, somebody who has heard that Musset wrote
such a book and (I regret to say) believes it.

There are copies of this book in the Bibliothèque Nationale, in the department known as l'Enfer; but there is
no evidence whatever that Musset wrote it. All likelihood
is quite to the contrary. He consulted the leader of the
Parisian bar with regard to bringing a suit against Jacquot; but the *Bâtonnier* wisely advised the irate poet to
do nothing, for any such action would give Jacquot the
very notoriety that he was seeking.

The scanty anecdotes concerning his last years show
that the lamp of life was burning low, they cry amen to
the words of *Proverbs*: Deliver us from the strange

woman, "for her house inclineth unto death, and her paths unto the dead. None that go unto her return again, neither take they hold of the paths of life." Maxime du Camp saw him at this time. Du Camp had gone to some fashionable *salon* after dinner in the evening. The chandelier and lamps were shining bright, and a group of ladies were listening to a discussion between Victor Cousin and Charles de Rémusat. Apart, by the hearth, sat Alfred de Musset. He looked bored, listless, with the air of a man obliged to perform a disagreeable task. He said little, but looked at the ladies as if he was making comparisons between them. There was no trace of youth or beauty left, nothing but his wonderful fair hair that still showed a golden glitter in the light. His face looked very long and thin, and precocious wrinkles emphasized all his features. His forehead had a noble look, but his lower lip was flabby and gave to his whole face a dull stupefied expression. His handsome hands, well cared for, adjusted from time to time his locks of hair. His dress and his way of speaking had a touch of past fashions, and indicated the antiquated dandy. He took out his watch, put it to his ear and shook his head; five minutes later he did the same thing, evidently annoyed to find that it had stopped. He spoke to nobody, merely addressed a few commonplace remarks to the lady of the house. At the end of half an hour he got up abruptly, stood motionless for a moment, then crossed the salon with a steady step, holding his head straight and his body very stiff. He walked on his heels and looked fixedly before him. A lady said, *Pauvre garçon,* but Victor Cousin uttered *un mot méchant* (something nasty), and the kind Maxime du Camp remembered the lines:

Dans ce verre où je cherche à noyer mon supplice,
Laissez plutôt tomber quelques pleurs de pitié,

Into the glass in which I strive to drown my woe,
Rather let fall some tear of pity.

Another anecdote that proves his loss of will, nevertheless shows the lingering of the poetic vision. In 1855 and in 1856 he had gone to Havre for his vacations; during the last he made great friends with an English family who were staying at the same hotel. He was ill and the two young English girls, in the earliest charm of womanhood, took a great liking to him, and were prodigal of little attentions. He delighted to play games with them or talk with them. One day he imprudently stayed out too late upon the dock, and the next day he was obliged to stay in bed because of fever. His bed was drawn near the window, and the girls placed their chairs on the veranda just outside. In short a delightful friendship arose between them. The poet got well, and all too soon it was time for him to return to Paris. He said good-by, climbed into the omnibus that carried him to the railroad station, and there he found that his trunk was no longer on top of the omnibus. Nobody knew what had become of it. He was vexed and indignant, but he could not go without it. He lost his train and returned to the hotel. The two girls had pulled the trunk off, in order to oblige him to stay longer. They danced and clapped and shouted triumphantly. So he stayed two days more. That autumn, but a month or two later, coming back of an afternoon to his apartment he found the English gentleman's card. He was delighted and next day walked out up the Champs Élysées toward their hotel. The day was fair, but his reflections were somber. He thought how different Paris was from a country town, how little really he and they had in common, that the girls would have young Englishmen about, perhaps courting them, perhaps accepted lovers, that the charming playful intimacy would be impossible, that his own spirits had been gay and boyish on the beach, but now they smacked of sobriety and town life. "If I go," he thought, "shall I not come back with that delightful picture tarnished, with an illusion lost, with a memory disfigured?" He reached their door; turned about, and never saw them again.

He may have been right, he may have been wrong, but he yielded to the poetical counsels of his imagination. He did so once more. He wished to say good-by to the pictures in the Louvre that he loved best; he did not know that he should never go again, but here he felt that none of the apprehensions that had drawn him away from seeing the English girls again, were relevant. He obtained permission to go alone by night into the galleries where the Italian masters were. Was he thinking of Venice, of its palaces and pictures, of the *Albergo Danieli* and the strange scenes enacted there? He carried a torch, and stopped before each picture that he loved best, and seemed to himself to be alive among the great masters of the Renaissance, to see them at their work, and wished that he might grind colors and sharpen pencils for Raphael and Leonardo da Vinci.

But he was not well. In March—we are in the year 1857—he was really ill. Then friendship made its last claim upon him. His friend Émile Augier, the playwright, had presented himself for election to the Academy. Augier begged Paul to see that Alfred went to vote. Paul found Alfred resolute to go, although palpitations of the heart bothered him extremely. It was raining in torrents. No carriage was to be had. He took Paul's arm and walked slowly under the arcade of the Rue de Rivoli, stopping every twenty steps for breath. At the corner of the Rue des Pyramides Paul hailed a passing cab. Alfred reached the *Institut* just in time to cast his ballot, and Augier was elected by one vote. Alfred was so elated that he insisted upon celebrating the success of his candidate, by dining at a restaurant and going to the theater. Mademoiselle Colin denounced this as most imprudent. "Don't be angry," he said, "it may be the last time; my friend Tattet is calling me, and I shall soon go to join him."

Tattet had died a few months before. And Alfred did not delay long to follow him. It was on April thirteenth that he played his last game of piquet with Uncle Desherbiers. From that time on palpitations of the heart were frequent, and sometimes he was delirious. Mademoiselle Colin attended him devotedly. At times he cried, "Oh, I am suffering Adèle, you know how to pray, pray for me." Madame de Musset was at Angers, but Paul was near by. Alfred kept saying that he was going to rejoin Tattet, and sometimes, that he was always afraid of being put into an asylum, and asked Adèle anxiously if he was at home. On May first he talked to Paul and thought over all the persons he cared for. Paul went off to bed at half past ten. Adèle took night watches. He died early in the morning of May 2, 1857, at the age of forty-six.

EPILOGUE

THERE were many people in the church at his funeral, but very few followed his coffin to its last resting-place in Père-Lachaise. There a tombstone was set up with his bust by Barre, and carved thereon the words,

> *Mes chers amis, quand je mourrai*
> *Plantez un saule au cimetière,*

as well as the names of several of his poems. After long years, a statue by Mercié was placed close to the entrance of the Théâtre Français, another at Neuilly, and a great memorial monument called *Le Rêve du Poète*, by Moncel, near the *Grand Palais.* And a South American colonel Tscasubi brought from the borders of the Paraná a weeping willow; and it was planted behind the poet's tomb. But these marble memorials are little compared to the monument raised to his memory in French literature. He had led the way by his *Confession d'un enfant du siècle,* in which he fulfilled his pledge to erect out of his stony griefs an altar to the nobility of George Sand's character. Two years after his death, probably because there was gossip running around among the literary circles in Paris, that recounted the episode in a form unfavorable to her, George Sand published in the *Revue des Deux Mondes* a version of the story unfavorable in great measure to Alfred de Musset. Thereupon Paul de Musset, who disliked George Sand and idolized his brother, immediately wrote an angry answer under the title *Lui et Elle.* Unwilling to be left out from a controversy that occupied so ample a space in the public eye, Louise Colet came out with *Lui,* in which, after telling how wildly in love with her the poet had been, she, too, narrates a version of the liaison between Alfred de Musset and George Sand, in the form in which, she says, he told it to her. Since then, as you may see by the long list of articles in reviews and newspapers, which Monsieur Clouard with great diligence compiled, the affair has been a subject of perennial interest to the public entertained by literary scandal. In due course, after many uncertainties, the whole correspondence between the two was published. George Sand, to whom Musset had given back her letters to him, left to her friend Emile Aucante all the letters of both to publish after her death, providing that if he should die before publication, Alexandre Dumas *fils* should act in his stead, and if Aucante should survive both George Sand and Dumas, that then he should nominate somebody to act if he himself had not. So, at last, another delegate, Félix Decori, consummated the publication in 1904. But already the letters had got out, and a number of books, in particular *La véritable histoire de Elle et Lui,* by Spoelberch de Louvenjoul, *Une Histoire d'Amour* by Paul Mariéton, and *Les Amants de Venise,* by Charles Maurras, had gratified the public's curiosity. Musset's prediction was fulfilled: their loves are more famous, and known in far greater detail, than those of Abélard and Héloïse.

Then, also, after considerable uncertainties, Musset's letters to Aimée d'Alton were also published. In 1880, two months before the death of Monsieur Paul de Musset, an old lady with white hair went to the Bibliothèque Nationale, told the librarian modestly that in her youth she had been the mistress of Alfred de Musset, and asked his advice whether she should burn his love-letters to her or keep them. He replied sagaciously: "Since you are proud to have been the mistress of Alfred de Musset, I do not see why you should be less proud of it after your death than during your life. Deposit the letters here to be published at a date you name." Madame Paul de Musset approved; so did Monsieur Paul de Musset, for he admired these letters of his brother. And so the letters were published in 1910. Probably there is little or nothing more that will ever be discovered about the earthly pilgrimage of Alfred de Musset.

It may be that it would be better—if one were sure of a measure for right and wrong—to be ignorant of poets' lives, and to content ourselves with their poetry. But most of us are made of common clay, we find poetry by itself a rarified diet, and when we read it, we try to picture to ourselves the nature of the man that wrote it, his disposition, his adventures in this work-a-day world, what it was that provoked him to write *Lycidas, The Ode to the West Wind, The Ancient Mariner, Les Méditations, Silvia mia,* or *Rolla* and *Les Nuits.* Once we start, we wish to know more and more; biographical seekers may find a great deal of scandal, but that does not prove that they go in search of scandal or that they would not much prefer heroism. There is nothing good or bad but thinking makes it so; and therefore the veritable life of a man, expressed in terms that connote praise or blame, is nothing but an exposition of our current notions of ethics. Musset's morals appear very different to a Parisian, and to a New Englander or to a Victorian Englishman. Nothing could well give more room to curious speculation about manners and customs than the contrast between the lives of the two poets, born within a year of each other, on opposite sides of the English Channel, Alfred Tennyson and Alfred de Musset.

As I was saying, the literary monument erected to the memory of Musset is far more magnificent in dimensions and in interest than monuments of marble, and the literary mausoleum is not yet complete. A Mussettiste Society was founded, and a magazine, *Le Mussettiste* was published, at least until the Great War, and in 1910 this Society celebrated the hundredth anniversary of the poet's birth with a great fête held in the *Trocadéro* in Paris. There were literary exercises, there was music, and a program of a length to satisfy the most exacting, and there was a banquet of which the following is the menu:

Menu

Consommé Sévigné
Bisque d'Écrevisses

Hors-d'Œuvre variés

Délices de Soles au Champagne

Cœur de Filet de Bœuf Rachel
Coupe à Foies gras au Porto

Granité Madarinette
Faisan rôti à la Broche
Salade

Petits Pois aux Laitues
Bisquits glacés Tortoni
Gaufrettes
Friandises

Corbeilles de Fruits

Médoc   Graves
Pommard
Champagne Frappé

Café   Liqueurs

One can only hope that Mademoiselle Colin and Marzo were looking down from the gold bar of heaven to see the memory of their beloved master fêted with such honors.

But let us take leave of our characters as we do in novels, with a glance at their later lives. Mademoiselle Colin, some three years after her master's death, married Monsieur Martellet a volunteer in the *gendarmerie de la garde*. It is said that she showed no vocation for married life, and yet after her husband's death, she kept his picture hanging on the wall. For a time she carried on a watchmaker's shop in a small way in the Faubourg Saint-Honoré. From there, possibly in consequence of losing her little property in the Panama Canal catastrophe, she moved to Rue Duras, where pilgrims, who honored Musset's memory, occasionally went to hear her reminiscences. She had some of her master's furniture about her, some portraits of him, a few of his books, in

especial a copy of *Lélia* in two volumes, a gift from George
Sand at the beginning of their acquaintance, each with its
inscription, the first *"À Monsieur mon gamin d'Alfred,
George,"* the second *"À Monsieur le vicomte Alfred de
Musset hommage respectueux de son dévoué serviteur,
George Sand."* She lived among these treasures and
her memories, a most respectable old lady, dressed always, as became her history, with shawl, ruffled collar,
and whatever else is necessary to constitute *l'ordonnance
sévère d'une toilette restée discrète,* and attained a ripe
old age.

Madame Allan-Despréaux, as I have said, died a year
before the poet. Her husband had forgiven her; probably of their mutual forgiveness to him went the far
larger share. He had stayed in St. Petersburg and he
knew well that *les absents ont toujours tort,* and even
when his wife was at the theater there he was off hunting
and what not; "Never marry a huntsman," she said.
Her brother appears to have been more rigid in his convictions than her husband, but that was of less consequence; for in spite of the embonpoint which made Musset unwilling to have her act the heroine in *Le Chandelier,*
she continued to obtain triumphs at the Théâtre Français, and her husband was well enough off to buy a *belle
propriété* near Nancy, delightful town, whose eighteenth-
century spirit must have been attractive to her. When she
died he burst into sobs of passionate grief: her fellow
players mourned her. One, Delaunay I think, a famous
actor in our fathers' time, said "With talents like that,
one ought not to die."

Rachel is immortal, as one can see by the statue in the foyer of the Théâtre Français. A strange spiritual sisterhood, Melpomene and the soul of a gutter-snipe in one frail body. Doctor Véron had acquired property by a quack medicine, I believe, and was a man of much *savoir faire*. From his protection the actress ran the gauntlet of many other protectors for longer or shorter periods; there was the Prince de Joinville, he who as a lad had clambered up on the elephant in the circus behind his brother; there was Count Walewski, the great Napoleon's son, and so on. The Melpomene in her, however, procured for her the society of the most respectable ladies. She was taken up by the *Faubourg Saint-Germain;* Madame Récamier received her at the *Abbaye-aux-Bois.* Some other *grande dame* and her daughters treated her with great distinction; "Madame," Rachel said with an obeisance, "these proofs of your regard are more precious to me than my talents," but as she was leaving the suite of mirrored salons, in which glass repeated to glass the gesture of a departing guest, thinking that she had reached covert, Rachel put her wide-spread fingers in that juxtaposition to her nose which though forbidden Melpomene is familiar to the gutter-snipe, and undid the gratification caused by her gracious words. In London she was brilliantly successful; she played before Queen Victoria in Windsor; "Such a nice modest girl," the Queen said. Rachel repressed expressions of relieved constraint, but outside the palace, exclaimed, *O mes amis, que j'ai besoin de m'encanailler!* Perhaps the reader will remember what Charlotte Brontë says

At top: George Sand
At bottom: Madame Allan-Despréaux

Rachel
Aimée d'Alton

ALFRED DE MUSSET
From the miniature by Mademoiselle Marie Moulin

of her when acting the part of Vashti in *Esther*: "Behold, I found upon her something neither of woman nor of man; in each of her eyes sat a devil. These evil forces bore her through the tragedy, kept up her feeble strength—for she was but a frail creature . . . they wrote HELL upon her straight haughty brow. . . . It was a marvellous sight, a mighty revelation. It was a spectacle low, horrible, immortal."

After London, there were triumphs in Vienna, Berlin, St. Petersburg. But the fragile body could not endure the flaming soul within. She was ill; she went to New York. George William Curtis records: "A sad solitary figure, like a dream of tragic Greece;" and never, perhaps, had a Hebrew such a Hellenic gift. Consumed by tuberculosis she sought health in Egypt, on the Riviera, but death followed at her heels. As she lay dying the rites of her forefathers were celebrated, and the Hebraic faith raised its torch over her:

God of our Fathers, revive in Thy mercy this soul that goeth to Thee; unite it to those of the holy Patriarchs, amid the eternal joys of the heavenly Paradise. Amen.

She died within a year after Musset, aged thirty-seven.

The Princess Belgiojoso continued her shining worldly course as revolutionary and blue stocking. Her essay upon Vico, the Neapolitan philosopher, who in his own country at least is regarded as one of the great precursors of modern thought, is said "to constitute a *tour de force* which few experts could hope to surpass"; and she wrote several volumes on various phases of the *Risorgimento* in Italy. Rumor says that there was talk of a feminine

Académie Française of forty *immortelles,* over which the
Princess, as a compromise candidate between George
Sand and Madame de Girardin was to preside. But
literature was much less interesting to her than life, especially political life. She loved Italy. When Louis
Napoleon escaped to England from his prison at Ham,
foreseeing his rise to power, she followed him. "Princess," he replied, "let us first arrange matters in France,
and then I will think of Italy." She went to Milan, eager
to guide or assist Cavour, Mazzini, Charles Albert. And
after Pio IX had been expelled from Rome and a republi-
can triumvirate set up, thither she went, and won praises
from Mr. and Mrs. W. W. Story. Reaction triumphed
in Italy; she went to Greece. At Marathon—perhaps
those who thought her cold except as to Italy were right
—she only "felt that the day was very warm." On to
Constantinople, and across the Bosphorus; she bought a
farm somewhere midway between Scutari and Angora.
Her experiences there were duly published in the *Revue
des Deux Mondes.* She went back in Paris in 1854; soon
Italy drew her away. But "Beauty vanishes, beauty
passes," and at fifty the Princess was prematurely aged,
her energetic spirit had exacted too much of her body
to spare its loveliness. She lived, however, to see a
united Italy.

Aimée d'Alton, as I have said, married, after mature
consideration of pros and cons, Paul de Musset, and in due
course, her interest again centering in the most romantic episode of her life, paid the visit to Monsieur Jules
Troubat at the Bibliothèque Nationale and deposited the

correspondence between herself and her posthumous brother-in-law, if that be the correct designation of her relationship to the poet. Monsieur Troubat is said to have turned the scales, as we know, when she hesitated whether to destroy the letters or give them publicity. Personally I think that the credit ascribed to Monsieur Troubat for saving the letters from destruction is scarcely deserved, as I do not believe that Madame Paul de Musset had the slightest intention of destroying them.

Madame Louise Colet did not, so far as *une vie tapageuse* goes, fall far behind George Sand, Rachel and the Princess Belgiojoso. *Lui* was written shortly after *Elle et Lui* and *Lui et Elle*. Fair criticism, more than fair it seems to me, says: "The book is a delicious exhalation of Madame Colet—with all her peculiar charm, her peculiar faults, the meridional exuberance and voluptuousness, the love of life and high spirits, the complete freedom from all restraints imposed by good manners, self-respect or respect for the feelings of others, and her incredible silliness." The book had a pecuniary success, but vexed a considerable number of literary people in Paris, and therefore, influenced also by love of novelty, as her husband was dead and her daughter in a convent, she went to Italy, to Milan for revolutionary thrills, to Venice for art. She piously visited the Hotel Danieli and saw the rooms of George Sand and Musset. More interested in agitation than in art, she went to Turin to see Victor Emmanuel open the Italian parliament; from there to Florence, and on to Naples to gaze upon the celebrated Garibaldi and his Red Shirts. She lived for a time at Ischia, and at Capri,

where she felt the same impelling constraint that has laid
hold upon other authors, and wrote *"The Courtesans of
Capri."* It is not worth while to record her noisy efforts
to obtain the public ear. She went to Egypt when Count
de Lesseps opened the Suez Canal. She was in Constantinople during the Franco-Prussian war. On her return
she stopped at Marseilles, harangued the crowd and
"tasted the intoxication reserved for orators." She
was back in Paris in time to sympathize with the Com-
mune for she had become very radical. She died in 1876,
old, ugly, disliked, and egotistical to the end.

Of all the women that troubled Musset's life she that
disturbed it most became the most serene. Let me quote
some witnesses to different phases of her life. In 1846
a young Englishman of genius, at that time aged twenty-
four, full of keen interest in Berry, Marche and Bour-
bonnais, old provinces made known by her novels, took
the train from Paris to Vierzon, where it ended, the diligence to Châteauroux, a humbler diligence to La Châtre,
coming close to the village of Nohant. Her château was
a plain house by the roadside, with a walled garden. He
wrote for permission to see her. This she granted. "I
entered with some trepidation . . . but the simplicity
of Madame Sand's manner put me at ease in a moment.
She named some of those present . . . her son and
daughter . . . and Chopin with his wonderful eyes. . . .
She conversed of the country in which I had been wandering, of the Berry peasants and their mode of life. . . .
She touched politely upon England . . . upon Oxford
and Cambridge, Byron, Bulwer. As she spoke, her eyes,

head, bearing were all of them striking; but the main impression she made was an impression of what I have already mentioned,—of *simplicity*, frank, cordial simplicity.'' After her death he wrote his opinion of the woman who for forty-five years had written and published, filling Europe with her name. Then he quotes a phrase from one of her last books: ''The sentiment of the ideal life is nothing else than the normal life, as we shall, following the inward voice within, some day know it.'' (The translation is mine.) That he says is the ground motive of all her strain; then adds, after naming some of her books, ''in these may be found all the principal elements of their author's strain: the cry of agony and revolt, the trust in nature and in beauty, the aspiration towards a purged and renewed human society.''

In 1868 Maxime du Camp saw the famous lady; they dined tête-à-tête in a restaurant in Paris. He was struck by her ''masculine smile in which pride at the domination that she had exercised, and a feeling of recognized superiority blended with an expression of contempt.'' They talked of her success; she said that her only wish was an assured income of three thousand francs a year. He exclaimed his astonishment that she had not laid up far more than that. No, she said, she had gained largely but had spent lavishly. They talked of her life. ''I regret nothing,'' she said. He does not explain how, but the words were suddenly luminous, and he felt that he understood how this *bonne bourgeoise* might become a terrible creature.

In 1872 the Goncourts dined with her and found her

"more and more mummified but *pleine de bonne enfance* and with the gaiety of an old woman of the eighteenth century." And Tourguéniev after her death wrote: "Madame Sand's death has caused me great sorrow. Poor dear Madame Sand, what a heart of gold she had! What absence of pettiness, of meanness, of deceitfulness! *Quel brave homme c'était et quelle bonne femme!*"

So it is in life, each one is the sport of what others may think; reputation but the sum of relations with other human beings; and fame dependent upon mood, whim, prejudice and local customs.

THE END

BRIEF BIBLIOGRAPHY

BRIEF BIBLIOGRAPHY

ALFRED DE MUSSET: *Oeuvres; Correspondance* (1827-1857), edited by Léon Séché (1907): *Lettres d'Amour à Aimée d'Alton*, edited by Léon Séché (1910): *Correspondance de George Sand et d'Alfred de Musset*, edited by Félix Decori (1904): *Oeuvres complementaires*, edited by Maurice Allem (1911).

PAUL DE MUSSET: *Biographie de A. de Musset* (1877).

GEORGE SAND: *Histoire de ma vie* (1854-5): *Lettres d'un Voyageur* (*Revue des Deux Mondes* 1834-5): *Journal intime* (1926).

MADAME MARTELLET: *Dix ans chez A. de Musset* (1899).

DR. CABANÈS: *Cabinet secret de l'histoire*—Vol. II, (1897).

LÉON SÉCHÉ: *Alfred de Musset*—Vol. I: *Les Camarades*—Vol. II: *Les Femmes* (1907).

CAROLINE JAUBERT: *Souvenirs* (1881).

MAURICE CLOUARD: *Documents inédits sur Alfred de Musset*: (1900).

ALTON-SHÉE: *Mes Mémoires*: (1869).

MAXIME DU CAMP: *Souvenirs litteraires:* (1883).

D. E. ENFIELD: *A Lady of the Salons (Louise Colet)* (1922).

H. LYONNET: *Les Premières de A. de Musset* (1927).

A. FEUGÈRE: *Un grand amour romantique* (1927).

FRANCIS GRIBBLE: Rachel, Her Stage Life and Her Real Life (1911).

PAUL MARIÉTON: *Une Histoire d'Amour* (1897).

ARVÈDE BARINE: *Alfred de Musset* (1893).

VICOMTESSE DE JANZÉ: *Études et récits sur Alfred de Musset:* (1891).

S. ROCHEBLAVE: *Lettres de George Sand à Alfred de Musset et à Sainte-Beuve:* (1897).

SPOELBERCH DE LOUVENJOUL: *La veritable histoire de Elle et Lui:* (1897).

A. LE ROY: *George Sand et ses amis.*

CHARLES MAURRAS: *Les Amants de Venise:* (1902).

A. AUGUSTIN THIERRY: *La Princesse Belgiojoso:* (1926).

ÉMILE HENRIOT: *Alfred de Musset:* (1928).

MAURICE DONNAY: *Alfred de Musset:* (1914).

MAURICE DONNAY: *La vie amoureuse d'Alfred de Musset* (1926).

H. REMSEN WHITEHOUSE: A Revolutionary Princess, Christina Belgiojoso Trivulzio (1906).

Romances based on fact

A. DE MUSSET: *Confession d'un enfant du siècle:* (1834-5).

GEORGE SAND: *Elle et Lui:* (1859).

PAUL DE MUSSET: *Lui et Elle:* (1859).

LOUISE COLET: *Lui:* (1859).

Criticism

LAMARTINE; SAINTE-BEUVE; BARBEY D'AUREVILLY; PAUL BOURGET; ANATOLE FRANCE; ÉMILE FAGUET; THÉOPHILE GAUTIER; M. L. PAILLERON; RENÉ DOUMIC; LEMAÎTRE; etc., etc.

INDEX

INDEX

333